Opportunity
Investing

Opportunity Investing

How to Profit When Stocks Advance,
Stocks Decline,
Inflation Runs Rampant,
Prices Fall,
Oil Prices Hit the Roof, . . .
and Every Time in Between

Gerald Appel

FT Press
FINANCIAL TIMES

An Imprint of PEARSON EDUCATION
Upper Saddle River, NJ • New York • London • San Francisco
Toronto • Sydney • Tokyo • Singapore • Hong Kong • Cape Town
Madrid • Paris • Milan • Munich • Amsterdam

www.ftpress.com

Vice President, Editor-in-Chief: Tim Moore
Executive Editor: Jim Boyd
Editorial Assistant: Susie Abraham
Development Editor: Russ Hall
Associate Editor-in-Chief and Director of Marketing: Amy Neidlinger
Cover Designer: Alan Clements
Managing Editor: Gina Kanouse
Project Editor: Christy Hackerd
Copy Editor: Keith Cline
Indexer: Larry Sweazy
Compositor: Moore Media, Inc.
Manufacturing Buyer: Dan Uhrig

© 2007 by Pearson Education, Inc.
Publishing as FT Press
Upper Saddle River, New Jersey 07458

FT Press offers excellent discounts on this book when ordered in quantity for bulk
purchases or special sales. For more information, please contact U.S. Corporate and
Government Sales, 1-800-382-3419, corpsales@pearsontechgroup.com. For sales outside
the U.S., please contact International Sales at international@pearsoned.com.

Printed in the United States of America

First Printing, September 2006

ISBN: 0-13-172129-1

Pearson Education LTD.
Pearson Education Australia PTY, Limited.
Pearson Education Singapore, Pte. Ltd.
Pearson Education North Asia, Ltd.
Pearson Education Canada, Ltd.
Pearson Educación de Mexico, S.A. de C.V.
Pearson Education—Japan
Pearson Education Malaysia, Pte. Ltd.

Library of Congress Cataloging-in-Publication Data

Appel, Gerald.
  Opportunity investing : how to profit when stocks advance, stocks decline, inflation
runs rampant, prices fall, oil prices hit the roof, . . . and every time in between / Gerald
Appel.
    p. cm.
  ISBN 0-13-172129-1 (hardback : alk. paper) 1. Investments. 2. Speculation. I. Title.
  HG4521.A655 2006
  332.63'2--dc22

                                                                        2006009655

*This book is dedicated
to my grandchildren—Emily, Caroline, and
Alexandra—and to all children across the globe.
May they grow up in an ever-better and peaceful
world.*

CONTENTS

Acknowledgments xvii

Introduction: New Opportunities xix

Chapter 1: The Myth of Buy and Hold 1

Variable Rates of Return from Stocks 3

Speculative Bubbles Are Often Followed by
Years of Below-Average Investment Performance 5

The Moral of the Story—Be a Flexible,
Opportunistic Investor 6

Growth Targets—"The Magic 20" 7

Growth Target Zone 8

Active as Opposed to Passive Management of Assets 9

Diversification—A Major Key to Successful Investing 10

   Geographic Diversification in the
   Developing Global Economy 10

   Diversifying Geographically in Foreign Bond Markets
   as well as in Domestic Income Investments 12

   Sector Diversification for Smoother
   Performance and Risk Reduction 13

Income Investing—Time Diversification 16

Creating a Bond Time Ladder 17

   Year-by-Year Management of the Bond Ladder 18

Increasing Returns from the Stock Market
while Reducing Risk 19

Useful Market Mood Indicators That You Can
Maintain and Use in Just a Few Minutes Each Week 20

Illustrations of Mood Indicators 20

Relationships of Price Movements on NASDAQ
and the New York Stock Exchange 23

How to Identify Periods When NASDAQ
Is the Stronger Market Area 25

General Suggestions 28

Chapter 2: Putting Together a Winning Portfolio 29

Which Investments Have Paid Off the Best? 30

Life May Not Be So Predictable After All 31

The Moral of the Story 31

And Perhaps Most Important 32

The Best Places to Put Your Money in Recent Decades 32

Implications for Mutual Fund Selection 33

Mutual Funds Provide Excellent
Vehicles for Your Diversification Program 34

Benefits of Using Mutual Funds for Both
Financial- and Nonfinancial-Based Investing 34

Mutual Fund Selections for All Seasons 35

Periods of Rising Interest Rates 35

Periods of Falling Interest Rates 36

A Quick and Dirty Way to Determine
Trends in Interest Rates 37

Summing Up 38

Creating and Measuring the Performance of
Well-Balanced Diversified Investment Portfolios 38

The Basic Portfolio Mix 39

Summing Up 41

Income Investing 41

Diversification Certainly Does Appear to Help the Cause! 44

Upping the Ante! Increasing Returns and Reducing Risk
through Active Management of Your Diversified Portfolio 45

Employing Mutual Funds to Carry Out Sector
Diversification   46

    The Selection of Specific Mutual Funds   47

Comparing Performance—The Diversified Portfolio,
Buy and Hold, Versus the Vanguard Standard & Poor's
500 Index Fund   48

Rebalancing the Portfolio to Improve Returns   49

    An Object in Motion Tends to Stay in Motion   49

    The Basic Procedure for Rebalancing
    Your Sector Portfolio   50

    Year-by-Year Comparative Results   52

A Final Thought   54

**Chapter 3: Selecting Mutual Funds Most
Likely to Succeed   57**

Myths and Merits of Morningstar   58

A Quick and Dirty Checklist to Locate the
Best Mutual Funds   60

    Expense Ratios and Portfolio Turnover—
    the Lower the Better   60

    No-Load Funds Are Likely to Outperform Load Funds   61

    Verify That Your Brokerage House Is Giving You
    the Best Deal, Not Just Upping Its Own Commission   62

    As a General Rule, the Lower the Fund Volatility,
    the Better   63

    With Excellent Market Timing, Some Higher-Velocity
    Vehicles in Your Portfolio Might Prove Advantageous   64

    Continuity of Management Is Important   64

Putting Together and Maintaining a Mutual Fund
Portfolio for Long-Term, Tax-Favored Holding Periods   66

    The TPS Strategy: Selecting Mutual Funds That
    Qualify for the "One-in-a-Thousand Club"   66

Managing Your Buy and Hold Portfolio   73

Putting Together and Maintaining a Portfolio of Strong
Mutual Funds for Intermediate-Term Investment   74

Rotating Your Portfolio at Regular Intervals to Maintain
a Portfolio of Market Leaders   74

Outperforming Typical Mutual Funds   77

Past Performance   78

Upping the Ante with Double-Period Ranking Model   80

Examining the Statistical Comparisons, Decile by Decile   82

Diversification Will Almost Certainly Help the Cause   84

Conclusion   86

Getting the Maximum Bang from the Bucks in Your 401K
Plan and Other Tax-Sheltered Investment Portfolios   86

Special Advantages of 401K Plans for Active
Mutual Fund Management   87

One Final Thought   91

One Final Test—Confirming with T. Rowe Price   92

**Chapter 4: Income Investing—Safer and Steady . . .
But Watch Out for the Pitfalls   95**

The Four Legs of Your Investment Portfolio   95

Dealing with Default Risk   98

Bond Duration as a Measure of Risk   100

Securing Higher Rates of Return from Lower-Quality,
Investment-Grade Bonds   101

Understanding the Total Income Return from Bonds   102

Investing in Bonds via Mutual Funds vs. Investing
on Your Own   105

Bonds and Bond Funds for All Seasons   109

Money-Market Funds   109

U.S. Treasury Bills   110

Short-Term Bonds and Bond Funds   111

Intermediate-Term Bond Funds and Individual Bonds   113

Long-Term Government and Corporate Bonds   115

Treasury Inflation-Protected Securities (TIPS)   118

Zero-Coupon Bonds   120

Municipal Bonds: Winning the Tax Game   122

High-Yield Bonds and Bond Funds   125

Summing Up   130

Chapter 5: Securing Junk Bond Yields at Treasury Bond Risk   133

The 1.25/0.50 Timing Model   135

    Signals   136

    Timing Decisions   137

    Tracking Total Return   138

Calculating Buy/Sell Levels for Funds with Prices That Are Reduced When Dividends Are Paid   141

    Example A   142

    Reviewing the Procedure One Final Time   143

Handling High-Yield Funds That Do Not Reflect Interest Income in Their Share Pricing   144

    Example B   145

    Performance of the 1.25/0.50 Timing Model   146

Comparing Results   148

Summing Up   150

Chapter 6: The Wonderful World of Exchange-Traded Funds   153

Enter the Exchange-Traded Funds (ETFs)   155

Pros and Cons of ETFs   156

    Pros   157

    Cons   160

A Closer Look at the ETF Universe   163

    Income ETFs   163

    Global Investment   163

    Domestic Market Indices   164

    Specific Overseas Countries   164

    Specific Industry Groups   164

Miscellanea   165

Creating Complete, Well-Diversified Portfolios 165

Creating and Maintaining Your ETF-Based Portfolio 167

Large Cap vs. Small Cap 168

Using ETFs as Hedges Against Inflation 171

Sample Portfolios 173

The Conservative Investor 173

The Moderate Investor 175

The Aggressive Investor 176

Summing Up 176

Chapter 7: A Three-Pronged Approach to Timing the Markets 179

Common Measures of Valuation 180

Company Earnings: The Core Fundamental 181

The Long-Term Correlation Between Corporate Earnings and Changes in Stock Prices 182

Opportunity Investing Strategy 1 184

Price/Earnings Patterns 184

Riskier Periods 185

Using Bond Yields to Know When to Buy Stocks 187

Earnings Yield 188

Opportunity Investing Strategy 2 188

Finding the Data You Need 191

Special Observation 192

Trailing Earnings vs. Forward Earnings 193

Indicator Implications 194

Bond Yield: Earnings Yield Comparisons Using Aaa Bond Yields 195

Stocks Bullish 1974–1980 196

A Significant Buying Opportunity? 197

Ten-Year Treasury Bond Yields vs. Earning Yields 197

Surprise! Buy Stocks When Earnings News Is Bad, Sell When Earnings News Is Best 200

Chapter 8: Time Cycles, Market Breadth, and Bottom-Finding Strategies 205

Market Cycles 206

The Granddaddy of All Key Stock Market Cycles:
The Four-Year (Presidential) Stock Market Cycle! 209

Confirming the Four-Year Cycle with Your Price/
Earnings Ratio Indicator 210

The Link Between the Four-Year Market Cycle and
the Presidential Election Cycle 211

Winning with Investments Based on the
Presidential Election Cycle 212

Market Breadth 214

Market Breadth and Major Market Indices 214

Capitalization Weighted 214

Confirming Price Action of Major and Less-Major
Market Indices with "Breadth" Indicators 217

The Advance-Decline Line 218

The New High–New Low Breadth Indicator—Including
the Major Bull Market Confirming 28% Buy Signal! 220

Bottom-Finding Parameters 222

Significant Buying Pattern 222

Cautionary Conditions Indicated by New High–New Low
Data 223

The 28% Major-Term New Highs Buy Signal 224

Summing Up 228

Chapter 9: Cashing In on the Real Estate Boom— Investing in REITs 229

REITs Provide Steady and High Rates of Ongoing Income 230

Types of REITs 232

Closed-End REIT Mutual Funds 232

REIT ETFs 235

Long-Term Performance of REITs 237

The Price Movement of the REIT Index Alone
Does Not Tell the Full Story 237

Dividend Payout by Type of REITS   241

Timing Your Entries and Exits   242

    Links Between REITS and Interest Rates   242

    For Long-Term Investment, Track the Major
    Channel of the REIT Sector   243

    Unfavorable Implications   245

Selecting the Best Apartments in the REIT
Apartment Building   245

    Technical Tactics   245

    Fundamental Strategies   246

    Further Information   248

Summing Up   249

**Chapter 10: Opportunities Abroad—
Investing from Brazil to Britain   251**

Emerging Markets   252

Many Overseas Markets Outperform the U.S.
Stock Market   254

    Long-Term Results Reflect the Potential in
    Foreign Stocks   256

Participating in the Growth of Overseas Stocks   256

    American Depository Receipts   257

    Overseas-Based ETFs vs. Open-Ended International
    Mutual Funds   261

    Closed-End Overseas Mutual Funds   265

When to Invest in Overseas Equity Mutual Funds
and ETFs   270

Which International Funds to Buy   271

Investing in International Bond Mutual Funds for Income and
for Currency Protection/Speculation   274

    Open-End International Mutual Fund Investment   274

    Higher-Quality International Bond Funds   275

    Lower-Quality International Bond Funds   275

    Closed-End Bond Funds   275

Balancing the Risks and the Potential Reward   276

Ongoing Currency Diversification Is a Useful
Strategy in and of Itself   278

Your Best Approaches to Overseas Opportunities   279

Chapter 11: How to Get the Most from Closed-End Mutual Funds   283

Open-End Mutual Funds   284

Unit Investment Trusts   285

Closed-End Funds   287

How to Buy $1 Worth of Stock or Bonds for Only 85 Cents!   288

    Discounts Mean Opportunity   290

    Finding the Special Bargains   290

    Larger-Than-Average Discounts from Net Asset Value
    Provide Increased Safety as Well as Increased
    Opportunity for Profit   293

    Taking Advantage of Premium-Discount Relationships   294

    Leverage Means Increased Opportunity but
    Also Increased Volatility and Risk   298

Strongly Performing Closed-End Mutual Funds   299

Chapter 12: Inflation—Coexisting and Even Profiting with Inflation   301

What Is Inflation?   301

The Benefits of Inflation   302

Runaway Inflation   303

Dealing with Inflation   304

    Income Investment—Borrow Long Term, Lend
    Short Term   304

Adjustable-Rate Bonds—Pretty Good, but Beware
of the Joker in the Deck   306

Commodity Investment—an Ongoing Hedge
Against Inflation   307

    Benefiting from Rising Commodity Prices   309

    Summing Up   313

Final Thoughts   314

Chapter 13: Reviewing Our Array of Opportunity Strategies 315

Ideally Achieved Investment Goals   315

Strategies to Control Risk   316

Investment Climates and Recommended Investments   319

    Periods of Sharply Rising Prices   319

    Periods of Steady but Moderate Inflation   320

    Periods of Deflation—Prices Decline   321

Specific Investment Strategies   322

    Timing the Stock Market   322

    Timing Investments in the Bond Markets   324

    Selecting Mutual Funds and Other Investments   325

The Basic Five-Step Investment Sequence   327

Suggested Reading   328

    Periodicals   329

    Books   330

    Newsletters   331

Index   335

ACKNOWLEDGMENTS

I would like to acknowledge all the many stock market technical and fundamental analysts from whom I have learned over the years and, in particular, those (such as Ned Davis, Yale Hirsch, and Jeffrey Hirsch, and others) whose research and knowledge have contributed to my understanding of the stock market and to the content of this work.

I also want to acknowledge the assistance of the research and portfolio staff at Signalert Corporation—Dr. Marvin Appel, Roni Nelson, Bonnie Gortler, Glenn Gortler, Arthur Appel, and Joon Choi—whose editorial and research contributions have been invaluable.

My thanks, too, to the editorial staff and book reviewers at Prentice-Hall for their encouragement and support and for their comments and suggestions, which have been very helpful in my efforts to produce a useful and readable work.

And finally, as always, my thanks to my wife of 50 years, Judy, for all she is and for all she has ever been.

Gerald Appel

INTRODUCTION: NEW OPPORTUNITIES

The world is changing.

If you have any doubt, just check out any major daily newspaper.

You will see the nexus of economic and political power shifting from Europe—possibly even from the United States—to China, Korea, South America, and other developing areas. You will see threats to world security emanating from such relatively minor powers as North Korea, Iran, and even Brazil, which has been contemplating its own nuclear development.

Some of this is bad news. Some not. Change is often associated with problems, anxiety, and fear. It is also associated with challenge. It may also be associated with progress, improvement, and opportunity.

Which is what this book is about. It is designed to help investors make the most of opportunities that lie within the United States and outside of the United States. Such opportunities include the usual—stocks, bonds, mutual funds, and money market instruments. Such opportunities also include areas with which most investors remain relatively unfamiliar—commodities, overseas bonds, foreign stocks, real estate–related instruments, and investments in developing countries. You will learn where such opportunities lie, of excellent vehicles in which to invest, how to time your purchases and sales, and how to create well-diversified and balanced portfolios that are appropriate to your stage of life and financial situation.

Perhaps even more important, you will learn how to contain and reduce risks associated with investing—timing techniques, diversification strategies, ways of recognizing "bargain-basement" prices, and strategies for profiting from inflationary trends as well as from deflation.

The Need for Active Management

The need for investors to be informed and active in their own management has, if anything, been increasing and is likely to continue to increase in the future. Movements are already under way to delay and/or reduce retirement benefits that accrue from Social Security, which would remove a major economic prop for many families. In addition, there have been initiatives to "privatize" Social Security, to make the individual beneficiaries rather than the government responsible for the financial growth of their Social Security assets, mirroring the responsibility for decisions that many investors now make within their 401K and other retirement plans. Many areas of decision making and risk are likely to be transferred from the government to the individual. The consequences of uninformed investing may well prove considerable.

Active, Informed, Self-Management

The passive investor may place his investment capital into one or two well-known mutual funds, hoping for the long-term best. Perhaps he may rely on his stock brokerage to select his investment portfolio. In both cases, he is likely to be relying on management whose interests almost certainly lie with encouraging investor passivity, in promoting buy and hold strategies through thick and thin, and who, because of the large amount of capital and large numbers of investors under their management, will tend toward investing conformity. This approach may have been fine during the 1980s and 1990s, two outstanding decades for the stock market. It has not worked well since then and may or may not serve investor purposes in the future.

The actively managing investor may seek information—and even some guidance—from many sources. Such investors, however, will process and evaluate such information themselves, will come to their own decisions, and will act based on long- and short-term plans for investment that are modified as new investment opportunities develop and as old ones recede.

They will adapt a true management style, establishing long- and shorter-term investment objectives, balancing potential reward and risks, remaining flexible—ready to change course if and when investment conditions change. They will learn and apply investment techniques that are useful in this regard.

The purpose of this book is to help *you* become one of the *they*.

How This Book Will Help

Opportunity Investing has been structured to provide benefit to readers who have only limited inclination/time to monitor their investments and even more benefit to investors who are willing to put additional time and effort into their investment programs.

The initial sections of *Opportunity Investing* show you a range of more familiar and basic investment areas, profit potentials and pitfalls, and strategies for constructing portfolios for greater returns at lower risk. We review which investments are likely to produce greater returns during periods of inflation and which during periods of deflation. You will learn where you can secure high levels of income commensurate with risk and the benefits of and strategies associated with diversification (including diversification by time, investment sector, and geography). You will learn how to select open- and closed-end mutual funds and exchange-traded funds (ETFs) most likely to succeed and will be provided with a "starter portfolio" of the less than 1% of mutual funds that have met certain criteria for long-term excellence in performance. You will also learn how you can improve your investing performance considerably—quite considerably—by the application of just one investment technique alone.

As the book progresses, more active and involved investors will learn general and investment-specific techniques of market timing—which are designed to help you know when to enter the various investment arenas and when to hold assets in cash and cash equivalents. You will learn how to measure the relative strength of different investments so that your portfolio may be rebalanced to emphasize those areas that are performing the best while de-emphasizing investment areas that are underperforming.

In short, you will first learn techniques designed to help you decide what to buy and how to structure your investment portfolio. This, alone, should improve your investment results. You will then learn when to invest and when to stand aside. This should further improve returns.

We live in a world of change, of challenges, and of opportunity. Let's move along now to enter into that world!

1

THE MYTH OF BUY
AND HOLD

What do the companies Radio Corporation of America (RCA), Cisco, General Motors (GM), Trans World Airlines (TWA), Admiral, and Pan American Airways (Pan Am), have in common? These are or were significant American, for the most part New York Stock Exchange listed, corporations that have, in years past, risen to and then fallen from grace. Shares of Cisco, for example, rose from a price of 4 in 1992 to 82 in early 2000 before falling back to 8 by the end of 2004. GM, once the granddaddy of all corporations and the largest employer in the country? Priced at 11 at the bottom of the great 1973–1974 bear market, GM recovered to a price of 94 at the start of 2000, before declining to 31 three years later, to lower still and near bankruptcy by the fourth quarter of 2005. Wal-Mart, with more than 1.1 million U.S. employees, has—of course—supplanted GM as the nation's leading private employer.

RCA, a pioneer in home radios and radio communication during the 1920s, rose from a price of 11 in the mid-1920s to 114 by

September 1929 before plummeting to 3 in 1932. Admiral, a hot television issue in the 1960s, met a similar fate—and never did recover. TWA and Pan Am, once investor favorites, both failed to survive shakeouts in the airline industry. The drug industry has generally been regarded as one of the more consistent investment sectors for investors, but this has not prevented Merck's roller coaster ride from 6 to 72 and down to 28. Another major *M*, Merrill Lynch, has seen its price range from 6 to 91 and then back to 26, like Merck within just one decade.

Such ups and downs are not limited to individual securities. The NASDAQ Composite of more than 3,500 issues rose from a price level of approximately 230 in 1984 to 5133 in 2000, before falling to 1108 at the bear market low in 2002. Even the more venerable Standard & Poor's 500 Index has recently given up as much as 49.7%, declining from 1,527.46 (2000) to 768.63 (2002).

The point of all this is simply that, regardless of what Wall Street and the mutual fund industry would have you believe, there are considerable risks to buying and holding stocks, even for long-term investors, and especially for investors who may need to draw on their assets during periods in which the stock market is showing significant cyclical weakness (for example, during the 1930s, 1973–1974, and more recently, between 2000 and early 2005).

Moreover, buy and hold strategies, which actually worked well during the 1980s and 1990s, the two strongest back–to-back decades in history, are not as likely to work as well in the foreseeable future. The economist Paul Krugman, writing in *The New York Times*, February 1, 2005, observed that whereas annual economic growth in the United States averaged 3.4% over the previous 75 years, it is likely to average only 1.9% between 2005 and 2080. Inasmuch as the progress of stock prices tends to reflect economic growth, investors who limit themselves to just the U.S. stock market may be placing themselves in a position from which it will be difficult to achieve the rates of capital growth required for expenses later in life.

Variable Rates of Return from Stocks

Figure 1-1 illustrates the variability in the performance of the stock market over the 75-year period of 1930 through 2004.

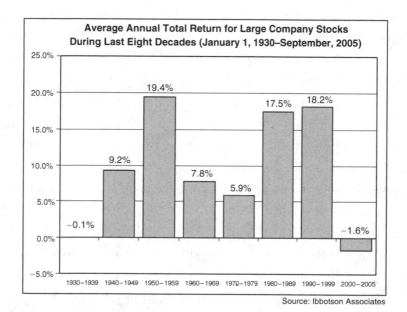

Average Annual Total Return for Large Company Stocks During Last Eight Decades (January 1, 1930–September, 2005)

Source: Ibbotson Associates

FIGURE 1-1   Strong decades tend to alternate with weaker investment decades.

As a general rule, rates of gain from stock ownership tend to fluctuate, decade by decade, with strong decades generally alternating with weaker decades. The favorable two-decade period from 1980 to 1999 was unusually long in this regard. The weakness between 2000 and 2005 represented the long period required by the stock market to readjust down to more normal valuations following the speculative excesses of the previous two decades.

Investor expectations of the stock market tend to follow rather than lead significant changes in the stock market climate. For example, if investors were "irrationally exuberant" during the 1920s (as Chairman Alan Greenspan of the Federal Reserve said they were during the 1990s), they became extremely cautious following the stock market crash of 1929— a caution fed by the great depression and by the fact that stocks did not do much more than break even during the 1930s. Stocks were priced to reflect the general pessimism, with "riskier" stock dividend yields higher than prevailing bond interest payouts.

Investors remained cautious into the 1940s, which did show marked improvements in the behavior of the stock market, with annual rates of return from stocks increasing to 9.2% for the decade, roughly average for the stock market during the twentieth century, and increasing still further to 19.4% during the 1950s.

Such growth rates helped to foster more optimistic expectations of the stock market—this was the period of front-end, multiyear, mutual fund purchase contracts; high entry commissions into load mutual funds; and a dramatic increase in the number of American families holding shares. It should not have been surprising then that bear markets developed relatively early during the 1960s—a short but serious bear market during 1962, another during 1966, and another yet as the decade drew to a close. As a whole, however, stocks were profitable during the 1960s.

Stock market instability did extend from the start of a bear market at the end of 1968 into the 1970s, with an ongoing bear market ranging into May 1970 and stocks declining between 1973 and 1974 (and again in 1977). These periods favored stock "traders" as opposed to long-term stock investors. And then came those two glorious decades, the 1980s and the 1990s!

The confluence of developing technologies, the passing of the depression generation, the end of the cold war, economic growth, falling interest rates, and rising speculation resulted in consistently rising stock prices (only occasionally interrupted by intermediate market declines). These gains were fueled by increasing speculation and by a general belief that rising stock prices were going to be forever. By the peak of the bull market in 2000, stocks in the Standard & Poor's 500 Index were, on average, yielding less than 1% in dividends and were selling at $46 per share for every dollar of company profits and at nearly $6 per share for every dollar of company assets—

all told, at the highest ratios of price to measures of actual share values since the early 1930s.

And then, in March 2000, reality returned.

Speculative Bubbles Are Often Followed by Years of Below-Average Investment Performance

The Japanese stock market has still not recovered following the market peak that developed between 1989 and 1990.

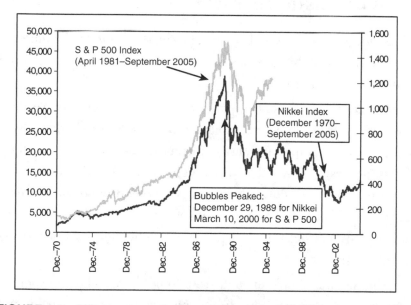

FIGURE 1-2   Fifteen years of underperformance following the peak of the Japanese bull market.

There have been numerous trading opportunities in the Japanese stock market since the peak of its speculative bubble as 1989 drew to a close, but longer-term investors have not had an easy time.

Figure 1-2 shows the Standard & Poor's 500 Index aligned below the Japanese Nikkei Index in such a way that their peaks and prepeak periods align. The similarity of these two markets is actually quite striking. If the Standard & Poor's 500 Index were to follow the path of the Japanese stock market, a full market recovery would not get under way until at least 2010.

This would not be unusual. Gold reached a peak level of approximately $800 an ounce during a final buying panic during the late winter of 1980. Prices remained below $500 an ounce through most of 2005—a full 26 years after—before rising during the first four months of 2006 to above $650 per ounce.

The Moral of the Story—Be a Flexible, Opportunistic Investor

Please forgive me if I have been belaboring the point, but so much of the "general wisdom" advises investors not to worry, to "stay the course," to trust in stocks.

I believe that the stock market offers fine opportunity. So does the bond market. So do commodities markets. So do markets overseas, coins, stamps, watches, antiques, art, and real estate. Opportunities for favorable investment occur frequently in some investor areas, less frequently in others. The best opportunities usually develop when the majority of investors are the most cautious or indifferent. They occur less frequently when the universal majority is the most optimistic.

The moral is simple enough. You do not have to be an expert in every area of potential opportunity. Or even in most. Probably not even in many. But you should be sufficiently familiar with at least a sufficient number of investment markets to be able to maintain diversified, flexible portfolios in a variety of investment sectors. In the process, you should be familiar enough with the behavior of the various markets in which you invest to be able to create and maintain exit strategies for when the time comes to cash in your chips.

Growth Targets—"The Magic 20"

Pretty much everyone likes to accumulate as much capital as possible. Some, obviously, succeed more than others. Spending patterns vary from individual to individual, family to family, and often by geographic location. However, the majority of families manage well if they accumulate an amount of capital that amounts to 20 times the amount of annual expenses that they incur—the "magic 20."

Why 20? Well, if you have 20 times as much capital as you spend each year, and you secure an annual rate of return on your investments of just 5% per year (generally achievable with minimum risk from instruments such as treasury bonds and the like), you will be able to maintain your ongoing living standard with minimal risk—at least for a relatively limited period of time (because a 5% rate of return is equivalent to one twentieth of your assets). It would, of course, be desirable to tack on something extra for the effects of inflation, at least until very late in life when you can allow your asset base to dwindle. It would be even more desirable if you could grow your assets after deductions for expenses, taxes, and inflation.

Inflation, incidentally, is no small matter. Money loses roughly one half its value every 16 years as a result of inflation. At age 60, Americans have an average life expectancy of approximately another 22 years. If you retire at 65, your retirement nest egg will be worth just about half its current value by the time you reach the age of 81. The income your assets produce, if they remain unchanged, will suffice to provide just about one half of the goods, services, travel, home expenses, and everything else that you could afford when you retired.

If we were to assume an average rate of inflation of 4% per year (actually higher than the past average) and an average tax bite of 20%, you would have to earn approximately 11.25% per year on your capital to make up for taxes and inflation if you require a true, inflation-adjusted 5% per annum stream of income.

Example

- $1,000,000 asset base (required living expense income = $50,000)
- You earn $112,500 or 11.25% on your investments.
- Your tax bill comes to $22,500 (20% of $112,500).
- This leaves you with $90,000 after taxes, of which $50,000 is used for living expenses.
- You add the difference, $40,000, (4% of your initial asset base) to your asset base to enlarge it to compensate for the 4% rate of inflation.

Looked at in this way, the "Magic 20" should be changed, perhaps, to something closer to the "Magic 40 or 45."

Growth Target Zone

Well, perhaps it comes down to this. Those of us who happen to be rich enough might well be able to settle for rates of return in the order of 5%. Such a return will probably result in some depletion of assets over the years, but if we are old enough or rich enough or both, this depletion can be tolerated with little risk of running out of money before we run out of time.

Those of us who are not fortunate enough to be that rich, or who are fortunate enough to have a longer-than-expected life span, may have to plan on either reducing our standard of living over the years or, preferably, increasing our rate of return. This second alternative is not necessarily an easy matter, but we will set as a general goal the achievement of rates of return in the order of 11.25% or higher by the use of the timing and asset-allocation strategies that you will be learning.

In short, the "Magic 20" will become the "Hoped-For 45."

Active as Opposed to Passive Management of Assets

The Wall Street establishment generally espouses the cause of passive investment management. Buy your favorite stocks or mutual funds or bonds, hold on through thick and thin, and hope that the stock and bonds markets are on upswings when you need the money. Not necessarily the worst of strategies—unless, of course, you happened to need to draw on your capital in mid-2002, at a time when stocks were more than 50%, on average, below their all-time peaks.

By the time you finish this book, you can be a successful active manager of your own investments and by so doing add to the returns available from the usual sources to passive investors. As an active manager, you will be able to do the following:

- Actively monitor the investment universe and select investment areas—and individual investments within those areas—likely to outperform the average investment of similar risk. In other words, you will have some idea as to when to emphasize bonds, stocks, gold, real estate, and international positions and when to opt for money market and other safe havens.

- You will have the ability to enter, and will enter, into investments relatively early in their rise and exit relatively close to their peak, either prior to or relatively soon after the final top is made. This does not mean that you have to be the first one in and the first one out. It does mean that you will be able to catch the major portion of up moves, while avoiding at least significant portions of the downswings that plague every investment at some time or other.

- And finally, you will be alert to special opportunities that develop from time to time in almost all investment areas and be able, ready, and willing to take advantage of such opportunities.

The benefits of active and successful management are self-evident.

Diversification—A Major Key to Successful Investing

If you do nothing else as part of your active management, you are likely to reduce risk considerably and probably even add to your returns by maintaining proper diversification in your investment account.

Diversification means allocating your investments in different areas so that your portfolio's various investment segments do not tend to rise and fall at the same time but instead, as a group, move more smoothly and with less volatility than any single investment alone. Mutual funds are popular because, to some extent, all mutual funds provide some element of diversification compared to the purchase of one or two single stocks and therefore involve less risk. You will learn more about diversification as you progress through this book. For now, let's just consider some ways in which you might diversify your portfolios.

Geographic Diversification in the Developing Global Economy

There have clearly been many changes in the balance of economies across the world. For years and years, the U.S. economy and, to a lesser extent, the economies of Europe were dominant in the world, reflected in the strength of the various stock and bond markets of the Western world. Japan eventually emerged, during the 1980s, as a major national success. The Japanese market soared into its own speculative bubble, which came to a conclusion at the end of 1989 and has not fully recovered since.

Figure 1-3 illustrates the significant shift that has taken place in the relative performance of the U.S.-based Standard & Poor's 500 Index and a cross-section of overseas stock markets as reflected in the EAFE Index.

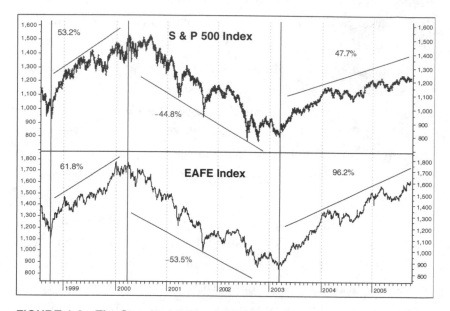

FIGURE 1-3   The Standard & Poor's 500 Index versus the EAFE Index, 1999–2005.

The U.S. market clearly led the EAFE (Europe, Australia, Far East) Index in its performance between 1995 and 1999, rising by 231% compared to 69% for the EAFE Index during this period. The performance of these two indices became more equal during the bear market, 2000–2002, with foreign markets clearly taking the lead in performance starting in 2003.

In recent years, particularly since 2002, economic strength has expanded from the United States to countries such as China (most obvious), India, New Zealand, Mexico, Brazil, and Australia (to name just a few). Whereas manufacturing nations led the world economically in the past, nations that provide the commodities needed by those manufacturing nations have risen more recently in relative

economic strength and power. As a result, the currency of New Zealand, which has a commodity-based economy, has become competitive over the years with the U.S. dollar. The New Zealand stock market, which generally lagged the American stock market in strength, has also, in recent years, become competitive with our own stock market, as have stock markets in many of the emerging nations previously mentioned.

Economic strength abroad relative to strength in the United States has been reflected in the relative strength of currencies as well as the relative strength of stock markets. The Canadian dollar, for example, has shown long-term strength superior to the long-term strength of the U.S. dollar. (We return to currency relationships when we consider investment opportunities in bonds issued by foreign countries.)

The moral of the story should be apparent enough. For decades, even though foreign stock markets did enjoy some periods in which they outperformed the U.S. stock markets, the name of the game was to buy American. This is no longer the case. The present strategy of choice is to keep track of stock markets across the world, identify the market leaders, and diversify at least a portion of your assets among the leading stock markets worldwide. You will learn how to do this and where you can readily find investment vehicles to employ.

Diversifying Geographically in Foreign Bond Markets as well as in Domestic Income Investments

In a similar vein, credit instruments issued by foreign governments often provide opportunities that are superior to domestic credit instruments. For example, at a time during 2004, when American 1-year Treasury notes were yielding approximately 2%, 1-year New Zealand Treasury notes, fully backed by the New Zealand government, were yielding in excess of 6% per year. There was virtually no

credit risk involved, although there were risks associated with currency relationships. Inasmuch as investors had to convert U.S. dollars into New Zealand dollars to make the purchase, and inasmuch as the investment remained denominated in New Zealand dollars, your income would be supplemented by currency gains if the New Zealand dollar continued to rise against the American dollar or would be offset by potential currency losses if the New Zealand dollar were to decline against the American dollar.

In effect, you were virtually guaranteed an extra 4% per year in interest income, and you might or might not improve this differential as a result of currency fluctuations. Given the weakness of the U.S. dollar at the time, the investment offered a double opportunity to aggressive income investors.

Many mutual funds—open-end as well as closed-end funds (funds traded on the various stock exchanges that have a fixed number of shares and that trade between existing shareholders and new shareholders)—provide access into foreign stock markets and into foreign income instruments. You will learn more about such funds throughout this book.

In the meantime, start to think globally. The diversification should reduce risk and, in many cases, will most likely improve opportunity and return, too.

Sector Diversification for Smoother Performance and Risk Reduction

Tables 1-1 and 1-2 illustrate the benefits of diversifying investment portfolios to include a variety of market sectors whose prices do not generally rise and fall simultaneously so that losses in some areas are generally offset by advances or by lesser loss elsewhere. The total portfolio, as a result, usually performs better than its parts taken separately.

TABLE 1-1   Nine Investment Classes*

Performance of Each Class of Investment Taken Separately
June 1980 through November 2004

Sector	Average Gain per Annum	Maximum Open Drawdown°°
Financials	17.1%	–35.1%
Health Care	16.0	–39.6
Real Estate	13.1	–21.9
Utilities	11.6	–45.3
Dow Jones Transports	11.2	–45.5
Energy	9.1	–46.7
Gold/Precious Metals	5.0	–68.9
Lehman Aggregate Bonds	9.5	–9.0
Global Bond	9.3	–9.1
Average, All Sectors	11.3%	–35.7%
Average, Excluding Bonds	11.9%	–43.3%

° The above table represents the average performance of universes of mutual funds that designate investments in these areas as their primary objective. The Dow Jones Transports and the Lehman Aggregate Bond Index are the exception. They reflect the performance of these price indices, including in the Lehman Bond Index, interest payouts from bond holdings, and the price movement of bonds included in the index.

°° "Maximum open drawdown" represents the largest decline in the value of investments in the above areas from a peak to a low point in value until new highs in equity value were achieved. This must be considered the minimum risk level of any investment because investors, during the period shown, did actually incur these levels of loss.

TABLE 1-2   Nine Investment Classes—as in Table 1-1—Grouped into One Portfolio

Starting with an Equal Amount of Assets in Each
June 1980 through November 2004°

Equal Starting Amounts, Including Bond Sectors, No Rebalancing	
Average Gain per Annum for Total Portfolio	12.6%
Maximum Open Drawdown	–22.4%

Equal Starting Amounts, Excluding Bond Sectors, No Rebalancing	
Average Gain per Annum for Total Portfolio	13.2%
Maximum Open Drawdown	–26.2%

Equal Starting Amounts, Including Bond Sectors.
Equalize Sector Assets at Start of Each Year, Including Bond Sectors

Average Gain per Annum for Total Portfolio	12.3%
Maximum Open Drawdown	–19.7%

Equal Starting Amounts, Excluding Bond Sectors.
Equalize Sector Assets at Start of Each Year

Average Gain per Annum for Total Portfolio	13.0%
Maximum Open Drawdown	–24.2%

° In portfolios that are not rebalanced, it is presumed that assets were equally divided at the onset of the study period (1980) and from that time forward assets were neither added to nor removed from any segment of the portfolio. At the end of the study period, then, some market sectors had increased in their proportionate size; some had decreased.

In the portfolios that were equalized at the end of each year, assets were redistributed at the start of the new year so that each sector started once again with the same-size portfolio.

Points of Special Interest

- Sectors, taken by themselves, produced an average annual rate of gain of 11.9% (no bonds) and 11.3% (with the two bond sectors). Maximum drawdowns were –43.3% (no bonds) and –35.7% (with bonds), respectively, for the average sector. The inclusion of bonds in the portfolio reduced the average rate of return from 11.9% to 11.3%, reduced the average maximum risk from –43.3% to –35.7% (a fair enough risk/reward tradeoff).

- A portfolio of the above sectors, invested as a portfolio, produced an average annual gain of 13.2% (no bonds) and 12.6% (with the two bond sectors). Maximum drawdowns were –26.2% and –22.4%, respectively. This portfolio was not rebalanced at any time. The inclusion of bonds in the portfolio reduced both average rates of return and risk.

- A portfolio of the above sectors, invested as a portfolio, assets rebalanced so as to start each year equally, produced an average annual gain of 13.0% (no bonds) and 12.3% (with two bond sectors). Maximum drawdowns were –24.2% and –19.7%, respectively.

> - Rebalancing portfolios at the start of each year smoothed out performance to some degree—reducing both the average rate of returns and the maximum risks associated with investing in diversified portfolios.
>
> This study illustrates the benefits of diversification. Rates of return generally show moderate rates of improvement. Risk levels generally improve significantly.

We return to issues regarding diversification, including additional ideas for portfolio structure, in Chapter 2, "Putting Together a Winning Portfolio."

Income Investing—Time Diversification

You will learn more about income investing along the way, particularly in Chapter 4, "Income Investing—Safer and Steady . . . But Watch Out for the Pitfalls," so at this time we limit the area of income investment diversification to issues involving time diversification in the establishment of a bond portfolio.

As a general rule—not always—the more distant the maturity of a bond (the date when the loan signified by the bond is due to be paid to bondholders), all else being equal, the higher the interest return you will receive as an investor. This should not be surprising. A bond represents a loan by the bondholder to the bond issuer, who is the borrower. A loan that is to be repaid in, say, 20 years, carries many more risks than a loan that is to be repaid in 20 days. Such risks include potential inflation over the life of the loan—the greater the inflation, the less will be the value of the repayment in today's dollar purchasing power, the higher will be prevailing interest rates in the future, and the lower will be the face as well as the real value of the bonds you own. There are also risks associated with the solvency of the borrower. (Who would have thought in 1985 that in 2005 bonds issued by General Motors would be down rated to junk status?)

Investors, therefore, must decide between the benefits of receiving higher rates of return from longer-term bond investments and the additional risks involved. As a general rule, it is probably better to purchase intermediate bonds—bonds whose maturities lie, say, between five and seven years—than to purchase longer-term bonds. Intermediate-term bonds pay approximately 80% to 85% the rate of interest of long-term bonds but are considerably more stable in price. For example, in mid-April 2005, 5-year Treasury notes provided yields of 4.13%, whereas 20-year bonds provided yields of 4.87%. The 5-year note's interest payments were as much as 84.8% the size of the 20-year bond, even though the implied loan was for only 25% the length of time.

Creating a Bond Time Ladder

It is possible for ongoing bond investors to gradually develop a portfolio that ultimately secures yields associated with longer-term bonds although the actual holdings of the portfolio are, on average, more intermediate term in nature. The strategy, which reduces many of the risks associated with bond investment, works like this.

Suppose that interest returns from U.S. government bonds, trading at par (face value), are spread so that 2-year Treasury notes are paying 3.7%; 4-year notes are paying 4.0%; 6-year notes are paying 4.2%; 8-year notes are paying 4.4%; and 10-year notes are paying 4.6%. These were rates actually available during the spring of 2005. You are attracted by the higher yields of the 10-year notes but believe that risks in the bond markets may be high and that it might be more prudent to concentrate your portfolio in the shortest-term area, the 2-year note. However, you would prefer returns that are greater than 3.7%. The issue might be resolved by the creation of a bond ladder.

Your bond ladder, in this case, might consist of the following:

20% of assets are placed into 2-year notes, yielding 3.7%.

20% of assets are placed into 4-year notes, yielding 4.0%.

20% of assets are placed into 6-year notes, yielding 4.2%.

20% of assets are placed into 8-year notes, yielding 4.4%.

20% of assets are placed into 10-year notes, yielding 4.6%.

The average yield for the entire portfolio comes to 4.18%. The average maturity is 6 years.

Year-by-Year Management of the Bond Ladder

You have established a portfolio that provides considerable safety, because of the time diversification that is built in to it. Suppose, for example, that interest rates rise during the first 2 years of ownership. Well, at the end of 2 years, your first set of notes will mature. The original 4-year notes now have 2 years of life left; the original set of 6-year notes now have 4 years of life left in them. The original 10-year notes now have 8 years of life remaining. You redeem your original 2-year notes—now matured, ready to be paid off—and use the proceeds to buy new 10-year bonds. Because interest rates have been rising, you will be able to reinvest to secure higher rates of interest for your new investment than were available when you first established your ladder.

If rates had declined instead, your total portfolio would have increased in value, reflecting the reduction in general interest rates, while you were receiving the higher levels of interest rates that prevailed when you first established the ladder.

Every 2 years, you cash in bonds due for redemption, for which you receive their face value, reinvesting in the new longest-term bonds that are coming out. Gradually, your original 10-year notes become 2-year notes, carrying minimum risk but paying a rate of return more typical of longer-term bonds.

If we assume that at the end of 10 years interest rates stand where they stood when you first established your ladder, your entire portfolio will be yielding 4.6%, the rate paid by the original 10-year note. However, the average maturity of your holdings will have become 6 years. If you go forward, maintaining the bond ladder, your portfolio will continue to produce rates of return associated with longer-term bonds, while it carries risks more associated with intermediate-term bonds.

This is not necessarily the most exciting of investment strategies, but it is a strategy that is relatively simple to follow (certainly so with the help of your brokerage bond department) and is excellent for conservative income investing.

Increasing Returns from the Stock Market while Reducing Risk

The strategies discussed so far relate only to the structuring of more efficient investment portfolios (and particularly to the benefits of various forms of diversification). We have not, as yet, even considered strategies associated with stock market timing, the attempt at least to make investments at the most appropriate periods in the investment cycle: to buy near market lows or at least relatively early in price up-trends and to sell near market highs or at least relatively early in price downtrends.

Successful market timing, like well-considered diversification, can help you to both increase returns from your investments and to reduce risks associated with buy and hold investments. If you are a typical investor, you are probably better off avoiding short-term trading, which places heavy demands on time, increases investment expenses, and which has become generally more difficult in recent years.

Useful Market Mood Indicators That You Can Maintain and Use in Just a Few Minutes Each Week

Market mood indicators are indicators that can help you identify the general outlook for the stock and bond markets—whether credit conditions, public psychology, and the behavior of the stock market itself are suggesting a generally favorable or a generally unfavorable outlook for stocks and bonds. Mood indicators do not provide precise entry and exit points into the stock market but do provide guidance as to how fully you may want to be invested and/or whether you want to emphasize aggressive or more conservative positions in your investment portfolios.

Illustrations of Mood Indicators

Public Psychology Mood Indicator

Probably the best mood indicator of all is the general mood of the investing public and particularly of the financial media. Reflections of public and media investment psychology should be approached in a contrary manner. The more bullish the general public, and especially the more bullish the articles appearing in magazines and newspapers, the closer we likely are to a significant market peak. Conversely, the most bearish articles regarding the stock market tend to appear on the front pages of newspapers *after* the stock market has undergone some serious decline, fairly close to the times that such declines are likely to come to a conclusion.

You can often secure an informal feel for public sentiment from conversations with your friends, family, and acquaintances. The more people who want to tell you how much money they have made and how smart they have been—it is very easy to confuse a rising stock market with being smart—the more likely that trouble is lurking on the horizon. Conversely, the more people hate stocks, the more fearful they are, the more likely are prospects for a market recovery. (Bad as public timing can be, the media is probably worse.)

Your emotional task, of course, is to avoid being swayed by the crowd and by the appealing newspaper and magazine crews and to be prepared to travel a more lonely, independent, and probably more profitable path to your own rather than the public drummer.

Interest Rate Indicators

As a general rule—not always—stocks tend to perform better during periods of declining interest rates compared to periods of rising interest rates.

It is often worthwhile to follow announcements and commentary from the Federal Reserve Board, which has the ability to control short-term interest rates directly and usually longer-term rates indirectly. In past times, two or three consecutive interest rate reductions by the Fed without intervening actions to increase rates would suffice to end bear markets, and two or three consecutive interest rate increases would suffice to end bull markets. In recent years, market responses to patterns of action by the Fed have taken longer to develop. The 2000–2002 bear market did not come to an end until the Fed reduced short-term rates 12 times in succession. The ensuing bull market did not seriously falter until seven consecutive rate increases were fostered by the Fed.

Significant actions by the Fed—which can include raising or lowering discount rates, setting maximum margin levels, and/or changing the federal funds rate—are reported in financial media such as the *Barron's Financial Weekly*. Television programs that concentrate on financial news report frequently on news releases from the Federal Reserve Board.

Seasonal Mood Indicators

The stock market tends to perform best between the start of November and the end of April, when almost all net gains for stocks take place. The period between May and October tends to do little better than breaking even on balance. The market also tends to perform best during the years immediately prior to years of presidential elections (for example, 1991, 1995, 1999, and 2003), well during the years of presidential elections, and worst during the two years following presidential elections. This pattern seems to be holding as we move into the twenty-first century. Stocks did very well in 1999 (year prior to election), topped a little early in 2000 (year of election), fell badly in 2001 and 2002 (years following election), and then recovered very strongly in 2003 (best year of cycle, year prior to the 2004 election).

These two seasonal indicators—best six months of the year and the presidential market cycle—have actually had a strong history of accurate past performance.

A Great Market Mood Indicator: The NASDAQ/NYSE Index Relative Strength Indicator

The oldest and most established trading exchange in the United States is the New York Stock Exchange, home to most of the largest corporations in the country. The American Stock Exchange lists somewhat smaller companies and has not been nearly as influential as the New York Stock Exchange. The NASDAQ Composite Index, home to over-the-counter rather than exchange-traded securities, used to be thought of as the home of small, emerging, and more speculative companies. This is still the case to some degree, but in recent years many companies listed on NASDAQ—such as Intel, Cisco, e-Bay, Yahoo!, Microsoft, and even Starbucks—have grown to be among the most prosperous of market leaders and technical innovators.

The NASDAQ Composite, like the New York Stock Exchange Index and the Standard & Poor's 500 Index, is weighted by capitalization. Larger companies are given more weight in the index than smaller companies. In fact, in April 2005, the five largest companies on NASDAQ—Microsoft, QUALCOMM, Intel, Apple Computer, and Cisco—represented 25% of the NASDAQ Composite Index. There were, at the time, approximately 3,500 issues listed on both the NASDAQ Composite Index and the New York Stock Exchange, with trading volume more or less equal on both exchanges, increasing on NASDAQ in recent years so that on most days trading volume there exceeds volume on the New York Exchange.

Relationships of Price Movements on NASDAQ and the New York Stock Exchange

Stocks on NASDAQ tend to move more rapidly than stocks on the more conservatively oriented New York Stock Exchange, so the NASDAQ Composite itself is approximately usually 125% to 150% as volatile as indices such as the Standard & Poor's 500 Index. Given this higher volatility, it is not surprising that the NASDAQ Composite often (not always) rises more rapidly than the New York Stock Exchange Index (a weighted average of all stocks on the New York Stock Exchange) when stocks are favorably trended and falls more rapidly during less-positive periods.

In addition, when investors are most optimistic, they are more likely to invest in speculative areas. When investors are most negative, they tend to turn to more defensive and conservative stocks.

For whatever the reasons—and there may be many—the stock market has tended to perform better when the NASDAQ Composite is leading the New York Stock Exchange Index in relative strength and to perform less well when the New York Stock

Exchange is leading in strength. It is not only the NASDAQ Composite that performs best when the NASDAQ is leading in relative strength; the New York Stock Exchange Index produces improved profit/loss relationships during such periods, too. Figure 1-4 illustrates these observations.

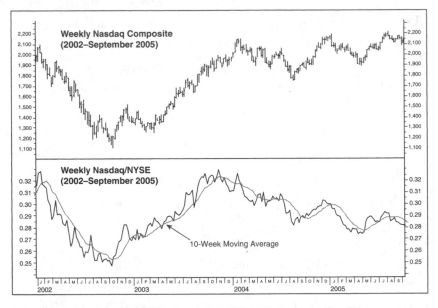

FIGURE 1-4   The NASDAQ Composite/New York Stock Exchange relative strength indicator, 2002–September 2005.

The price movements of both the NASDAQ Composite and the New York Stock Exchange Index have tended to show rising prices during periods that the NASDAQ Composite leads the New York Stock Exchange in strength and to decline when the relative strength indicator suggests that NASDAQ is the weaker market sector.

The stock market does not necessarily decline in price when the New York Stock Exchange Index leads the NASDAQ in relative strength. There are times when stocks advance, nonetheless. However, on balance, net gains take place when NASDAQ leads, again not just in NASDAQ but in other market sectors, too.

The NASDAQ/New York Stock Exchange relative strength indicator is designed to help investors identify in an objective manner periods in which NASDAQ is leading in strength (and therefore periods when the stock market is most likely to succeed).

How to Identify Periods When NASDAQ Is the Stronger Market Area

The steps involved have to be taken only once each week, after the close of the final trading session of the week. The entire process should take just a few minutes. Signals, created at these times, carry for the entire week following, until the next calculation takes place. Here are the procedures involved:

1. Secure at the end of each week the closing levels of the NAS-DAQ Composite and the New York Stock Exchange Index. These are readily available in *Barron's,* in the financial pages of virtually any major newspaper, and on almost any Web site relating to the stock market.

2. Divide the weekly closing level of the NASDAQ Composite by the closing level of the New York Stock Exchange Index to secure a weekly NASDAQ/NYSE Index relative strength ratio. For example, on April 22, 2005, the NASDAQ Composite closed at 1932.10, and the New York Stock Exchange Index closed at 7015.85. The weekly ratio, therefore, stood at .2754. (1932.10 divided by 7015.85 = .2754.)

3. Each week, calculate the average of the most recent 10 weekly ratios that you have calculated, as per Step 2. To do this, you add the most recent 10 weekly ratios and divide the total by 10. On the eleventh week, you drop the furthest week back so that you are always totaling and then averaging the most recent 10 weeks in your calculation. This is called a moving average.

Weekly ratios will increase if NASDAQ is rising more rapidly than the New York Stock Exchange Index. They will decrease if NASDAQ loses strength in relationship to the New York Stock Exchange Index.

4. Compare the most recent reading of the NASDAQ/NYSE Index relative strength ratio to its 10-week moving average. If the weekly relative strength ratio is greater than its 10-week moving average (for example, if the latest weekly ratio stands at .2750 and the 10-week moving average is .2746), consider the NASDAQ to be leading the New York Stock Exchange Index in relative strength. This will usually carry positive implications for the stock market. If the weekly relative strength ratio is below its 10-week moving average (for example, the ratio is .2745 and the 10-week average is .2750), consider the NYSE Index to be the stronger market area. This does not necessarily carry bearish implications but does indicate that the most favorable market climate, at least based on this indicator, is probably not in effect.

The following tabulations in Table 1-3 are hypothetical, based on retroactive research employing the parameters set forth above, and do not represent real-time performance for the entire period. The presumption is that investors would be invested in stocks only during favorable market periods (weekly NASDAQ/NYSE Index ratio above its 10-week moving average) and would be in cash at other times. No allowance is being made for commission and other transaction expenses or for tax consequences. Nor is any allowance being made for interest returns while in cash or for dividend payouts while in stocks.

TABLE 1-3   A 34-Year Historical Performance Record of the NASDAQ/NYSE Index Relative Strength Indicator, February 1971–April 2005*

Performance of the NASDAQ Composite Index

Buy and Hold	Average Gain per Annum	8.98%
	Maximum Open Drawdown	–77.42%
	Invested 100% of time	

Trading By The NASDAQ/NYSE Index Relative Strength Indicator

	Average Gain per Annum	11.28%
	Percentage of Time Invested	–54.6%
	Rate of Return While Invested	20.65%
	Number of Round-Trip Trades	–141 (4.1 per year)
	Maximum Open Drawdown	–39.72%

For the New York Stock Exchange Index

Buy and Hold	Average Gain per Annum	7.60%
	Maximum Open Drawdown	–49.78%
	Invested 100% of time	

Trading By the NASDAQ/NYSE Index Relative Strength Indicator

	Average Gain per Annum	7.59%
	Percentage of Time Invested	–54.6%
	Rate of Return While Invested	13.9%
	Number of Round Trip Trades	–141 (4.1 per year)
	Maximum Open Drawdown	–23.72%

° The employment of the NASDAQ/NYSE Index relative strength indicator, even as a sole determinant for stock market investment, would have improved both rates of return while invested as well as risk levels for the NASDAQ Composite, more than doubling rates of return achieved while investor capital was at risk in stock portfolios that replicated on a buy and hold basis the performance of the NASDAQ Composite Index. No credit has been given for income received while in cash.

The performance of the NYSE Index improved, too. This index produced almost identical returns when invested all the time as it did when it was invested only when the NASDAQ/NYSE timing indicator was favorable. However, rates of return while invested were clearly superior during periods that this model was favorable (+13.9% rate of return versus +7.59% for buy and hold). Risk levels were lower, too (–23.72% versus –49.78%).

No allowance has been made for trading expenses, but these would almost certainly be off-set by additional interest earned while in cash positions.

General Suggestions

Although the NASDAQ/NYSE Index relative strength indicator has been quite useful, and may be beneficially employed by investors who want to spend just a minimum of time in tracking the stock market, you will be learning other, somewhat more time-consuming, timing models that have been more efficient in the past when tracked in a very formal manner.

The NASDAQ/NYSE Index relative strength indicator is a fine "mood indicator," an indicator that reflects general levels of investor optimism and speculative interest (which usually favor stocks when they are high, if not too exuberant). Although the indicator does have its formal parameters, you might want to also evaluate trends. Is the indicator showing increasing or decreasing strength in NASDAQ versus the NYSE Index, even if no moving average reversal crossings have taken place? Does a crossing of the moving average by the weekly ratio seem imminent? Favorable buying junctures frequently take place when the NASDAQ Composite has been lagging the NYSE Index in relative strength but is showing signs of catching up. You probably have the idea by now.

We return to the matter of market timing in due course. Let's move along at this time to the creation of efficient investment portfolios.

2

Putting Together a
Winning Portfolio

More often than not, the typical investor's portfolio has been gradually assembled over diverse market climates, with the help of diverse
stockbrokers and an advisor, influenced by diverse fads and fashions,
and possibly is cluttered with diverse losing investments. ("It's not a
loss if I don't take it.") Sometimes such portfolios include long-standing favorites that have had their best days.

Some investors, often specialists regarding industries in which
they work and/or about which they are knowledgeable, do assemble
productive stock portfolios, based on their familiarity with the funda-
mentals of certain industries. However, many such portfolios, insufficiently diversified, sometimes meet with trouble when their narrow
industry bases falter.

It has been my experience—based on contacts with many clients
of my investment company over the years—that relatively few
investors operate with balanced, thought through investment portfolios that actually match their financial situation and life circumstances, not to mention good principles of capital management.

29

Which Investments Have Paid Off the Best?

Average rates of return over the years are by no means the entire game, but are, nonetheless, a good starting point for considering the composition of your investment portfolio. Two major issues are involved: the average rates of return you might expect to secure over the years, and the amount of variability or risk that you might expect to incur along the way. As you can see from Table 2-1, performance may vary considerably from period to period.

TABLE 2-1   Performance of Different Investment Classes over Different Periods of Time

Investment Area	Compound Annual Rate of Return
1963–1982	
Large company stocks	8.3%
Small company stocks	16.9
Long-term corporate bonds	4.5
Long-term government bonds	4.0
Intermediate government bonds	6.3
U.S. Treasury bills	6.5
Rate of inflation	6.0%
1983–2002	
Large company stocks	12.7%
Small company stocks	11.6
Long-term corporate bonds	11.0
Long-term government bonds	11.1
Intermediate government bonds	9.2
U.S. Treasury bills	3.1
Rate of inflation	3.1%

Source of data: Ibbotson Associates

Life May Not Be So Predictable After All

Here we have two 20-year periods, the one following the other. What might have happened to the investor who had created and maintained for 20 years a portfolio at the start of 1983 simply based on the market action of the previous 20 years?

- He would have overweighted his portfolio with smaller capitalization stocks, which for the next 20 years underperformed larger capitalization stocks.

- He would have overweighted his bond portfolio with shorter and intermediate-term bonds, which for the next 20 years underperformed longer-term corporate and government bonds.

- You might notice that high rates of inflation were favorable for stocks and for short-term bonds but bad for long-term bonds, which did not even keep pace with rising prices between 1963 and 1982. Low rates of inflation, 1983–2002, were favorable for long-term bonds but did not favor shorter-term bonds.

The Moral of the Story

Over the long run, most investment areas associated with the stock market have proven to be profitable. However, there have been periods, sometimes as long as several years, during which this has not been the case. For example, in March 2006, a full six years following the start of the 2000–2002 bear market, the NASDAQ Composite remained approximately 60% below its 2000 previous bull market peak.

Rates of returns have not necessarily been predictable, either year by year or decade by decade. Investors tend to be excessively optimistic following strong decades, excessively pessimistic following weak decades.

Returns, however, are likely to be more consistent for investors who maintain balanced portfolios (diversification again) rather than focusing solely on narrow investment areas based on historical past returns.

And Perhaps Most Important

You may well be able to improve your rates of return by actively managing your portfolio so that, though diversified, it is overweighted in the best-performing areas, quarter by quarter, year by year.

The Best Places to Put Your Money in Recent Decades

We have seen that the stock and bond markets do not perform with uniform consistency, that rates of return vary over periods of time, that different areas lead and lag in strength at different times. That said, certain trends in performance appear to have been relatively consistent over the decades, and you may want to consider these in establishing your investment portfolios.

The stock market universe may, by one form of measure, be roughly divided into two categories: growth stocks and value stocks.

Growth stocks are stocks of companies that are generally showing higher than average growth of sales and earnings. Such companies generally pay low rates of dividends and sell at high price/earnings ratios (price per share divided by the amount of earnings or profit per share) and/or at high book value to price ratios (the total net value of assets of the company per share divided by share price). Such company shares are selling on future prospects, hopes, and often glamour.

Value stocks are shares of generally more stable companies whose shares generally sell at lower price/earnings ratios, lower book/share price ratios, and which usually provide higher dividend payouts. The price levels of value shares are based more on present and tangible levels of earnings and company assets rather than on hopes and expectations for the future. Such stocks are generally less glamorous than shares of growth companies but tend to be less volatile and more stable in price.

Ibbotson Associates (*SBBI 2005 Yearbook*) makes the following observations:

- Large-cap (larger capitalization—high company total value) value stocks generally outperform large-cap growth stocks and are usually more stable and less risky.

- Mid-sized (mid-cap) value shares generally outperform mid-cap growth shares while being generally more stable and less risky.

- Small-cap value stocks considerably outperform small-cap growth stocks and are more stable and less risky.

- Micro-cap (very small company) value stocks outperform micro-cap growth stocks by a large margin and are more stable and less risky.

You are likely, on balance, to show little net gain by taking large chances. We shall be returning to this point many times. The secrets to investment success are consistency and capital preservation.

The value area of small company stocks, incidentally, has been the best area, over the long run, in which to invest. In recent years, this sector lagged the large-cap growth area during the mid- to late 1990s, but far outperformed during the 2000–2002 bear market, which essentially left the small-cap value asset sector unscathed.

Implications for Mutual Fund Selection

These seem obvious enough. It will not be the case in each and every year, and your portfolio should still be well diversified, but if you have to overweigh any area of your portfolio, you want to at least consider mutual funds that specialize in small-capitalization value companies that, preferably, carry a relatively low level of price volatility.

Mutual Funds Provide Excellent Vehicles for Your Diversification Program

Many investment areas provide excellent investment potential and, in combination, would constitute a nicely diversified investment portfolio. These include, again, among others, domestic and foreign stocks, bonds, commodities, precious metals, and real estate.

Many investors are familiar with one or the other of these areas, but relatively few investors are likely to be familiar enough with enough of these areas to be able to profitably invest across the spectrum. However, the mutual fund industry does provide a plethora of specialty mutual funds that you may employ for broad diversification.

Benefits of Using Mutual Funds for Both Financial- and Nonfinancial-Based Investing

Mutual funds do provide expert management in many diverse areas of investment. For example, some mutual funds offer specialized management of commodity assets, bonds, stocks, overseas investments, real estate, precious metals, and specific industry sectors.

Mutual funds generally provide for ready liquidity of assets in investment areas in which liquidity is frequently limited. For example, it can take several months or even years to sell actual homes or apartment buildings, but shares of real estate income trusts (REITs) that represent investments in real estate can be sold on almost any day that the stock market is open.

Mutual funds provide a means of establishing well-diversified portfolios representing many asset classes with limited amounts of capital. For example, even smaller investors can participate in real estate via REITs or in commodity investment via mutual funds.

A portfolio of mutual funds representing diverse investment areas may be readily rebalanced, reapportioned, partially or fully sold, augmented, and otherwise adjusted in accordance with changes in market conditions or the personal circumstances of investors. (It is generally better to be in investments from which you can exit than to be in investments into which you are locked, through thick, thin, or changing life needs.)

And finally, inasmuch as mutual funds are priced and valued daily, investors can readily keep track of the value of their holdings, the performance of their portfolios, and of changes that need to be made. We return to strategies of mutual fund selection in Chapter 3, "Selecting Mutual Funds Most Likely to Succeed." For the moment, however, we just assume that the mutual fund industry will be playing a large part in your investment planning.

Mutual Fund Selections for All Seasons

Periods of Rising Interest Rates

Long- and intermediate-term bonds and related mutual funds are likely to decline in price. Income portfolios should be placed into mutual funds whose income holdings are relatively short term in nature, and/or in income mutual funds whose holdings feature adjustable rate bonds—bonds whose rate of interest payout varies with the general level of interest rates. Adjustable rate bonds tend to be less volatile than fixed-interest long-term bonds.

The stock market has the ability to perform well during periods in which interest rates rise providing that rates are rising at only a moderate pace. In general, stocks perform better when interest rates decline than when they advance.

Rising Interest Rates Often Coincide with Inflationary Price Pressures

The stock market tends to like moderate inflationary pressures in the economy, which often stimulate business activity—better to buy today if prices are going to be higher tomorrow. However, more extreme inflationary pressures, which result in significantly higher interest rates, usually exert negative pressures on stocks as well as bonds.

Places to Put Your Money When Prices Are Rising Rapidly

Precious metals, mining, energy development, food and agriculture, forest and lumber, raw materials, short-term bonds, and money market funds all represent investments suitable for periods of inflation.

Energy issues tend to rise with increases in oil prices, as do many utility stocks.

Commodity and raw material based investments benefit from rising prices. Two mutual funds involved in natural resources which have had fine long-term performance records are the RS Investment Trust: Global Natural Resources and the Van Eck Global Hard Assets Fund/Class A.

The RS Investment Trust has holdings in aluminum, oil, and forest products such as timber. Van Eck is similarly diversified with more emphasis on oil-related issues. You can access further information regarding these funds at www.rsfunds.com and from www.vaneck.com, respectively.

Mutual funds that invest in raw materials tend to be average or slightly above average in volatility (extent of price movement or risk) but do represent some hedge against inflation and to some extent against bear markets in other stock areas. For example, both the RS and Van Eck natural resources funds held their prices very well during the 2000–2002 bear market, both performing profitably during 2003 and 2004, as well.

Periods of Falling Interest Rates

These are generally good periods to buy stocks in general, longer- and intermediate-term bonds and bond funds, and invest in interest-rate-sensitive industries such as real estate. Precious metal stocks usually underperform during periods of declining interest rates.

A Quick and Dirty Way to Determine Trends in Interest Rates

Interest rate trends tend to last for fairly long periods of time, so you do not have to be the first one into and out of the bond and related markets to benefit from the identification of changes in such trends.

Here is a quick way to at least usually be on the right side of interest rate changes in direction:

1. Each week, secure the weekly closing levels of the 3-year and 5-year U.S. Treasury notes. These are available in the Market Laboratory section of *Barron's Financial Weekly* as well as elsewhere.

2. Average these two yields each week. For example, for the week ending April 22, 2005, the 3-year note paid 3.81% and the 5-year note paid 4.02%. The average yield, (3.81 + 4.02)/ 2 came to 3.915%. Compare the latest average yield with the average yield of the 3-year and 5-year notes 33 weeks previous. Thirty-three weeks prior to April 22, 2005 was September 6, 2004. That week, the average yield of the 3-year and 5-year notes (2.86% and 3.45%, respectively) was 3.15%.

3. If the current average yield of the 3-year and 5-year notes is *higher* than the average yield 33 weeks previous, consider the trend in short-term interest rates to be rising, which means that price trends of related bonds are declining and that the interest rate climate is not favoring the stock market.

   The stock market tends to achieve almost all of its gains on balance during periods that short-term interest rate trends are favorable, rates declining.

4. Although stocks do sometimes rise when rates are rising, such periods usually carry more risk and less reward than when rates are falling.

5. If you make the same comparison employing yields of the 20-year Treasury bond, you can get an assessment of yield trends in longer-term bonds, which do not always move in the same direction as shorter-term bonds. For example, the yield of 20-year Treasury bonds was 5.05% on September 6, 2004, and stood at 4.79% on April 22, 2005. Short-term yields were higher in 2005 than in 2004, but longer-term rates were lower. The stock market is usually more influenced by the direction in shorter-term rates than by longer-term rates.

Summing Up

If you can spend just a few minutes each week tracking the direction of trends in shorter- and longer-term interest rates, you will be able to readily monitor changes in price trends in the bond markets and, indirectly, probably in the stock market, too.

Remember, falling short-term interest rates are bullish for the stock market, bullish for short- to intermediate-term bonds. Rising interest rates are bearish.

Creating and Measuring the Performance of Well-Balanced Diversified Investment Portfolios

We have already considered one variation and have seen the benefits that can accrue as a result of diversification. Let's examine other portfolio mixes, ranging from the rather conservative to moderately aggressive, all well balanced.

The Basic Portfolio Mix

Our portfolio will consist of the investment sectors listed below, represented by mutual funds with coinciding investment objectives. The source of data represented in this discussion is the "Steele Mutual Fund Expert" database, an excellent reference for the past history of mutual fund prices and for current rankings of mutual fund performance:

- **Financials.** The financial sector of the stock market, which includes industries such as banking and brokerage houses, has been among the strongest of market sectors over the years. Its performance correlates closely with the Standard & Poor's 500 Index, which it often leads at market turning points.

- **Utilities.** A more conservative market sector, whose performance generally runs somewhat below more aggressive investment sectors, utility stocks pay above-average dividends and are often favored by income-oriented investors who prefer to invest for total return rather than with an emphasis on aggressive capital gain. Despite their reputation as conservative vehicles, however, utility stocks have, in the past, been subject to market declines as severe as those that have befallen other investment sectors. Utilities often do rise and fall at times other than groups such as the financials. In recent years, the price movement of utility issues has become more correlated with the price movements of investments related to energy.

- **REITs.** Real estate mutual funds tend to show price movements that are relatively uncorrelated with other sectors of the stock market (for example, those represented by the Standard & Poor's 500 Index). Their annual returns during the period from January 1996 to early 2005 were approximately equal to the financials, but risks were lower during this period for the high-dividend-paying REITs. This is a fine sector to include in any diversified portfolio because of its high dividend payout, its

emphasis on real estate (a diversified investment arena), and its
tendency to rise and fall at times that are different from most
stock sectors.

- **Energy.** This sector includes oil producers, refineries, drilling
  companies, coal producers, and related industries. Although
  energy stocks are periodically the subject of much publicity,
  depending on the state of oil supplies, their long-term rates of
  return have actually slightly lagged those of the financials and
  real estate sectors. The energy sector represents some hedge
  against oil shortages and attendant rates of inflation and, if you
  believe (as I do) that energy shortages are likely to prove peren-
  nial, probably represent a fine long-term area for investment.

- **Materials.** This area, which includes, for example, gold, silver,
  aluminum, various minerals, and their related industries, is
  another hedge in the portfolio against inflation. The materials
  sector tends to be fairly volatile with very strong periods, very
  weak periods, and larger drawdowns than other industry sectors. This sector is somewhat marginal as an inclusion in a balanced portfolio but is one of the few stock market areas that
  does have strong potential during periods of runaway inflation.

- **U.S. small-capitalization value sectors.** This has, historically,
  been among the very strongest of investment sectors, featuring
  historical rates of return generally above average, with relatively
  favorable risk characteristics. Representing small companies,
  this area offsets investments in the financial, utility, and energy
  areas, which generally involve larger companies.

- **International equity.** This sector includes diverse international stock and balanced mutual funds, representing large- as
  well as smaller-capitalization stocks of foreign countries. This
  area has, historically, lagged the U.S. stock market in performance but, inasmuch as this may not be the case in the future,
  is being included in our diversified investment portfolio.

- **International small-capitalization companies.** No stronger than many other investment sectors in years past, the foreign small-cap area demonstrated excellent strength during and following the 2000–2002 bear market. With emerging countries showing rising economic growth, this sector is likely to perform well in the years ahead.

Summing Up

This eight-sector portfolio shows balance in many ways. Two of its sectors (real estate and utilities) provide above-average dividend payout—real estate, in addition, providing participation in real estate as an area for investment. The financial sector represents corporations involved in stocks and finance, and the energy and materials areas represent companies involved in commodities and other raw materials. Large-capitalization, small-capitalization, domestic and foreign corporations are represented as well—all within only eight investment sectors.

Income Investing

Income investments (various forms of bonds and such) are likely to add benefit to the majority of balanced investment portfolios and should be included in such portfolios by all but the most aggressive of investors. Income investments generally provide less in the way of return than most stocks but are safer. These include, among others, the following:

- **Corporate high-yield bonds.** Lower quality, often below investment grade (BBB) ratings. These bonds, nonetheless, have generally provided higher rates of total return than higher-grade debt instruments. High-yield bond funds tend to provide interest returns between 3% to 5% above those provided by long-term Treasury bonds, sometimes even more. The price movement of high-yield bonds is often more correlated with the price movement of the NASDAQ Composite Index (and small businesses in general) than with general credit conditions that affect other forms of income investments.

As of March 31, 2005, high-yield bond funds in the Steele database had shown annual rates of returns of 9.2%, 5.1%, and 6.1% for the 3-, 5-, and 10-year periods, respectively. Their worst year was 2000, when the group showed a loss of 6.5%.

- **Short-term corporate bonds.** A low-risk, relatively low-return investment sector, short-term income instruments are good havens for income capital during periods in which interest rates are rising. Short-term bonds are less affected by interest rate trends than long-term bonds. And, although they do carry more risk than money market funds, high-quality short-term bonds are basically an almost riskless investment for investors with a two- to three-year time horizon. Most bond mutual funds that invest in this area employ AA-rated bonds of a high, though not the very highest, investment quality.

  Short-term corporate bonds in the Steele database showed, through March 31, 2005, annual rates of return of 2.7%, 4.2%, and 5.1% for the previous 3-, 5- and 10-year periods, respectively. There were no full years in which they incurred a net loss.

- **Global bonds.** Bonds issued by foreign countries generally (not always) provide higher rates of interest return than domestic bonds, with no particular increase in credit risks (risks of default) but carry a certain amount of risk based on the fluctuations of other currencies compared to the U.S. dollar. Such bonds, therefore, do provide an additional element of diversification in a balanced portfolio, providing some insurance against an ongoing weakness in the U.S. dollar, such insurance coming at the expense of possible loss if the U.S. dollar gains in strength against the currencies represented by such bonds.

• **Intermediate corporate bonds.** Bonds with about 5 to 7 years maturity provide what is probably the best compromise between the higher yields offered by longer-term bonds and the safety provided by short-term corporate bonds. Taken all in all, intermediate bonds may be the area of choice for most income investors.

TABLE 2-2 Average Annual Investment Returns—Mutual Funds Representing Eight Equity and Two Income Investment Sectors Listed Above, Moderate Balanced Portfolio, 1996–March 2005*

Sector	3-Year Return	5-Year Return	10-Year Return	Worst Year
Financials	6.7%	10.1%	14.9%	−10.2%
Utilities	6.7	0.5	9.8	−23.6
REITs	17.6	19.2	14.5	−16.6
Energy	17.8	14.9	14.4	−22.8
Materials	17.2	19.0	4.5	−32.2
U.S. small cap	11.0	13.9	14.0	−11.4
International equity	9.2	−2.5	6.5	−20.9
Inter. small cap	18.6	1.6	12.3	−18.7
Inter. corp. bonds	5.4	6.2	6.3	−1.2
Global bonds	11.4	8.3	7.9	−1.5
Average	**12.1%**	**7.2%**	**10.5%**	**−15.9%**

Vanguard S & P 500

| **Index Fund** | **2.6%** | **−3.2%** | **10.7%** | **−22.2%** |

° The above performance results are based on mutual fund performance as reported in the Steele Mutual Fund Expert database, classified according to investment objectives that coincide with the sectors above.

The sectors employed were selected on the basis of a combination of balance and historical performance and do not necessarily reflect the very strongest of market sectors during the periods shown. The average sector performed essentially as well as the Standard & Poor's 500 Index (reflected in the Vanguard Index Fund) during the 1996–2005 period, better than the Standard & Poor's 500 Index, during the 3-year and 5-year periods ending March 31, 2005. The average sector demonstrated less risk than the Standard & Poor's 500 Index, though some sectors did show slightly greater risk.

**TABLE 2-3   Average Annual Investment Returns of Diversified
Portfolios Invested as Full Portfolios—Equal Dollars
Placed at the Start, No Rebalancing, 1996–March 2005***

Portfolio Style	3-Year Return	5-Year Return	10-Year Return	Worst Year
Aggressive	13.1%	9.6%	11.4%	–4.2%
Moderate	12.5	9.5	9.7	–1.9
Conservative	11.4	8.7	9.0	–0.8

° The aggressive portfolio includes the eight equity sectors discussed above but *none* of the bond sectors. This is a purely equity mutual fund–based, but nonetheless diversified, portfolio.

The moderate portfolio includes the eight equity sectors discussed above and two bond sectors—the corporate intermediate bond sector and the global bond sector.

The conservative portfolio includes the eight equity sectors and two bond sectors that exist in the moderate portfolio and also bond funds representing the corporate high-yield and the corporate short-term bond areas—eight equity areas, four bond areas.

The aggressive portfolio is divided into eight sectors, equally represented so that each represents 12 ½% of the portfolio at the start.

The moderate portfolio is divided into ten sectors, equally represented so that each represents 10% of the portfolio at the start.

The conservative portfolio is divided into 12 sectors, equally represented so that each represents 8 ½% of the portfolio at the start.

No rebalancing of assets is assumed to have taken place so that by the end of the relevant test periods, the better-performing portfolios occupy larger percentages of the portfolio, whereas the poorer performers occupy smaller percentages of the portfolio. Investors may want to rebalance to start each year with equal dollar amounts in each sector. This practice appears, in my own testing, to add slightly to returns and to reduce risk slightly but not by large amounts in either case.

Diversification Certainly
Does Appear to Help the Cause!

Again we see that the maintenance of fully diversified portfolios improved risk/reward ratios, seriously reduced risk, while outperforming the Vanguard Standard & Poor's 500 Index Fund, usually taken as a very difficult benchmark for investors to outperform. The inclusion of bonds in portfolios did reduce returns but also reduced risks.

The tables above probably underestimate investment risks!

The results shown in the tables above do not fully reflect investment risks (and interim returns) both within and outside of the diversified portfolios. These results reflect end-of-year to end-of-year performance and do not reflect periods within each year when interim losses greater than year-end losses might have taken place. This extra amount of risk that is not reflected in year-end to year-end calculations is often significant. Table 2-4 illustrates this point, among others.

TABLE 2-4   Performance of Diversified Portfolios, Calculated Based on Monthly Performance Data, January 1989—March 31, 2005*

Portfolio Style	Average Gain per Annum	Maximum Open Drawdown
Aggressive	11.6%	–21.1%
Moderate	10.9%	–18.3%
Conservative	10.4%	–16.5%
Standard & Poor's 500 Index	11.7%	–44.7%

* A review of performance results based on monthly rather than year-end annual data does not produce much change in average rates of return—this particular study covered more than 15 years—but does reflect higher levels of interim investment risk, not just for the diversified portfolios but for the Standard & Poor's 500 Index on its own.

It should also be noted that Tables 2-2 and 2-3 reflected only the worst single-year drawdowns, whereas Table 2-4 reflects cumulative drawdowns that during the 2000–2002 period spread over 3 years.

In evaluating your likely risk levels, you might think of both—what is the worst likely to happen in any given year and what is the worst likely to happen if investment markets undergo protracted declines.

You may notice that the inclusion of bonds to the extent of 33% of the portfolio (conservative portfolio) reduces risk by about 21.8% (21.1% to 16.5%) compared to the aggressive portfolio. This is consistent with other research my staff has carried forth, and similar to the previous diversified portfolio presented in Chapter 1, "The Myth of Buy and Hold."

Upping the Ante! Increasing Returns and Reducing Risk through Active Management of Your Diversified Portfolio

So far, we have pretty much confined our discussions to strategies that basically involve passive management of your investment portfolios—we have assumed that once your diverse portfolio is established, you pretty much allow it to operate on its own, simply reinvesting dividend and interest payments as they come through.

You will be learning various strategies to improve returns as we move along—strategies for selecting superior mutual funds, strategies that will help you adjust the amounts and types of positions in your portfolio. We have already considered the NASDAQ/NYSE Index relative strength mood indicator and the 3- to 5-year Treasury rate indicator, which have done a fine job over the years of separating low-risk from high-risk stock market investment climates.

At this time, we are going to discuss a relatively simple to apply strategy that should require just a small investment of time once every six months that is likely to both increase your rates of investment return and to reduce the risks involved in your diversified investment portfolio.

My research staff has assembled a different portfolio mix to demonstrate this strategy and to demonstrate that the principles and benefits of diversification apply to various portfolio combinations.

Employing Mutual Funds to Carry Out Sector Diversification

Here are a group of U.S. stock market sectors, along with a selection of well-performing mutual funds that may be employed as representative investments in these sectors:

- **Real estate.** Fidelity Real Estate Investors Class (FRESX)

- **Food and agriculture.** Fidelity Select Food and Agriculture (FDFAX)

- **Financials.** Fidelity Select Insurance (FSPCX)

- **Utilities.** Franklin Utilities (FKUTX)

- **Energy.** Vanguard Energy/Inv (VGENX)

- **Health.** Vanguard Health Care (VGHCX)

- **Leisure.** AIM Leisure/Inv (FLISX)

The letters in parentheses are the ticker symbols of the funds, which would be entered in brokerage or computer buy-sell instructions.

This particular portfolio includes no bond funds and no international funds, and to that extent is not as diversified as previous portfolio structures that we have evaluated. It does include, however, representation in the real estate, financial, utility, and energy areas with which you are already familiar. The food and agriculture area, like the raw materials sector, tends to relate in its price movement to inflationary trends, with less price volatility than precious metals. The leisure sector, which includes, for example, companies such as Disney, is closely correlated with the Standard & Poor's 500 Index. Health-related stocks represent an industry group that often marches to its own beat, apart from other sectors that are more associated with the general economic outlook.

As portfolios go, this is not a particularly volatile portfolio and can be made safer by the addition of income positions and which may be more geographically diversified by the addition of international holdings.

The Selection of Specific Mutual Funds

The particular mutual funds employed in this portfolio were selected because of their above-average historical performance. The Fidelity and Vanguard families are broad and frequently will find representation in well-established portfolios. Mutual fund selection is discussed in greater detail in Chapter 3.

For purposes of simplicity, this sample portfolio is employing only one mutual fund to represent each market sector. It is often a better idea to employ more than one fund for this purpose (diversification of another sort), particularly if your portfolio has sufficient size so that

the extra commissions that might be involved do not become oner-
ous. The use of two to four mutual funds per sector is likely to be sufficient in this regard and is recommended for portfolios of perhaps
$100,000 or more (and for smaller portfolios if they are not going to
be actively managed).

Quick Cost-Saving Tip!

Shop around brokerage houses for the best commission deals. It
will generally be a better idea to purchase long-term positions via
single-payment commissions rather than in wrap-fee accounts in
which you pay a percentage of assets, generally 1% to 2% per
annum, for unlimited trading. You will be paying these amounts
each and every year in a wrap account—not a good idea for holdings that will rarely be traded and whose values are likely to rise
year by year.

Comparing Performance—The Diversified Portfolio, Buy and Hold, Versus the Vanguard Standard & Poor's 500 Index Fund

**TABLE 2-5   Comparative Performance, Total Return, Seven Sector
Portfolio, Buy and Hold, Versus the Vanguard S & P 500
Index Fund,* 1989—November 30, 2004**

Investment Vehicle	Gain Per Annum	Open Drawdown	$700 Becomes
Seven Sector Portfolio	15.2%	−15.9%	$6,638 (848.3%)
Vanguard Index Fund	11.8%	−44.8%	$4,155 (493.6%)

° It is interesting to observe that the securing of what appears to be a moderate improvement
in return, 15.2% compared to 11.8%, results in a more than 70% increase in profit and nearly
a 60% increase in the final value of an account after 16 years. There really is considerable
power in compound interest.

Returns shown reflect both capital gain and dividend streams, which are considered to be
reinvested.

Commission costs are not included in the above tabulations.

Rebalancing the Portfolio to Improve Returns

Well, we have seen one more example of diversification in action, outperforming the usual benchmark of the stock market, the Standard & Poor's 500 Index, and with less risk at that. Let's consider now some concepts and a specific strategy that you can employ in many different ways to improve your investment results.

An Object in Motion Tends to Stay in Motion

This is a basic principle of physics. If an object is in motion, it takes force to keep it from remaining in motion. That is why satellites continue to orbit the earth. In space, there is no resistance. Nothing to end the motion. That is why your automobile needs strong brakes—to stop a heavy vehicle that has momentum and motion.

Stocks do not reside in outer space, so that even stocks in strong motion tend to meet resistance—bad news, sellers cashing in, rising interest rates, changes in industry conditions. Strong stocks do not remain strong forever. However, they do often retain strength for considerable periods of time. Stocks, mutual funds, and industry sectors that lead the stock market in any particular month, quarter, or even year tend to lead in performance for subsequent periods, not forever, but for at least some period of time after they attain leadership. This does not mean that all leading stocks will continue to outperform indefinitely. It does not mean that all leading stocks will outperform for even the next weeks or months. It does mean that, on average, market leaders will outperform the average stock, mutual fund, or market sector for at least a period of time, and that you are likely to do better following market leaders than investing at random. Investments that are leading in relative strength are likely to continue to lead until proven otherwise.

Given these premises, your investment strategy appears clear enough. You get on the leading horse, you ride that horse until you can see it tiring, and then you jump onto the next leading horse. There are many ways that this concept can be applied. You will see how it can be applied to mutual fund selection as we move along. Let's see how one variation can be employed to improve the performance of your sector portfolio.

The Basic Procedure for Rebalancing Your Sector Portfolio

1. You first establish the Seven Sector Portfolio by placing equal amounts of money in each of the seven sectors.

2. After six months you do the following:

   a. Check the performance of each of the sectors (as measured by your portfolio of representative mutual funds) in which you are invested over the previous 6 months. The data is readily available, for example, in the *Barron's Financial Weekly*.

   b. Rebalance the total assets in your portfolio so that each of the top two sectors start the new 6-month period with 28.6% of your total portfolio assets, each of the next three sectors start the new 6-month period with 14.3% of your total portfolio assets, and each of the last two sectors in performance start the new 6-month period with no assets.

   c. Hold positions for 6 months. At the end of six months, again rebalance so that the two sectors that led in performance over the most recent 6 months receive a double allocation of capital, the lowest performing two sectors receive none.

   d. Once again, at each 6-month interval, place 28.6% of your assets in each of the top-performing two sectors, 14.3% of assets into each of the next-performing three sectors, no assets into the two worst-performing sectors.

> Rankings are based on the performance of all sectors
> during the 6-month periods prior to the date of ranking.

As you can see, you are constantly re-weighting your portfolio so
that the best-performing sectors start each 6-month period with the
most assets, the average sectors will start each 6-month period with
an average amount of assets, and the worst performers will start each
6-month period with no assets.

Figure 2-1 illustrates the performance of the Seven Sector
Rebalanced Portfolio compared to the same portfolio on a buy and
hold basis, and the Vanguard Standard & Poor's 500 Index Fund.

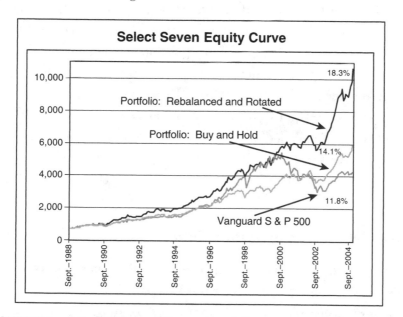

**FIGURE 2-1   A Comparison of Sector Portfolios to the Vanguard
Standard & Poor's 500 Index Fund (January
1989–November 2004)**

This figure compares the performance of the Seven Sector
Rebalanced portfolio with the Seven Sector Buy and Hold portfolio
and the Vanguard Standard & Poor's 500 Index Fund. The
Rebalanced Sector Portfolio, as described above, achieved a compound rate of return of 18.15% per annum. The Seven Sector Buy and
Hold Portfolio achieved a compound rate of return of 15.18%. The
Vanguard Standard & Poor's 500 Index Fund achieved a compound
rate of return of 11.84%. Results are derived from hypothetical back
testing and cannot be assured in any way for the future.

Table 2-6 shows the comparison numerically.

**TABLE 2-6   Comparative Performances, Seven Sector Rebalanced and
Buy and Hold Portfolios, Vanguard Standard & Poor's 500
Index Fund, January 1989–November 2004**

Investment Vehicle	Gain per Annum	Maximum Open Drawdown	$700 Becomes
Rebalanced Seven Sector	18.3%	−13.9%	$10,172
Unbalanced Seven Sector	15.2%	−15.9%	6,638
Vanguard S & P Index	11.4%	−44.8%	4,155

Because the Vanguard Health Fund requires a 1-year holding
period to avoid redemption charges, the presumption has been made
in the back testing that this fund position was not involved in the
rebalancing process as described above and was held undisturbed
from the beginning of the portfolio (1989) until the end of the study
(November 2004). In effect, then, rebalancing procedures in this
study actually included only six of the seven funds in the portfolio. I
do not believe that this affects the implications of the study in any significant manner.

Year-by-Year Comparative Results

Table 2-7 compares the performance of the Rebalanced Seven Sector
Portfolio to the performance of the Vanguard Standard & Poor's 500
Index Fund on a year-by-year basis from 1989 through November 2004.

TABLE 2-7 **Year-by-Year Comparison, Rebalanced Seven Sector Portfolio, Versus Vanguard Standard & Poor's 500 Index Fund, January 1989—November 2004**

Year	Performance Rebalanced Seven Sector Portfolio	Performance Vanguard S & P 500 Index Fund
1989	34.4%	31.6%
1990	5.1	−3.1
1991	41.2	30.4
1992	14.9	7.6
1993	20.3	10.1
1994	6.8	1.3
1995	30.2	37.5
1996	20.3	23.0
1997	26.3	33.4
1998	19.9	28.6
1999	13.3	21.0
2000	27.3	−9.1
2001	−2.1	−11.9
2002	−4.7	−22.1
2003	27.8	28.7
2004 (11 mos.)	**21.2**	**7.2**
Average	**18.9%**	**13.4%**

° The Seven Sector Rebalanced Portfolio outperformed the Vanguard Standard & Poor's 500 Index Fund during 10 of the 16 years included in the study.

You might notice that the average annual gains were above the compounded rates of return shown in Table 2-6. Compounded gains are not the same as average annual gains. For example, if your portfolio started with $100, gained 100% the first year and then lost 100% the second year, its average annual return for the 2-year period would have been 0 ((+100 − 100) / 2 = 0). However, the actual end result would be that your portfolio would have been totally wiped out.

You should also notice how well losses were contained during this period by use of the rebalanced sector portfolio. Diversification, again, definitely provides significant benefits in regard to risk reduction.

A Final Thought

I hope that I have not confused you by demonstrating, between Chapter 1 and Chapter 2, three differently diversified portfolios, although there are common elements among them. I did this to demonstrate that many variations are possible in portfolio construction and that diversification is the key factor in this strategy, not a particular combination of sectors that may or may not prove the best combination over the years.

My staff and I have by no means completed all the research that might be conducted regarding the construction and rebalancing of market sectors, but I am, on faith at this point, recommending the following procedure for investors who might want to make use of a broader roster of investment sectors than are employed in models I have already described.

A Broader Active Management Plan for Sector Diversification

Here is a step-by-step plan for the creation and maintenance of a broader diversified sector portfolio, adjusted at regular intervals to be invested in the strongest of market sectors and within the strongest of mutual funds within those sectors:

1. List and maintain a roster of diversified market sectors that should be tracked for quarterly performance. Tracking may be initiated based on general sector performance or based on the performance of individual mutual funds or an average of a few mutual funds that represent each sector.

   Your universe of sectors might include, for example, the following:

   • Small-cap U.S. value funds

   • Energy funds

   • Small-cap international value funds

   • Utility funds

- International equity funds

- Financials

- REITs

- Transportation-based funds

- Health-related mutual funds

- Food and agriculture

- Natural Resource mutual funds

- Precious Metals

- Mid-cap value mutual funds

- Equity income mutual funds

Every six months (could also be annually, but you will probably do better on a pretax basis if you do this every six months), rebalance your portfolio so that it is invested in the top-performing 7 of the 14 sectors shown here, based on the performance of each sector the six months prior to the time of rebalancing. You might provide some additional weight to the top two sectors in your roster so that the top two sectors each are assigned 25% of your total assets, with the remaining five sectors each assigned 10% of assets.

2. Maintain a roster of several, preferably more than several, mutual funds that represent each sector. At the time you select the sectors in which you want to invest, also select the mutual funds that you will employ to represent these chosen sectors.

It will probably prove worthwhile to have each sector in your portfolio represented by at least two or three mutual funds (second level of diversification). These would be chosen in a similar manner as you chose the sectors—the funds in each sector that performed the best in the quarter prior to rebalancing are the funds you would employ for the next six months. (This form of mutual fund selection will be further discussed in Chapter 3.)

If you follow this plan, you will be starting each 6-month period in the best-performing mutual funds in the best-performing stock market sectors with a well-diversified stock market portfolio.

This portfolio should, in and of itself, provide a high level of safety as well as rate of return. However, depending on your emotional and financial risk tolerances, you may choose to allocate a certain portion of your assets to a diversified income portfolio, an example of which we have already seen. A default proportion of your assets that would be placed into income investments might be 20 to 30%. More-conservative investors might opt for as much as 40% (or even 50% or 60% or more). More-venturesome investors might opt for an all equity-based portfolio.

We move along now to consider issues regarding the selection of mutual funds in which to invest, closing with just five final words: *Diversification. Diversification. And more diversification!*

3

SELECTING MUTUAL FUNDS MOST LIKELY TO SUCCEED

Mutual funds, initiated during the 1920s, enable investors to invest in large and diverse portfolios of stocks, bonds, and often other investments (such as real estate and precious metals), with relatively small amounts of capital. In theory, for each share of a mutual fund that an investor purchases, he secures a portion of a portfolio of domestic and/or foreign stocks, bonds, or other investments (investment selections made by "trained" and "professional" managers, "experts" in their fields of investment).

Moreover, risks (and potential rewards) are at least theoretically reduced by the diversification inherent in broad mutual fund portfolios, and transaction costs are reduced by the relatively large size of mutual fund purchases and sales.

Offsetting the advantages of diversification and professional management are various, sometimes hidden, costs to investors in mutual funds. Apart from management fees, which vary considerably, mutual funds involve other expenses, such as the following:

- Commission costs incurred by the funds, particularly if portfolio styles involve active trading

- Administrative costs, frequently more or less hidden (back end and front end)

- Early-redemption fees

- Ongoing "12b-1" charges to investors, the payments of which often accrue to selling brokerage houses and salespeople

Largely as a result of such expenses, approximately 80% of mutual funds underperform market indices such as the Standard & Poor's 500 Index—a fact to a large extent unnoticed by the millions of investors who have placed capital into more than 17,000 mutual funds within the United States alone.

If mutual funds are not necessarily the best investment for everyone, and even if most do not perform as well as a broadly held portfolio of stocks held by individual investors (which involve less expense), these facts remain: A select group of mutual funds have had outstanding long-term performance records; many funds, for shorter periods of time, outperform the general mutual fund universe as well as the stock market; and many funds provide access into investment arenas in which most investors are insufficiently familiar to invest on their own.

Countless books, advisory services, brokerage recommendations, and magazine articles are devoted to the selection of the "best" mutual funds in which to invest. I recommend sources of further information, but essentially in this chapter you get my personal take on the subject—what to look for, investment strategies to follow, and specific recommendations of mutual funds to purchase.

Myths and Merits of Morningstar

Mutual fund management companies as a group tend to use a number of favorite advertising ploys. One is to present in their advertisements performance results for the most recent year, 3 years, 5 years, 10 years, or even 20 years of the mutual funds they are plugging. This strategy proves most popular following long periods of rising stock prices and was a particular advertising staple during the late 1990s, just prior to the onset of the 2000–2002 bear market. (The 1980s and 1990s were the most profitable consecutive decades of the twentieth century, with annualized rates of total return for the Standard & Poor's 500 Index of 17.5% and 18.2%, respectively. Between 2000 and May 2005, however, stock investments produced average annual losses of 2.3% per year.)

Another favorite advertising ploy is to trumpet the "star ratings" of mutual funds as determined by Morningstar, a widely followed publisher of mutual fund data, including performance. Morningstar assigns a past-performance rating to mutual funds, which ranges between one star and five stars, a five-star rating the highest. Given this spread, one might assume that the average mutual fund receives a rating of three stars. This does not seem to be the case. The average rating of listed funds in the 2005 edition of "Morningstar Funds 500" actually came to 3.76—closer to four stars than to three stars. As we know, four- and five-star ratings carry favorable implications for restaurants and hotels. Although the four-star rating is only about average for mutual funds, the advertising obviously implies superior performance.

Morningstar, incidentally, states that "the star rating isn't predictive" (2005 edition), which then raises the issue of why they exist in the first place. That said, it should also, in all fairness, be noted that Morningstar's annual and other publications (www.morningstar.com) do provide a considerable amount of useful information regarding mutual funds, including past performance, investment style, expense ratios (very significant), portfolio weightings, measures of risk and performance, general commentary, and fund evaluations.

I have already mentioned the Steele Mutual Fund Expert database (www.steelesystems.com), which provides considerable data regarding mutual funds, too, but is not quite as comprehensive as Morningstar. I have found the Steele ratings of historical mutual fund return, risk, and risk-adjusted performance helpful.

If the future does not lie in the stars, where does it lie?

A Quick and Dirty Checklist to Locate the Best Mutual Funds

Here are a few quick and readily available items to check out in your selection of mutual funds. Some are widely available in publications such as the *Barron's Financial Weekly* and/or on brokerage Web sites such as www.schwab.com. On the Schwab site, clients can click Advice & Research, Mutual Funds Research, and then Try Our Research Tour to find considerable amounts of data. Other brokerage houses provide similar information to clients.

Expense Ratios and Portfolio Turnover— the Lower the Better

Expense ratios, which include a mutual fund's transaction fees as well as management expenses, represent the cost of participating in the stock market via mutual funds and, thereby, represent a definite handicap in the quest to outperform the stock market as a whole, or more specifically, the benchmark (market sector or combination of sectors in which the fund invests) of each mutual fund.

The average expense ratio for equity-related mutual funds usually runs in the area of 1.25% of assets per annum (for bond funds closer to 0.75% of assets). This means that if everything else is equal, the fund must outperform its related market benchmark by at least 1.25% each year (if the market makes 10%, the fund must make 11.25%) to provide returns equal to the stock market on an unmanaged basis. Some expenses are always involved in owning stocks, but

for a buy and hold investor, these are essentially limited to initial purchase commissions and bid-asked spreads, after which a portfolio
may be maintained with minimal, if any, expense. The mutual fund
investor pays the expense ratio every year, an expense that can easily
amount to 10% or more of average annual profit.

The lower the expense ratio, the better. Index funds, mutual funds
whose portfolios are designed to reflect the composition and performance of one market index or another, and which do not involve the
analyses or trading of many securities, generally carry the lowest
expense ratios. The Vanguard Standard & Poor's 500 Index Fund has
been a leader in this regard, with expense ratios since 1997 in the
order of just 0.18% of assets per annum. (Fidelity has since initiated
a Standard & Poor's 500 Index fund with an expense ratio of just
0.10%, but this low level of expense is not guaranteed for the future.)

Because index funds cost investors less, they do tend to outperform the average more-actively-managed mutual fund—the
Vanguard Standard & Poor's 500 Index Fund, for example, has outperformed approximately 80% of all equity mutual funds.

Still, some funds have outstanding performance histories. Such
funds tend to be characterized by relatively low expense ratios as well
as relatively low portfolio turnover (the percentage of the portfolio
changed during the year), thus limiting expenses. (The average portfolio turnover for equity stock mutual funds is about 85%.)

No-Load Funds Are Likely to Outperform Load Funds

Load funds are mutual funds that charge some form of sales fee (the
load) at the time of purchase or at the time of redemption (at
redemption if not held for a certain period of time—often 60 to 90
days, sometimes years). Such fees may vary with the size of purchase;
the larger the purchase, the smaller the fee. Front-end loads, fees
charged at the time of purchase, are often waived for purchases of

$1 million or more but may rise to 5% of the purchase value, or even more, for smaller purchases.

There are no reasons to assume that a typical load fund will outperform the typical no-load fund and many reasons to assume that the presence of a front-end load will simply place your investment at an immediate handicap with no offsetting benefit.

Back-end loads are not much better. These fees are charged to investors who want to redeem assets before certain specified times pass, which can run into years, such fees declining year by year until they vanish. Such funds, often marketed by brokerage houses, also tend to involve above-average 12b-1 fees charged annually to investors.

Many brokerage houses also use the "C" share as a way of charging investors high levels of fees in an indirect way. This particular charge works like this: The investor is offered C shares of a fund rather than A shares (A shares having a front-end load). C shares do not involve a front-end investment fee but do charge investors higher ongoing investment expenses, often in the order of an extra 1% per year, which, over the years, can add up to more than the initial sales commission charged for A shares. C shares also often involve redemption (again, based on holding for a specific time period, usually 1 or 2 years) fees that do not apply to A shares.

Mutual fund performance summaries often show A shares of a particular mutual fund regularly outperforming that same fund's C shares.

Verify That Your Brokerage House Is Giving You the Best Deal, Not Just Upping Its Own Commission

It is not unusual for brokerage houses to recommend mutual fund shares that involve high initial loads, high back-end loads, high expense ratios, and/or high 12b-1 fees, while charging annual wrap fees for maintaining investor accounts that hold mutual funds for which transaction fees have already been charged. Wrap fees can easily add an additional annual 1% to even 2% to maintaining positions in mutual funds.

Financial planners are also often prone to recommending mutual funds that impose front-end loads, for which the planner receives compensation, rather than no-load mutual funds, which are likely to be of greater benefit to the client. Planners are sometimes paid on commission. However, clients may be better off paying hourly consultation fees to the planner rather than mutual fund commissions, which negatively impact performance.

I am emphasizing the need to monitor investment expenses—which are often neglected by investors—because each percent of expense that you can avoid represents an additional percent of profit that you can secure from your investments. The compounding effect of even just a percent or two a year can be considerable.

As a General Rule, the Lower the Fund Volatility, the Better

Rapidly moving mutual funds—often associated with higher-velocity market sectors, growth stocks, speculative issues, and more-concentrated portfolios with fewer issues—can be joyous to own during the right market climates. Over the long run, however, most investors gain little by taking the risks associated with such vehicles. When all is said and done, lower-volatility mutual funds have, over the long run, secured more favorable risk/reward ratios, and end returns equal to more-volatile and higher-risk mutual funds.

Volatility of a mutual fund is often expressed as its "beta," or volatility compared to its benchmark market index (the Standard & Poor's 500 Index for many funds). The beta of the Vanguard Standard & Poor's 500 Index Fund is 1.00, reflecting the fact that the fund is designed to replicate this index. Beta levels above 1.00 indicate that the fund is more volatile than its underlying index. Betas below 1.00 indicate that the fund is less volatile or risky.

Research carried out by my firm suggests that the mutual funds with the best long-term risk/reward relationships (also known as the *gain/pain ratio,* my term) are funds whose beta is less than 1.00, often in the 0.60 to 0.80 range, indicating risk levels 60% to 80% those of the Standard & Poor's 500 Index. This is not to say that a fund is necessarily inferior because its volatility is greater than the Standard & Poor's 500 Index. It is to say that the lower levels of risk associated with less-volatile mutual funds usually works to the advantage of investors rather than against.

With Excellent Market Timing, Some Higher-Velocity Vehicles in Your Portfolio Might Prove Advantageous

Although most investors, particularly buy and hold investors, will secure more consistent rates of return with mutual funds of no greater than average volatility, investors with a good sense of stock market timing may be able to achieve greater profits if they do, indeed, ride the high flyers during periods of market advance and exit in time to avoid serious market decline.

Chapter 7, "A Three-Pronged Approach to Timing the Markets," covers some excellent market-timing techniques that have fine historical records of avoiding weaker stock market periods. Investors who apply these tools may find it worthwhile to place some capital into more-aggressive mutual funds and other stock market vehicles. However, for the most consistent investment performance, aggressive positions should probably be limited to no more than 20% to 25% of your portfolio, give or take.

Continuity of Management Is Important

Check out asset size, too. The larger the fund, the more likely it will just reflect major market benchmarks.

If you are attracted to a mutual fund because of its long-term performance and/or because of a characteristic management style, verify before purchase that the management team that produced that success remains essentially intact.

In a similar vein, smaller mutual funds are generally more able to outperform their benchmarks than larger mutual funds, which have less ability to locate outstanding developing companies with enough shares available to produce significant benefit to a large fund of capital. Larger funds find it necessary to emphasize larger, highly liquid companies that tend to be more widely followed by market analysts and that essentially mirror, before expenses, market indices such as the Standard & Poor's 500 Index. Smaller funds are naturally more maneuverable and provide greater opportunity, for better or for worse, to their managements to carry forth their own specialties.

A situation that illustrates both of these concepts has been the Fidelity Magellan Mutual Fund. The fund, under the management of Peter Lynch, outperformed its Standard & Poor's 500 Index benchmark for many years, its best performance taking place in the years shortly following its inception when the fund was relatively small. In the 1990s, Peter Lynch retired, and the succession of managers who followed never matched his success. The fund, at the same time, grew to a behemoth $63 billion in assets by 2005, by which time its performance had deteriorated to below average.

Magellan has been the victim of both changing management and of growing so large as to become an investment dinosaur.

It is not surprising then, that many of the very best long-term mutual fund performers—funds such as Fidelity Low Priced Fund, Aegis Value, and Dodge and Cox Balanced Fund—were closed to new investors by the end of 2005, management opting to keep assets within bounds to maintain performance.

Putting Together and Maintaining a Mutual Fund Portfolio for Long-Term, Tax-Favored Holding Periods

More gain, less pain! This section covers favorable tax treatment as well as how to accomplish above-average rates of return!

The TPS Strategy: Selecting Mutual Funds That Qualify for the "One-in-a-Thousand Club"

Only 20 of approximately 19,000 mutual funds in our long-term database met, in mid-2005, the criteria for risk-adjusted performance listed here for inclusion in the one-in-a-thousand club.

The Triple-Period selection (TPS) strategy represents a simple screening strategy designed to identify mutual funds that have a long-term history of consistently outperforming the Standard & Poor's 500 Index while, at the same time, involving less risk than this popular stock market benchmark.

You will now learn a relatively easy-to-follow model for selecting mutual funds for long-term investment, a simplified variant of a model that my management company uses for the investment of capital in its own staff-pension portfolio and in client-managed accounts.

Performance Criteria

1. The mutual fund's average performance over the most recent 3 years must have surpassed the average performance of the Standard & Poor's 500 Index, including dividends.

2. The mutual fund's average performance over the most recent 5 years must have surpassed the average performance of the Standard & Poor's 500 Index, including dividends.

3. If the mutual fund has been in operation for at least 10 years, the average performance of the fund must have surpassed the average performance of the Standard & Poor's 500 Index, including dividends, for the most-recent 10-year period.

The concept underlying this first set of criteria is straightforward: We look for mutual funds that have consistently outperformed the most widely accepted benchmark of stock market performance over varying time periods.

These rules, in and of themselves, will go a long way toward nullifying the advantage that more-volatile mutual funds have during rising market periods when more aggressive mutual funds might be expected to outperform an index such as the Standard & Poor's 500 Index (inasmuch as at least some of the comparative time frames are likely to involve periods of market decline).

Risk:Adjusted Performance Ratio—Superior Sharpe Ratio Levels

This section is a little complicated, but you do not have to carry out these mathematical processes to secure significant benefit from the Sharpe ratio measure of risk:adjusted performance.

Basically, the Sharpe ratio (derived by Professor William Sharpe) levels the playing field between higher-risk investments (for example, volatile mutual funds) and lower-risk investments (for example, mutual funds of lower volatility) so that investors can determine whether the amount of historical gain has been worth the level of historical pain for these classes of investment, or for specific mutual funds that can be compared against each other. (The Sharpe ratio can, of course, be applied to other investments, too.)

Use the following formula to calculate the Sharpe ratio:

$$\text{Monthly Sharpe Ratio} = \frac{\text{Average Monthly Return} - \text{Monthly Risk-Free Return}}{\text{Monthly Standard Deviation of Returns}}$$

For an annualized reading, multiply monthly returns by 12 and multiply the monthly standard deviation of returns by the square root of 12 (3.4641).

Do not be concerned with the need to actually do these calculations yourself. Sharpe ratios for mutual funds are readily accessible. I am showing you the formula as a means of explaining the basis of the ratio.

The formula subtracts returns that you can achieve with no risk (the risk-free return that you might be able to secure from 90-day Treasury bills, for example) from returns that have been achieved by your contemplated investment.

The average monthly return is the average monthly return that your mutual fund (or other investment) has actually received for the period of time you are evaluating.

The difference, average monthly return minus monthly risk-free return, is called the excess return—the extra return that you have secured by taking investment risk.

Have Your Investment Returns Been Worth the Risk?

This is the key question, which is answered by relating the excess return to the amount of risk of the investment, which is reflected in the standard deviation of monthly returns (The standard deviation is the range of monthly fluctuation above or below the average monthly change that contains two thirds of all monthly swings.)

For example, a standard deviation of 5% means that two thirds of the time, monthly changes were 5% or less away from the average or mean monthly change, regardless of direction. The standard deviation is one measure of the range of monthly performances, including the best months and the worst months. Ninety-day Treasury bills show minimal variation in performance; they pay the same interest month in and month out for the short life of the bill and show only minor price volatility. Mutual funds may show a range of results ranging from gains of, for instance, 8% to losses of 8% per month— greater potential gain than Treasury bills, but certainly with greater potential pain. The higher the standard deviation of return, the more investment results vary for the good or the bad, and the greater the risk of the investment.

Caveat

This concept has one weakness: the possibility that the range of movement may lie either consistently to the upside or consistently to the downside. The concept of standard deviation as applied to the Sharpe ratio presumes equal excursions above neutral (no change) as below. This potential shortcoming notwithstanding, the Sharpe ratio has been widely accepted as a useful reflection and measure of risk.

Understanding Excess Return Compared to Risk Levels

A mutual fund that shows an excess return of, say, 5% per year compared to Treasury bills but whose standard deviation of annual returns has been 10% may be a poorer risk:adjusted investment than a mutual fund whose annual excess return has been just 3% compared to Treasury bills but whose standard deviation of annual returns has been just 2%. The latter mutual fund has secured 60% of the excess return of the first fund but has had just a small fraction of the risk.

The Sharpe ratio, again, may be used as a quick way to compare the risk/reward qualities of alternative investments. It is a useful tool, but not perfect. To the extent that the Sharpe ratio depends on historical data for its calculation, an implicit assumption holds that future performance will reflect past performance—which, of course, is not always the case. Readings of the ratio may change rapidly (for example, as a result of rapid changes in the short-term interest structure, which will affect Treasury bill yields). And again, there is that issue of whether maximum excursions from the mean monthly change are really balanced between gains and losses.

For Further Information Regarding the Sharpe Ratio

If you perform a search on Google or MSN for "Sharpe ratio," you will be directed to numerous articles and commentaries relating to the subject.

You can find Sharpe ratios for individual mutual funds on www.Morningstar.com, www.Yahoo.com (look under Financial), and in the financial areas of www.MSN.com. Refer to the areas that relate to investment risks. The Steele database, referred to previously, carries Sharpe ratios for as long as 10 years; other sources may not maintain that long a database, but 5-year ratios will probably serve the purpose.

Sharpe Ratio Levels Required to Qualify a Mutual Fund for the One-in-a-Thousand Club

In addition to the performance criteria cited previously, for a mutual fund to qualify for membership in the one-in-a-thousand club, it must also meet the following Sharpe ratio criteria:

- The Sharpe ratio of the mutual fund must have been at least 0.75 for the most-recent 3-year period.

- The Sharpe ratio of the mutual fund must have been at least 0.75 for the most-recent 5-year period.

- The Sharpe ratio of the mutual fund must have been at least 0.75 for the most-recent 10-year period.

As an alternative, the Sharpe ratio must have been at least 0.30 higher than the Sharpe ratio for the Standard & Poor's 500 Index for each of the periods listed here. For example, if the Sharpe ratio for the Standard & Poor's 500 Index has been 0.30 over the past 3 years, the Sharpe ratio for a mutual fund during this period must have been at least 0.60 (0.60 − 0.30 = 0.30).

This alternative parameter has been somewhat easier to achieve and is likely to provide a larger number of mutual funds from which to make your selections. (See Table 3-1.)

The One-in-a-Thousand Club Selections

The bear market of 2000–2002 affected the majority of stock market sectors—the Standard & Poor's 500 Index losing nearly 45%, and the NASDAQ Composite Index giving up more than 77% of its value during the market decline. As a result, relatively few market sectors were able to both maintain positive Sharpe ratios and to outperform the Standard & Poor's 500 Index.

Real estate market sectors, along with small-capitalization value companies, were among the few groups that bucked the negative trends of the bear market, as reflected in their relatively longer-term dominance as of mid-2005, the time at which the preceding selections were screened. Small-capitalization value issues have had a fine long-term historical performance, with real estate strong enough over the years as well during most market periods. During favorable market climates, additional investment sectors would be likely to achieve representation in this select buy and hold group, too.

The 20 mutual funds that met both selection criteria all produced profit for the 3-year, 5-year, and 10-year periods of the study, even during the 5-year period during which the Standard & Poor's 500 Index declined by 2.37%.

The average Sharpe ratios for these 20 mutual funds were 1.24 for 3 years, 1.23 for 5 years, and 0.87 for 10 years—all high and excellent readings.

Table 3-1 The 20 Contenders—July 26, 2005

Fund	Objective	3-Yr GPA	5-Yr GPA	10-Yr GPA	3-Yr Sharpe	5-Yr Sharpe	10-Yr Sharpe
AIM Real Estate/c	Real estate	22.75	20.72	14.37	1.46	1.37	0.77
Alpine US Real Estate	Real estate	34.35	34.06	21.36	1.47	1.41	0.82
Amer Century Equity Income	All cap	10.56	12.56	13.55	0.87	0.99	0.89
Ariel Fund	Small cap value	13.07	15.11	15.57	0.94	1.02	0.82
CGM Realty Fund	Real estate	32.62	27.81	20.54	1.29	1.23	0.94
Cohen & Steers Realty Fund	Real estate	23.01	20.78	15.81	1.32	1.23	0.84
Columbia Real Estate Equity	Real estate	19.37	17.55	15.59	1.28	1.13	0.92
DFA Real Estate Sec.	Real estate	20.81	20.46	15.22	1.23	1.27	0.86
Fidelity Real Estate Inv.	Real estate	20.98	20.15	15.51	1.28	1.28	0.87
First American Real Estate	Real estate	21.94	21.16	15.52	1.33	1.36	0.91
Heitman REIT/PBHG	Real estate	20.85	19.66	15.70	1.21	1.19	0.88
Loomis Sayles Bond/1st	Global income multisector	16.49	11.41	10.30	2.01	1.25	0.88
Loomis Sayles Fixed Income	Global income multisector	16.73	11.92	10.28	1.93	1.26	0.89
Loomis Sayles InvGrFXInc.	Global income multisector	13.37	12.17	10.14	1.52	1.41	0.95
M Stanley Inst: US RE/A	Real estate	22.79	20.44	17.56	1.38	1.28	1.03
MainStay Balanced	Asset allocation balanced	10.87	10.69	10.31	1.10	1.04	0.77
Mairs & Power Growth	All cap	11.52	11.16	15.47	0.89	0.75	0.87
Royce Total Return	Small cap value	13.09	15.15	14.38	0.97	1.00	0.93
Russell Real Estate Sec/S	Real estate	21.90	20.20	15.50	1.31	1.24	0.86
T. Rowe Price Cap. Apprec.	Asset allocation balanced	12.62	13.64	12.68	1.22	1.24	1.06
Fund average		**21.85**	**20.91**	**16.25**	**1.24**	**1.23**	**0.87**
S & P 500 total return		**8.28**	**-2.37**	**9.94**	**0.49**	**-0.30**	**0.39**

Managing Your Buy and Hold Portfolio

Although strong and well-managed mutual funds tend to retain strength for many years, sooner or later even the best of funds may lose strength relative to the market as a whole and/or to other mutual funds.

Review your portfolio annually to make certain that your holdings continue to meet the basic criteria required for long-term investment positions of this nature. You can review positions at 6-month intervals, if you like, which may be suitable for tax-sheltered holdings such as those maintained in an IRA account, for example. However, if positions are taxable, a procedure of holding positions for at least 12 months may prove beneficial with regard to after-tax returns because a 1-year holding period is required to qualify an investment for long-term capital gain tax treatment.

Therefore, do the following:

1. Establish your portfolio of mutual funds designated for long-term holding. Such funds should essentially meet the criteria designated for membership in the one-in-a-thousand club and may be held until they no longer meet the criteria. In general, avoid funds that charge front-end loads, as well as funds that incur back-end charges for holding periods of longer than 1 year.

2. At annual intervals, sell those holdings that no longer meet the buy and hold criteria and replace them with new qualifying positions.

3. When assembling your portfolio of buy and hold mutual funds, remember to apply the concepts of diversification. This would have been possible even with the relatively small group of 20 mutual funds that met the one-in-a-thousand club criteria with its emphasis on real estate mutual funds. You might select a real estate, a small-cap value, a global

income, an asset allocation, and an all-cap mutual fund for a five-fund diversification.

4. For most investors, this segment of your investment portfolio may well occupy approximately 35% to 50% of your stock market investment assets, representing a fine, tax-favored core position in your total portfolio.

Putting Together and Maintaining a Portfolio of Strong Mutual Funds for Intermediate-Term Investment

More gain, less pain!

Responsive to changing market leadership!

Relatively few transactions each year!

Rotating Your Portfolio at Regular Intervals to Maintain a Portfolio of Market Leaders

Mutual funds meeting the criteria required to be held on a long-term, essentially buy and hold, basis offer many advantages: low transaction costs, favorable tax treatment if held outside of tax-sheltered accounts, outstanding risk/reward characteristics, and generally fine long-term performance.

However, because this portfolio emphasizes consistency and risk reduction, there are times when investors using buy and hold portfolios alone may not participate with the strongest industry groups during favorable market periods or during periods that are unfavorable for most industry groups but possibly favorable for a more select number.

Lower-volatility buy and hold portfolios are not always positioned to reflect changes in market leadership that take place not just year by year, but often month by month—certain industry groups and individual funds rising to the leadership fore, others dropping from the top ranks.

You can derive definite benefits from identifying and investing in mutual funds that have consistently produced long-term above-average performance, especially when favorable risk levels accompany such performance. You can derive other benefits from identifying and investing in mutual funds that are outperforming 90% of other mutual funds for somewhat shorter periods of time, shifting assets so that your capital starts each investment period in funds that represent the top 10% of mutual funds in terms of market strength.

The four-step "follow-the-leader" strategy presented here has shown excellent past performance, including a fine record of producing superior gain with smaller pain than the average mutual fund:

1. Identify the leaders.

2. Buy the leaders.

3. Hold the leaders until they stop leading.

4. Change to new, emerging leadership.

For our purposes, I define a mutual fund as a market leader if its performance over the most-recent 3 months has been more favorable than 90% of all mutual funds. In other words, funds that are in the top 10% (decile) in market performance are considered as members of the elite top decile of all mutual funds.

Why 3 months? Well, actually it is not a magical period. You might use a 2-month period for measurement. Or a weighted combination of 3-month and 1-year holding periods that provides a blend of measures of near-term strength and longer-term strength.

The 3-month period, however, has many advantages. For one, quarterly mutual fund performance data is readily available—

Barron's Financial Weekly, for example, publishes mutual fund performance on a quarterly basis, as do many other financial publications. You will shortly see why this is useful. For another, many mutual funds charge fees to investors who sell mutual funds within 90 days of purchase. If you rank funds at 3-month intervals, and transact at such intervals, you can avoid many fees that might accrue were you to trade more frequently. Relatively few mutual funds have a problem with the number of trades that the intermediate mutual fund relative-strength investment model involves.

Isolate the Safer Group of Mutual Funds in Which to Invest

Separate the normally volatile mutual funds from those funds that normally demonstrate below-average volatility.

Volatility may be expressed as the standard deviation of monthly returns, but may also be expressed as a fund's "beta" or amount of fluctuation compared to its benchmark, the usual benchmark for stock market comparisons, the Standard & Poor's 500 Index. Volatility ratings for mutual funds may be found in the Morningstar publications or on their Web site, on the Steele Web site, and from many other sources. A search of the Web for "mutual fund volatility" will produce a number of relevant sites.

Unless you are making use of a viable and generally reliable stock market timing model that reduces risk in its own way, confine your mutual fund selections to those that are no greater than the Standard & Poor's 500 Index in their longer-term volatility ratings! Forget about the imaginary and often-illusory potential gain of the "hot mutual fund universe." Remember that the secret to success in the stock market is minimization of pain.

I do not take the space and time to dwell on this point further. The simple fact, again, is that for the most part, investors who have invested in quieter, less-volatile mutual funds have come out over the long run with as much net profit as those who have taken the risks associated with higher-risk and more-volatile funds. *Equal long-term gain, less pain.*

Again, you will see how you can up the gain while minimizing the pain with a strong stock market timing model, but for now we will assume that you do not want to become involved with procedures that require daily tracking of the stock market and that risk control is properly high on your priority list.

Ranking the Funds for Performance

Obtain a source of mutual fund quarterly performance. Many financial publications provide such data. A search of the Web for "mutual fund performance, quarterly" will turn up numerous services that provide reports of mutual fund performance. Morningstar's Web site (www.morningstar.com) provides a free membership that includes considerable information and news about the mutual fund industry. MSN.com, in their Money section, provides performance rankings and data for the mutual fund industry, including funds that have been leading in performance for the most-recent 3-month period. The Steele database, already cited, is also a good source for information you may require.

Outperforming Typical Mutual Funds

1. Separate mutual funds of less-than-average volatility (less risk) from mutual funds of greater-than-average volatility.

2. Isolate within the lower-volatility universe those mutual funds that have shown the best performance over the previous calendar quarter, funds whose performance exceeds that of 90% of the total fund universe you are examining.

You do not really have to review all the thousands of mutual funds that now exist. For practical purposes, you should do just fine selecting the top 10% or top decile of a universe of perhaps 250 to 500 mutual funds. This range will provide you with a selection of between 25 and 50 candidates for purchase.

3. Establish your portfolio with a selection of perhaps four to seven different mutual funds in the top decile. Remember the principles of diversification! Spread your holdings over a variety of market sectors. Be certain to check out front-end and back-end transaction fees. This program should involve minimum commission costs.

4. At 3-month intervals, review your portfolio and the universe of mutual funds from which you have been making your selections. If any of your holdings have dropped out of the top performance decile, sell them and replace them with mutual funds that have risen to or remain within the top 10% of your mutual fund universe in terms of performance.

You will, thus, always start each new quarter with a portfolio of mutual funds that have been outperforming 90% of mutual funds within your volatility group (below-average volatility to average volatility). As a general rule, your selections will fare well over the long run with relatively low risk levels against even the most glamorous and "hot" aggressively oriented mutual funds.

Past Performance

Figure 3-1 shows the relative performances of mutual funds of average to below-average volatility, including the top-performing 10%, the average-performing 10%, and the lowest-performing 10%, 1990 to mid-2005.

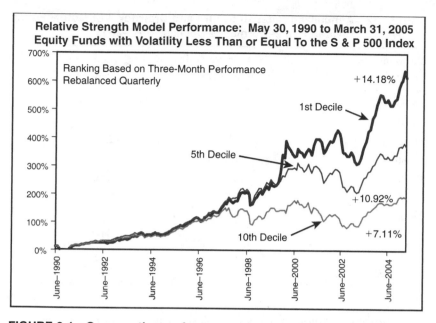

FIGURE 3-1   Comparative performance of mutual funds ranked by relative strength and rotated on a quarterly basis, 1990–2005

Mutual funds whose performance was in the top decile achieved a compounded annual rate of return of 14.18%. The average mutual fund (average of deciles 5 and 6) achieved a compounded annual rate of return of 10.84%. Funds in the lowest decile produced annual returns of just 7.11%.

As you can see, funds in the highest-performing decile have consistently outperformed funds of lower rank while at the same time showing lesser drawdowns. Table 3-2 lists the annualized gains per annum for each decile as well as the maximum drawdown for each decline. The presumption is that your mutual fund universe is divided into ten deciles that are rebalanced at quarterly intervals so that your capital starts each quarter with a diversified portfolio of only mutual funds that have led in performance (top 10%) during the previous quarter.

TABLE 3-2   Annualized Rates of Return and Drawdown of Mutual Funds Divided into Performance Deciles, 1990–2005

Performance Decile	Average Gain per Annum	Maximum Drawdown
Decile 1	+14.18%	–23.33%
Decile 2	+13.32	–20.28
Decile 3	+12.58	–22.83
Decile 4	+11.50	–25.27
Decile 5	+10.92	–26.04
Decile 6	+10.76	–28.46
Decile 7	+9.49	–31.19
Decile 8	+8.76	–34.87
Decile 9	+8.38	–34.66
Decile 10	+7.11	–37.07

There are almost perfect correlations among performance, risk levels, and decile rank. The higher in rank the decile, the higher the rate of return and, with two exceptions, the lower the drawdown. The difference between gain per annum of +14.18% (decile 1) and +10.84% (average of deciles 5 and 6) can be quite considerable, especially when compounded over a long time. For example, a starting amount of $100,000, growing at a compound rate of 14.18% would be worth $730,888 after 15 years, $2,752,650 after 25 years. The same starting amount, $100,000, compounding at a rate of 10.84% per year would grow to $468,218 after 15 years, to $1,310,427 after 25 years.

The long-term differential in asset growth is striking, not to mention the risk reduction.

Upping the Ante with a Double-Period Ranking Model

Although ranking funds each quarter based on their performance the previous quarter does improve both total and risk:adjusted performance considerably, this is actually not the best set of parameters to use—just one of the simplest because quarterly performance data is so readily available.

You can achieve a clear improvement in investment results by using the following double-period ranking model:

1. Isolate your fund universe so that you are investing only in funds of average to below-average volatility, when compared to other mutual funds.

2. Secure the performance of each fund in your universe for the previous 3 months (prior quarter) *plus* the previous 12 months. You need the most recent 3-month investment performance *and* the most recent 12-month investment performance. Both are actually readily available from various sources, including some already listed.

3. For each fund, add the 3-month performance to the 12-month performance to secure a combined performance total for ranking. For example, if a fund has gained 5% over the previous 3 months and 12% over the previous 12 months, its combined performance total would be +17% (5% + 12%). If the fund gained 5% over the previous 3 months but lost 2% over the previous 12 months, its combined performance total would be +3% (5% – 2%).

4. At 3-month intervals, rank funds based on their combined performance total.

5. Invest only in those funds whose combined performance total lies within the top 10% of all funds in your universe.

By using multiple time periods in your ranking process, you are giving weight to both long-term (12 months) and shorter-term (3 months) action of the mutual funds that you are tracking in contrast to just assigning weight to one period alone.

Once again, ranking and rebalancing takes place at 3-month intervals, but in this case the ranking is based on the total of each fund's 3-month and 1-year performances, not on the basis of the 3-month performance alone.

Figure 3-2 shows the performance of the first decile of mutual funds ranked quarterly based on the combined performance of the most recent 3- and 12-month periods.

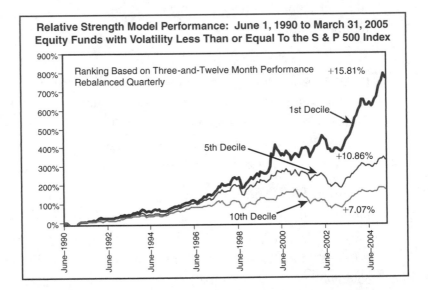

FIGURE 3-2   Mutual fund performance based on decile rank of performance for the most-recent 3-month and 12-month periods

This chart shows the relative performance by deciles of funds in the top decile (10%) in performance, decile 5, and decile 10 (the lowest). The correlations between decile rank at the start of each quarter, gain per annum, and risk levels are almost perfect insofar as long-term performance is concerned.

Examining the Statistical Comparisons, Decile by Decile

Table 3-3 shows the mutual fund performance by deciles based on the ranks of the combined 3-month and 1-year performances of the funds.

TABLE 3-3   Annualized Rates of Return and Drawdown of Mutual Funds Divided into Performance Deciles, Based on a Combination of 3-Month and 12-Month Performance, Rebalancing at Quarterly Intervals, 1990–2005

Performance Decile	Average Gain per Annum	Maximum Drawdown
Decile 1	+15.81%	–17.16%
Decile 2	+13.85	–19.36
Decile 3	+12.94	–21.34
Decile 4	+11.90	–24.07
Decile 5	+10.86	–28.88
Decile 6	+10.05	–31.87
Decile 7	+9.34	–35.18
Decile 8	+8.05	–37.11
Decile 9	+7.46	–36.54
Decile 10	+7.07	–36.42

As a comparison of Table 3-2 to Table 3-1 indicates, using a combination of 3-month and 12-month performance and rebalancing quarterly rather than using just the performance of the 3-month performance rank alone in conjunction with quarterly rebalancing appears to have had the following effects:

- Returns for mutual funds in deciles 1, 2, 3, and 4 (particularly decile 1) improved, whereas returns in the lower decile groups appear to have deteriorated.

- The additional parameters seem to produce more clear-cut distinctions between mutual funds that are likely to succeed and those more likely to lag in performance.

- Of particular note have been the improvements in the performance of funds ranked in the first decile when ranking is based on two criteria rather than just one.

- Of lesser practical significance, lower-ranked groups lagged higher-ranked groups by greater amounts.

- The performance of groups near the universe midpoint was relatively unchanged. The greatest impact seems to be on funds at the extremes in relative strength.

> ### Recommendation!
>
> If at all possible, given your temperament and time, try to use a combination of time frames for the ranking of mutual funds in your database. This is almost certain to improve performance with just a moderate additional expenditure of time and effort (although the 3-month period may be used alone to good benefit).

Diversification Will Almost Certainly Help the Cause

At the risk of beating a dead horse, I want, once again, to restate the benefits of *diversification* in the construction of your mutual fund portfolios.

With proper diversification, you should be able to expand the universe of mutual funds that may be used in your holdings to include at least some of greater volatility, if they happen to be leading in relative strength, while still retaining desirable risk characteristics.

Table 3-4 illustrates again the risk-reducing abilities of diversification. Volatility in this table refers to the extent of price movement for each market sector in comparison to the Standard & Poor's 500 Index. The greater the volatility, the riskier the investment.

The "ulcer index" is a reflection of risk, a measure of the amount of loss any investment might incur during the life of its holding. The lower the ulcer index, the less risk incurred by an investment. One good gain:pain measure can be secured by dividing the annualized rate of return of any investment by its ulcer index (gain/ulcer index), which provides a meaningful reflection of risk/reward characteristics of that investment over the period of time measured.

Table 3-4, created via research carried forth during August 2005, shows the effects of creating a portfolio of six mutual funds representing five industry sectors—Aim Energy (IENAX), Fidelity Select Energy (FSENX), Fidelity Select Brokerage (FSLBX), Alpine US Real Estate (EUEYX), Jennison Utilities (PRUAX), and Schwab Health Care (SWHFX). There are two representatives, a double weighting of assets, from the energy sector in this portfolio because of the high relative strength of this market sector at the time.

TABLE 3-4   Volatility Effects of Sector Diversification

	Average	IENAX	FSENX	FSLBX	EUEYX	PRUAX	SWHFX	Volatility of Blended Total Porfolio
90-day volatility	2.219	2.048	1.227	1.890	1.051	1.266	1.617	1.330
1-year volatility	2.138	1.961	1.332	1.958	1.071	1.300	1.630	1.307
3-year volatility	1.374	1.306	1.408	1.449	0.921	1.105	1.261	1.043
3-year ulcer index	**5.21%**	**4.83%**	**8.90%**	**5.59%**	**4.65%**	**5.12%**	**5.72%**	**3.81%**

Volatility levels are in relation to the volatility of the Standard & Poor's 500 Index. For example, for the 90 days preceding the calculations for this study, the Aim Energy Fund had a volatility of 2.048, which means that the fund's price movement was 2.048 times that of the Standard & Poor's 500 Index. This tabulation does not reflect that direction of movement.

We can readily see that the average volatilities of the components of this portfolio, taken separately and averaged, have been far greater than the volatility of the total portfolio, when the individual sectors are combined. For example, the average volatility for the 3-year period of the separate components was 1.374 times that of the Standard &

Poor's 500 Index, whereas the total portfolio had a volatility only 1.043 times that of the Standard & Poor's 500 Index.

Perhaps more to the point, the ulcer index of the separate sectors as represented by the listed mutual funds, taken separately, came to an average of 5.21%. The ulcer index of the total portfolio, taken as a portfolio, was only 3.81% (another reflection of the reduced risk involved in proper diversification).

Conclusion

Diversify! Diversify! Diversify!

Getting the Maximum Bang from the Bucks in Your 401K Plan and Other Tax-Sheltered Investment Portfolios

We have now considered three types of mutual fund investment programs—the "buy and hold" portfolio which provides excellent opportunities for favorable long-term capital gain tax treatment, the "diverse sector mutual fund portfolios," which provide some but probably lesser opportunity for favorable tax treatment in unqualified or unsheltered accounts, and "mutual fund portfolios, traded on intermediate term measures of relative strength," which are relatively unfriendly from a tax point of view.

Many 401K plans provide the best of many worlds. Such plans are often created to provide participants with access to the entire universe of major mutual fund families—for example, Fidelity, T. Rowe Price, or Vanguard. If you are reading this book, there is at least a fair chance that you, yourself, are participating in such a plan or that you can structure your IRA account so that it may be flexibly invested within a large mutual fund family.

Special Advantages of 401K Plans for Active Mutual Fund Management

Many mutual fund families have become skittish regarding active trading of their funds. This is understandable. Large amounts of trading in and out by shareholders create unstable portfolios, extra expenses that have to be borne by all shareholders, problems for portfolio managers, as well as clerical and other expenses and difficulties. For the most part, however, most mutual fund families accept trades that follow on minimum holding periods of investments of at least 90 days, in some cases 6 months.

It often happens, moreover, that 401K plans that use the rosters of specific mutual fund families arrange for participants to have the right to make *unlimited trades* or movements of assets from one mutual fund within the family to another. You should not have to alter your investment posture nearly that often—but it can be nice to know that the flexibility is available if market conditions suddenly change.

Trading flexibility apart, trading in mutual funds via 401K plans has the potential to provide the opportunity to benefit from active portfolio management at no tax penalty.

If you study and act on the following procedure, you will have a well-tested strategy for reallocating assets in your 401K and other tax-sheltered investment milieus on a regular and consistent basis.

We have already discussed the basic concepts underlying your 401K maximization strategy, so much of what follows is already familiar. Here are the steps involved:

1. Secure the full roster of equity mutual funds in the fund family to which you have access via your 401K plan. (Bond funds may be used, too, but should probably be carried in their own universe in a proportion to stock funds that would be based on your total investment portfolio, including assets outside of the 401K plan.)

In mid-2005, the Fidelity family offered more than 100 equity-oriented mutual funds from which selections might be made. We use this family as the prototype example.

2. Inasmuch as this is likely to be an equity fund only portfolio (no bonds) and inasmuch as we are presuming a minimum of protective market timing activity in this account, you should reduce risks in the portfolio by selecting for investment consideration only those Fidelity funds which lie *in the lowest third of all Fidelity funds in terms of market volatility and risk*. (Relevant data may be secured from Fidelity, Morningstar, Steele and/or a variety of other sources of mutual fund data.)

3. At the end of each quarter, review all the Fidelity funds in your lower-volatility universe, ranking the roster of funds in the lower-volatility universe based on their performance over the most recent *12-month* period. Start by purchasing those funds that stand in the top 10% based on these rankings (the familiar top decile in performance). In mid-2005, the top decile of the lower-volatility group included three funds—the top 10% of the 33 funds out of 100 that carried the lowest volatility.

4. Re-rank each quarter, based on fund performance over the previous 12 months. Remove from your portfolio funds that have dropped out of the top 10%. Retain funds that remain in the top 10% of performance.

Unless you are certain that a broad and durable stock market advance is under way, emphasize lower-volatility funds in your 401K portfolio. This should be a conservative area of your general investment portfolio—money you are setting aside for retirement.

You might be able to improve performance somewhat by using more-complex ranking criteria such as the combination of 3-month and 1-year performance discussed previously. There is nothing sacrosanct in using just a 1-year "look-back" period, which I am using as an example of how even simple ranking criteria can prove viable.

Figure 3-3 shows the growth of assets, using only the Fidelity roster of funds, a low-volatility sector derived from the total Fidelity universe, and quarterly updating based on 12-month performance.

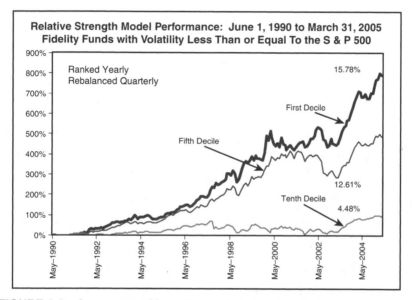

FIGURE 3-3   **A program of investing only in the top decile of lower-volatility mutual funds in the Fidelity family would have produced favorable results compared to random investing in the total family, 1990–2005. (Results based on hypothetical back testing.)**

Table 3-5 presents these results in tabular form.

**TABLE 3-5   Annualized Rates of Return and Drawdown of Lower-
Volatility Fidelity Mutual Funds Divided into Performance
Deciles Based on 12-Month Performance, Rebalancing at
Quarterly Intervals, 1990–2005**

Performance Decile	Average Gain per Annum	Maximum Drawdown
Decile 1	+15.78%	–15.2%
Decile 2	+12.43	–21.4
Decile 3	+13.63	–25.7
Decile 4	+10.47	–31.8
Decile 5	+12.61	–26.7
Decile 6	+9.57	–35.5
Decile 7	+7.54	–30.6
Decile 8	+8.61	–31.0
Decile 9	+9.32	–37.7
Decile 10	+4.48	–37.9

As you can see, investing only in those Fidelity funds that stand in the top decile, rebalancing quarterly based on one-year performance, produced an average annual rate of return of 15.8% compared to the average Fidelity fund (the average of the fifth and sixth deciles) which produced an average annual rate of return of 11.1%.

Even more significant have been the reductions in risk levels associated with investment only in the top decile of even the lowest volatility group in the Fidelity family. Risks in an unmanaged portfolio can be far greater than many investors assume, ranging to as high as 37.9% for poorly performing funds on a past basis—no guarantees that greater losses will not take place in the future.

You might notice that, while there are clear correlations among decile performance rank, average annual rates of return, and risk, relationships have not been quite as linear as we have seen in earlier studies that include a much broader universe of mutual funds than is available within any single mutual fund family. The larger the available universe, the more likely results are to prove predictable in the same way that political polls narrowly taken are likely to prove less reliable than more broadly sampled polls.

Caveats of this nature aside, the evidence does appear to clearly indicate that portfolio returns may be augmented, risks reduced, even within single mutual fund families, by the application of relative strength strategies, carried out in a consistent manner.

One Final Thought

Life being what it is, many, many families find it difficult to set aside retirement capital earlier in life. There are often simply too many expenses for your homes, child care needs, college expenses, travel, rising energy costs—to easily maintain life styles, much less to save for retirement, as desirable as that might be.

However, even if families cannot readily save after tax dollars, many do make regular contributions to their IRA accounts, or to their 401K plans, all the more so because most such plans involve employer contributions, too.

Well, let's suppose that by the age of 45, you have been able to accumulate $100,000 in your 401K plan or IRA account and from that time forth until the age of 65, you have been able to compound capital at a rate of 15.8% per year (decile 1). Because your gains are tax sheltered, you have no tax obligations along the way.

Final total value of assets in the account, based only on those assets with which you started, not including the growth in value of contributions that might be made on an ongoing basis between ages 45 and 65?

Your original $100,000 would grow to $1,880,057 or to approximately 18.8 times your starting capital!

The opportunities involved certainly do seem to be worth the effort of reviewing and rebalancing your investments four times each year.

One Final Test—Confirming with T. Rowe Price

I spare you further detailed charts and tables, but as just one final test to see how our ranking techniques would have fared with a mutual fund group other than Fidelity, my research team took a similar approach with the T. Rowe Price family of mutual funds, another highly regarded and diverse mutual fund family.

The following research assumptions applied to this hypothetical study:

1. At quarterly intervals, the performance of each equity fund in the T. Rowe Price family was measured for periods of 1 year and of 3 months. The performances for the 3-month and 1-year periods were added together to secure a composite 3-month, 12-month total. For example, if a fund shows a gain of 10% for the past 12 months and 5% for the past 3 months, its composite performance is +15%.

2. At quarterly intervals, all capital was placed into T. Rowe Price funds whose composite performance lay in the highest 10% of the fund family. As funds dropped out of the top 10%, they were sold and replaced with funds currently in the top decile. The test period covered the period from 1997 through 2005.

3. Investments were limited to funds in the T. Rowe Price family that were no more volatile than the Standard & Poor's 500 Index.

Results—Fine discrimination, better returns, risk reduction:

- T. Rowe Price equity funds in the top decile showed an average annual rate of return of 13.2% per year, with a maximum drawdown of 18.3%.

- T. Rowe Price equity funds in the fifth decile showed an average annual rate of return of 8.8%, with a maximum drawdown of 29.2%.

- T. Rowe Price equity funds in the tenth (the lowest) decile showed an annual rate of return of 7.1%, with a maximum drawdown of 32.5%. The tenth (lowest) decile actually outperformed deciles 7, 8, and 9, which produced annualized rates of return of 4.4%, 3.5%, and 2.6% and maximum drawdowns of 33.9%, 48.1%, and 34.7%, respectively.

We will review additional ways to achieve profit from various segments of the equity arena. However, inasmuch as investment portfolios do not usually grow value from capital gains alone, perhaps the time has come to return to the many opportunities provided by income instruments.

4

INCOME INVESTING— SAFER AND STEADY . . . BUT WATCH OUT FOR THE PITFALLS

The Four Legs of Your Investment Portfolio

Suppose that we think of your investment portfolio as a solid, firm table—a table meant to support your assets, financial needs, and retirement income with relatively small risk of overturning or collapsing.

Such a table could not stand at all if it had only one or two legs. It might be able to stand on three legs, but would almost certainly be unstable and prone to accident should the weight of its burden shift (and especially if one of its legs gave way).

However, a properly built table with four strong legs can safely support considerable weight and can withstand shifts in the weight of its burden and vibrations in the floor below. It might vibrate a bit if bumped, but can carry forth its tasks for many, many years, providing support with relatively little risk.

So far, we have discussed three legs of the four required for your investment table:

- The first leg is *diversification,* diversification in the type of investments you are making as well as diversification within each asset class. You have seen how you can increase return while reducing risk by creating and maintaining portfolios that represent diverse industry groups and geographic areas. Diversification in general, and that portion of your equity (stock) portfolio that has been specifically designed for diversification and sector rebalancing, is the first leg of the table that supports the burden of your investments.

- The second leg is represented by those mutual funds that have had *outstanding long-term performance histories* as well as favorable risk/reward characteristics. Such funds provide stability in investment portfolios; and for unsheltered accounts, tax benefits often accrue from profits taken over long-term periods. (These portfolios should be well diversified, too.)

- The third leg is represented by those mutual funds (and exchange-traded funds [ETFs] to be discussed in forthcoming chapters) purchased and held for intermediate (usually several months) periods, whose selections are based on intermediate-term relative strength. These represent funds *purchased and held for only as long as they remain in the top tier of mutual fund performance.*

These three legs provide a fine balance among long-term investments, intermediate-term investments, and representatives of the strongest of diversified sectors—all of which may be supplemented by market timing strategies, some of which have already been discussed, others of which will be.

The fourth leg of your investment portfolio table should include areas previously alluded to but not yet pursued in detail: *areas of income investment,* that portion of your investment portfolio structured to provide safety of principal and relatively predictable ongoing cash flow (as opposed to less-certain capital gain). The presence of a certain portion of income components within a total investment portfolio considerably reduces the risks associated with an all-stock portfolio, improving the risk/reward or gain/pain ratios that accrue from portfolios that hold stocks alone.

This fourth leg of your portfolio should, for most investors, occupy generally between 20% and 30% of investment assets—more for investors whose financial situations suggest prudence, the avoidance of risk, and high current and predictable income streams; possibly somewhat less for younger, aggressive, well-earning investors, whose investment objectives strongly emphasize asset growth rather than safety.

A Quick and Dirty Glossary of Income-Related Terms

A *bond* is a loan that a bondholder makes to a corporation, to the government, or to other organizations for which the borrower agrees to pay a certain amount of interest (*coupon*), usually expressed as an annual percentage of the *face value* of the bond, the amount of the loan, generally $1,000. In addition, most bonds are issued with a *maturity date,* the date when the loan signified by the bond is scheduled to be paid back in full. Many bonds allow for an early prepayment of the loan by the bond issuer, under specified conditions.

A bond, therefore, provides a *fixed amount of income, a fixed date at which your investment capital is pledged for return,* and a *fixed amount of repayment,* usually the face value of the bond. Sometimes, if the loan is paid back (*called*) prior to its maturity date, an extra premium is paid to the bondholder in addition to the face value of the bond.

So far, so good. You know how much you are investing. You know how much interest you are scheduled to receive. You know when you are supposed to get your money back. Where are the potential problems?

Well, for one—and this is probably the *major long-term risk*—some borrowers, even well-known corporations, run into hard times and do not pay their debts. When a company fails to meet its interest payments or cannot repay some or all of its bonds' face value on maturity, it is said to be in *default,* a definite risk to bondholders. Well-known companies that have defaulted on their debt have included TWA, Pan-American Airlines, Enron, and WorldCom. As I write, the ability of companies such as even General Motors and Ford to meet payments on long-term bonds is under question. At different times, large municipalities such as New York City have found their credit-worthiness to be in question. Only bonds issued by the U.S. government are considered to be free of default risk (because of the government's power to tax to meet payments), but it is conceivable that conditions might arise that could prevent even the U.S. government from paying its bills.

Dealing with Default Risk

The creditworthiness of the issuers of bonds of various sorts are rated by five major rating agencies (nationally recognized statistical ratings organizations [NRSROs]) designated by the Securities and Exchange Commission—AM Best, Dominion Bond Rating Service, Fitch Ratings, Moody's Investor Service, and Standard & Poor's.

Ratings are broadly divided into two categories: *investment grade* and *noninvestment grade.* Using the Standard & Poor's ratings, investment-grade ratings include AAA (highest creditworthiness), AA, A, and BBB (BAA when rated by Moody's). Bonds rated AAA are considered to have minimal risks of default, whereas bonds rated as BBB are considered to be of adequate credit quality but susceptible to default risk at future times.

Noninvestment-grade ratings (S & P) include BB, B, CCC, CC, C+, C, C−, and D (each level down implying successively greater risk). Ratings of CCC and below are considered highly speculative, although many high-yield bond funds tend to carry large amounts of C-rated bonds in their portfolios, along with bonds in the B to BBB category. (High-yield bond funds typically find 3% to 5% of their holdings in default each year, a percentage that ranged up to 10% and even more during the 2000–2002 economic recession.)

For safety purposes, bond investments should be confined for the most part to investment-grade holdings. High-yield bond funds, despite the lower quality of their holdings, have performed well enough during most years, and generally do hold well in diversified portfolios. The best of such funds evaluate their holdings carefully on an individual basis and purchase only bonds that their managements consider to hold better prospects than their ratings might imply. High-yield bond funds that invest in lower-quality bonds do tend to be rather volatile in their price movement. They may have their place in but should not occupy a major portion of most investors' portfolios.

Bond ratings can be secured from rating services as well as from brokerage houses and other sources. The quality of holdings of bond mutual funds can be secured from these mutual funds, which will generally provide, on request, average yields, ratings, and maturities of their portfolios.

Risks can also be contained in your bond portfolio *by diversification, diversification, and more diversification.* Remember, even the best-known companies get into trouble, and if a bond is providing an extremely high yield there is probably a reason for it.

Shorter maturity bonds, all else being equal, carry less risk than longer-term bonds. As mentioned in Chapter 1, "The Myth of Buy and Hold," intermediate-term bonds generally provide better yield/risk relationships than longer-term bonds. They are less subject to risks of default because their holding period (period of risk) is less than long-term bonds—less time for the condition of issuers to deteriorate. They are also less subject to damage arising from changes in the general interest rate climate because of their relative closeness to maturity and payback in full.

Bond Duration as a Measure of Risk

The length of time until the maturity of a bond is one factor in the risk involved in that bond. Another measure is also widely used as a measure of risk: the duration of the bond.

Duration is a fairly complex concept. In basic terms, *duration* differs from *maturity* in this way: A bond's maturity tells you when you will receive full repayment of the bond's face value. A bond's duration is a weighted measure of when you will get your investment back from a bond investment, including the stream of interest payments that you receive during the time that you hold these bonds.

For bonds that mature at the same time, the bond that pays the higher rate of interest each year has the lower duration, or lower risk. It is easy enough to see why. If you purchase a bond with a 20-year maturity that pays 10% per year in interest, you will receive your entire investment back within 10 years (one tenth repayment per year), not including potential reinvestment of interest payments. If the bond pays 5% interest, it would require a full 20 years for you to receive in interest alone the cost of the bond, so your invested capital would remain at least at some risk for the full 20-year period.

The higher the duration of a bond, the greater the risk. Bonds with higher durations are more subject to price fluctuations arising from general changes in interest rate levels than bonds of lower duration. When considering the purchase of bonds, evaluate their duration in comparison to other bonds that you might be considering. When evaluating bond mutual funds for purchase, secure the "average duration" of the mutual fund holdings you are considering, generally available for mutual funds. Again, the lower the average duration, the safer the bond.

For more information about bond duration, check out www.luhman.org and www.finpipe.com/duration.htm; you can also use your favorite Internet search engine to guide to relevant Web sites.

Securing Higher Rates of Return from Lower-Quality, Investment-Grade Bonds

Although for the most part the additional yields available from lower-quality bonds do not particularly justify the risks involved, sometimes yield spreads (BAA bonds minus AAA bonds) are sufficiently wide to suggest the purchase of lower-quality issues.

Lower-grade investment bonds tend to pay the most in relationship to higher-grade bonds during periods of economic uncertainty. Such a period occurred during 1980 to 1981, a period marked by high spreads in yield between BAA and AAA bonds, and also by sharply rising inflation and vacillating stock prices. Previous peaks in these spreads had also taken place during 1970 and 1974, bear market periods for stocks.

Figure 4-1 shows the yield spreads between BAA 30-year corporate bonds (low investment grade) and AAA 30-year corporate bonds. As a general rule, BAA bonds provide approximately 1% to 1.5% per year in extra interest income, in comparison to the highest investment-grade issues. Venturesome investors may place some capital into lower-grade bonds for this extra gain, but for most investors this should not be an area for speculation.

Figure 4-1 pretty much tells the story. It is usually best to take investment risk during periods of the greatest investor pessimism—in this case, when fears of bond default are the greatest.

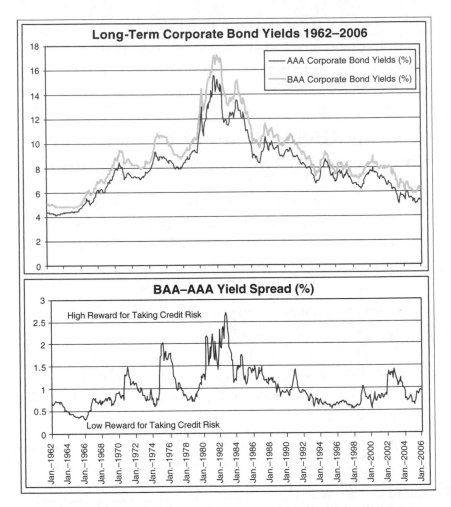

FIGURE 4-1   Yield spreads, lower versus higher investment-grade 30-year bonds, 1962–2006

Spreads in yield between BAA and AAA bonds tend to peak in the area of between 2% and 2.5%. When final peaks are achieved, lower-grade bonds tend to advance in price more rapidly than higher-grade bonds. Based on past history, bond investors may want to emphasize bonds of slightly below maximum investment grade when their yields rise disproportionately compared to the highest quality of bonds.

Understanding the Total Income Return from Bonds

Many investors contemplating the purchase of a bond think only of the *current yield* or interest payout of that bond in relation to its current price. For example, if a bond is selling at $1,100 and its coupon is 7% (based on $1,000 face value), the current interest return would be 6.36% ($70 interest divided by current price of $1,100). However, although you are paying $1,100 for the bond, you will receive back only $1,000, the bond's face value, at maturity. There is, therefore, a capital loss of $100 built in to this bond's ownership, which should be included as an offset against the bond's interest payments in your consideration of this bond for purchase.

The *yield to maturity* (YTM) of a bond is the *total rate of return* you receive if you hold a bond to maturity *and* reinvest all the interest payments at the yield to maturity rate. It takes into account all the interest payments you will receive until maturity, the price you actually pay for the bonds, the period of time until maturity, and the face value you will receive back at maturity. The assumption that you will and can reinvest all interest payments at any particular rate of return is, of course, an assumption. Nonetheless, the yield to maturity better indicates the true rate of return from a bond than the amount of current interest alone.

For example, suppose that the current interest rate is such that 1-year Treasury bills are providing yields to investors of 3%. If you purchase a newly issued 1-year Treasury bill, you would pay $1,000 (par face value) and receive two semiannual interest payments of 1.5% for a 3% total payout. At maturity, you would receive the amount you paid for the bond, $1,000.

Let's suppose instead that you are considering the purchase of a 30-year Treasury bond, due to mature in 1 year, with a 6% coupon. This bond would, in such an interest rate climate, sell at above its face value of $1,000 because its interest payout (6% or $60 per year) is greater than the prevailing 1-year loan rate of 3%. Perhaps the bond would sell at approximately $1,030 per bond, or $30 above face value to neutralize the extra $30 in interest that buyers would receive if they purchased new 1-year bonds paying 3%.

The coupon of the 30-year Treasury bond is 6% based on its face value, 5.8% based on its current selling price of $1030. It will, however, lose 2.9% of its current price ($30 divided by $1,030) when it is redeemed at $1,000 face value at maturity—essentially providing the same total dollar return and yield to maturity as the 1-year Treasury note (which has a lower coupon but which does not sell at a premium [price above] of its face value).

Bonds whose coupons are less than prevailing interest rates will tend to sell at prices below their face value (at a discount). Bonds whose coupons are above prevailing interest rates for bonds of similar maturity will tend to sell at amounts greater than their face value (at a premium).

It is not necessary for you to know how or to actually calculate yields to maturity; these calculations are available from any broker listing bonds for sale. If you are investigating mutual funds, the fund will provide the average yield to maturity of its holdings. An easy-to-use yield to maturity calculator is available online at Morningstar.com (www.morningstar.com; in the section "Investor Tools and Calculations").

The true (or actual) total return you receive from a bond, including its interest payout and gain or loss that will result from the difference between your purchase price and the bond's face value, adjusted for the time remaining until maturity, is the yield to maturity.

If current income is of most importance, you might look for bonds that are selling at a premium but that have the largest current interest payout as a percentage of the price you pay.

If current income is not important, you might look for bonds that provide the highest yields to maturity, even if current income is somewhat lower.

Special Note of Caution

If you are buying bonds through a broker, make certain that the current yields and yields to maturity that the broker is quoting include any adjustments for brokerage commissions or bond markups that are going to be charged to you.

Investing in Bonds via Mutual Funds vs. Investing on Your Own

Advantages of bond mutual funds include the following:

- **Ready diversification**

  Bond mutual funds can provide, at reasonable cost, a higher level of bond diversification for smaller investors than they would be able to assemble themselves. Investors can diversify further by simply taking positions in a few such mutual funds that have varying investment objectives and which hold different types of securities in different market segments.

- **Specialized portfolio management**

  Although in many cases, a bond is a bond is a bond (for instance, most government and high-grade corporate issues), there are areas of bond investment about which the typical investor is likely to be unfamiliar (for example, foreign bonds, individual low-quality bonds, bonds issued by distressed companies, adjustable rate issues). Many successful bond mutual funds that invest in such specialized areas represent convenient vehicles for investors seeking ways to expand their investment opportunities.

In addition, certain bond fund managers add value by having a better-than-average ability to predict interest rate trends and to create portfolios in harmony with such predictions. For example, if higher interest rates are correctly anticipated, such managers may reduce longer-term bond positions, move assets to shorter-term holdings (which are less susceptible to higher interest rate driven declines). Conversely, if such managers correctly foresee trends toward lower interest rates, they may alter their portfolios to lengthen the average maturity of their holdings.

Managers of global funds, which invest in foreign as well as domestic bonds, potentially add value by forecasting and operating portfolios in accordance with anticipated changes in currency relationships as well as interest rate trends and general economic developments.

- **Investing in small increments**

  Many bond mutual funds enable investors to initiate and to supplement existing bond portfolios with relatively small amounts of capital, whereas the purchase of small amounts (less than $10,000) of individual bond purchases may involve higher commission costs and wider bid-asked spreads, presuming even that very small-size bond lots are available for purchase.

  In addition to higher commission costs, the need to purchase bond positions in small lots may limit the choices you have available for purchase and may result in poorer executions in addition to higher commission costs. As a very low-volume bond investor, your account may not receive much in the way of attention from your bond broker.

  Bond mutual funds, in addition, generally allow investors to automatically reinvest interest from existing bond holdings in additional mutual fund shares as such interest is paid—providing a ready ability to compound income from your holdings. Interest payments from a diversified portfolio of actual bonds are not as readily reinvested.

- **Simplified recordkeeping**

   Mutual funds keep track of your dividend (actually interest) payments for tax purposes and provide year-end reports for this purpose. The recordkeeping for your initial bond fund purchase prices and dates is likely to be simpler than for a broad portfolio of bonds. However, reinvestments of dividends can be difficult to track for tax purposes, especially if holding periods involved stretch into several or more years. We'll give the edge in this area to investing via mutual funds, but it is not a clear call.

All this considered, it is probably more convenient to invest in bonds by way of mutual funds (not necessarily more profitable, not necessarily safer, just more convenient—a decisive element for many people).

There are, however, advantages to owning a portfolio of specific bonds rather than bond mutual funds. For example, individual bonds have a specific maturity date on which you are guaranteed repayment in full of the loan signified by your bonds. Bond mutual funds have no such date of maturity for their portfolio. This is a significant advantage to portfolios of individual bonds and a significant disadvantage to bond mutual funds.

A major reason to invest in bonds at all is that, in addition to fixed-interest payouts, bonds provide the safety inherent in the pledge by the bond issuer to return to owners of bonds a specified amount of repayment (usually the $1,000 face value) at a specified time. These pledges, which are almost always honored by issuers of very high-grade corporate and government bonds, allow investors to create their own timelines of investment, to plan ahead with relative certainty, and to monitor and control the risks of their portfolios.

Although there are some bond unit trusts that have scheduled termination dates, the typical bond mutual fund has no specific date of maturity and redemption for its portfolio. Whereas individual bonds in a mutual fund portfolio will have specific maturity dates, the portfolio as a whole does not, because the proceeds of bonds that are sold are generally rolled into new bonds (if not immediately, then eventually). This process results in a perpetual portfolio of bonds rather than in a portfolio that will automatically convert to cash at a predictable value at a predictable time.

A portfolio of individual bonds is likely to be marked by diminished risk as its holdings draw closer to maturity, a quality that does not generally exist in bond mutual funds. The differential between the fixed maturities of individual bonds and the perpetual maturity of bond funds (although, again, individual components do have fixed maturities) does add to the risk of bond funds, and to greater price variability of many bond funds as interest rates in general fluctuate.

A portfolio of individual bonds can be more closely tailored to the life situation of the investor. For example, portfolio risk may be more tightly controlled at or following retirement by converting a longer-term bond portfolio to a shorter-term, more-price-stable income portfolio. Mutual fund holdings can be altered in the same manner, but without the precision.

The expenses of maintaining a portfolio of individual bonds are likely to be considerably less than the costs of maintaining a portfolio of bonds based in mutual funds. This can be a significant advantage to holders of individual bonds rather than bond mutual funds. The typical bond mutual fund charges approximately 0.75% per year in management fees to its investors. For a bond fund whose portfolio holdings average 7.5% in average interest payout, a management fee of

0.75% per year represents an expense that is 10% of the income flow derived from its investments, leaving the investor with only 6.75% in net annual income after fund management expenses. This is equal to a tax of 10% on your bond interest income, paid this time to your fund management company rather than to a government—not a one-time commission hit, an expense levied against your income each and every year, the cost of which compounds over time. (Verify the expense ratio of any bond fund you are considering—the lower, the better.)

Unless you have a special reason for not wanting to assume management of your own bond portfolio, large investors who invest in portfolios of high-grade domestic corporate, municipal, or federally issued bonds are probably better off investing in actual bonds than in bond mutual funds. This is not necessarily the case for investors in specialized bond areas, however.

Bonds and Bond Funds for All Seasons

The financial "powers that be" are nothing if not creative insofar as generating new products to foist on investors. That bit of cynicism aside, the fact is that there are numerous incarnations of income instruments available for investment, many of which have special features of appeal depending on your investment purposes. We do not have the space to discuss all possibilities or to provide the final word on any, but the review that follows should provide useful introductions, at the least, as well as sources for further investigation.

Money-Market Funds

Money-market funds are popular depositories for safe, short-term investment capital and as an interest-paying refuge for assets between more long-term investments. Although money-market funds are not insured by the U.S. government, they have had, as a group, an excellent record for safety, generally using investor capital to invest in short-term debt instruments, with management skimming off for their expenses and profit the difference between what the fund receives for its various investments and what it pays to shareholders.

Positive

Very high grades for liquidity, safety, and convenience.

Negative

With a little effort, it is often possible to secure higher rates of return with no greater risk. For example, in August 2005, at a time when the typical money-market fund was paying approximately 2.5% to 3% in interest, bank certificates of deposit that paid up to 4% and more in interest for holding periods of less than 1 year were available, as were debt obligations that paid up to 5% for minimum holding periods of just 1 month. These vehicles were not as absolutely liquid as money-market funds, but many investors maintain capital in money markets for long periods of time and do not really require immediate liquidity.

When to Buy

Money-market funds are safe harbors during periods of interest rate instability, especially when rates are still rising, as a cash haven during weak stock market periods, and as a holding area for personal capital awaiting use. Their safety is a good feature, but their relatively low payout argues against long-term use.

U.S. Treasury Bills

U.S. Treasury bills, the ultimate in safety, are short-term securities that do not pay interest as such but are, instead, sold at a discount to their face value but then redeemed at face value—the difference between the purchase cost and face value repayment representing the income received by investors.

For example, a 90-day Treasury bill, with a par or face value of $1,000, might be sold at initial auction for a price of $990. The $10 difference between what the investor pays ($990) and the $1,000 that is received at maturity represents an interest return of 1.01% for the 90-day period, which would represent a 4.04% rate of return on an annual basis.

Treasury bills, issued in maturities of 90 days and 6 months, are useful as short-term depositories for cash and are acceptable as collateral for almost any collateral purpose. T-bills, fully guaranteed by the U.S. government, are considered to be the safest of investments. The income they provide is exempt from state and local income taxes.

You can purchase these instruments directly from the U.S. Treasury, via many banks, and through brokerage houses.

Positive

Absolute safety, some tax protection, highly liquid, predictable return.

Negative

Not all that much in the way of return.

On Balance

Safe havens during periods that interest rates are volatile and during periods that long-term interest rates are very low.

Short-Term Bonds and Bond Funds

This category includes income mutual funds whose holdings may range up to 3 years or so in maturity, longer-term bank certificates of deposit, short-term Treasury notes with up to 3 years maturity, and long-term bonds in their last years prior to maturity. This category also includes funds that invest in relatively short-term mortgages or short-term corporate loans, which may provide interest payouts that adjust frequently, and individual notes that represent short-term loans made by individual investors to businesses and/or municipalities through brokerage houses.

Positive

Relative price stability, high ratings for safety, higher yields than Treasury bills and money market. Generally high levels of liquidity, minimal risk of default (although there may be some price fluctuation in accordance with movements of short-term interest rates in general). Short-term bond funds and equivalents generally provide better returns than money-market funds, albeit with some element of risk. *These instruments proved to be fine safe havens for capital during the bear market, 2000–2002.*

Negative

Income returns are generally only moderately higher than money market, although surpluses were as much as 3% or so higher during the period between 2000 and 2004. After allowances for inflation and taxes, returns are unlikely to match rates of inflation. *Price stability of related mutual funds is not totally firm, so there are periods when total return (the net return from interest payout and price movement) actually turns negative.*

When to Buy

Buy during periods when longer-term interest rates are rising more rapidly than short-term rates, long-term bond prices are declining more rapidly than short-term bond prices, or, if you are purchasing actual Treasury notes (which carry no real risk to capital if held to maturity), during periods of interest rate uncertainty (for predictable income). Actual 3-year Treasury notes or short-term, high-grade corporate debt instruments are likely to provide returns essentially equal to short-term bond mutual funds with less risk. You can purchase Treasury instruments commission free directly from the U.S. Treasury. For further details, visit www.Treasurydirect.gov.

Intermediate-Term Bond Funds and Individual Bonds

Intermediate-term bonds are debt instruments whose maturities range from 3 to 10 years—the range of maturity periods often favored by managers to provide a suitable balance between the more-or-less absolute safety of short-term bonds (especially government bonds) and the higher returns available from longer-term income instruments.

As a general rule, interest yields available from intermediate-term bonds range from 80% to 90% of yields available from long-term bonds. In August 2005, 5-year Treasury notes provided a yield of 4.21%, 91% of the 4.62% yield provided by 20-year Treasury bonds. An investment of $1 in long-term government bonds, 1926–2004, would have grown to $65.72, an annual rate of growth of 5.4%. An investment of $1 in intermediate-term bonds over the same period would have grown to $61.83, also a compound annual rate of growth of 5.4%. Returns were essentially similar.

Total annual returns for long-term bonds ranged from a high of 40.4% (1982) to a low of –9.2% (1967). Total annual returns for intermediate bonds ranged from a high of 29.1% (1982) to a low of –5.1% (1994). Long-term bonds are more affected—for the good or bad—by changes in the general direction of interest rates, rising more in price than intermediate bonds when rates fall, falling more in price when rates rise. On balance, however, these bond segments have tended to produce similar returns over longer-term periods. (As with stocks, there is, over the long run, little to be gained from extra risk.)

Positive

The safety of intermediate bond funds is considerably greater than the safety of longer-term bonds. Between 1930 and 2004, intermediate-term government bonds showed only about 60% of the price volatility (a measure of risk) of long-term government bonds. Although the risk of default by U.S. government bonds is minimal, intermediate corporate bonds will generally have less risk of default than longer-term bonds because of the shorter times that capital is at risk of default. Intermediate bonds lie in the maturity periods that are most conducive to bond laddering.

Negative

Yields do lie below those of longer-term bonds, which may reduce the potentials of profit for investors who take positions at a time when interest rate levels are starting a serious decline (for example, 1982). For instance, long-term bonds provided a protracted period of price gains to long-term bond investors, in addition to higher yields, in the years following 1982.

When to Buy

Buy when interest rates in general are flat to declining. Although risks involved in intermediate term bonds are considerably lower during periods of rising interest rates than the risks involved in longer-term bonds, there are risks during such periods when investments are better made in shorter-term debt instruments.

Bond ladders may be favorably established with intermediate-term bonds at almost any time. Related mutual funds tend to show more stability than longer-term bond mutual funds.

Well-diversified portfolios of intermediate bonds or bond funds are not likely to outperform portfolios of well-performing stocks over the long run, but on a risk-adjusted basis represent a fine investment base for conservative investors and a solid sector of income investment for investors whose primary investment commitments lie with the stock market.

Long-Term Government and Corporate Bonds

These are bonds with maturities of 10 years or longer. High-quality long-term bonds have provided long-term rates of growth of 5.4% since 1925, with annual risk levels as high as –9.2%, which is not necessarily the maximum level of potential risk.

Numerous long-term bond funds are available, representing corporate, U.S. government, and tax-exempt bonds, all of which may be purchased individually.

Positive

If purchases are well timed (that is, interest rates are at very high levels), high-grade long-term bonds can provide a long-term flow of high income with relatively low risk. Such bonds may be suitable for pension portfolios, for which they provide prudence and predictability, and as investments for trust and other fiduciary accounts for which active management is not desired.

From time to time, extremely fine opportunities develop in the long-term bond market, usually at some climactic turning point in the interest rate or psychological climates. For example, a fiscal crisis in New York City and elsewhere in the mid-1970s provided to astute investors the opportunity to purchase tax-exempt bonds that provided double-digit tax-exempt yields. The winter of 1980, during which interest rates reached a climactic peak, provided the opportunity to purchase long-term U.S. Treasury bonds at a time when yields lay in the area of 15%.

The Media Indicator

The secret of profiting from such opportunities usually lies with the courage and ability to swim against the popular tide. In this regard, one of the best market indicators I know relates to the tone of the general news, magazine, and television media, which is often very wrong at key investment turning points. For example, when you see a flood of media articles relating to how high the markets have risen and how much further pundits are predicting additional rise, it is a pretty good bet that stocks will turn down. Similarly, when the popular press—including new books at the bookstore—feature predictions of interest rates rising further, especially after a period of recent advance, the odds are that we are at or very close to a peak in interest rates—*a great time to buy long-term bonds.*

Why does it happen this way? Well, let's consider the publishing cycle, for example, during bear markets. As the stock market declines, with public pessimism rising, interest increases regarding ways to profit from ongoing market declines, in ways to survive economically during market decline, and with regard to how much further prices are likely to drop. Book publishers begin to turn to authors for books on "Surviving Depressions," "Profiting from Falling Stocks," and so forth. It takes at least some months for such books to be written, printed, and distributed. Books of this nature are finally ready for sale at just about, if not already after, the time that stocks have reached their lows. The cycle for magazine publication is, of course, much shorter, but in general this sort of article follows on public psychology rather than leads. The "media indicator" is one of my favorite investment forecasting tools. I suggest that you consider moving against the general crowd whenever investing sentiment becomes very one sided, particularly when the normally optimistic public media turn bearish.

Negative

Longer-term bonds are more susceptible to declines created by rising interest rates than intermediate-term bonds, without providing commensurate increases in return—unless they are purchased at or very close to significant peaks in the interest rate cycle. Longer-term corporate bonds are also subject for longer periods of time to risks associated with deteriorating corporate fortunes.

Risks of Bonds Being Called

Many bonds are issued with provisions that allow the issue to "call" or to "redeem" bonds at a date or different dates prior to the maturity of the bond. This is referred to as the "call feature" or "call provision"—and represents a real risk to the bond purchaser.

Why should this be considered a risk? After all, initial investors at par get all their money back, ahead of schedule, and usually with a little extra premium to boot. This sounds all right. Suppose, however, that you purchase a high-grade corporate bond at a time when interest rates are high, and you are able to secure a 10% coupon or yield from a 15-year maturity bond. Three years pass, during which time you have secured this return, even as general interest rates have declined. Interest rates decline, to the point where 15-year high-quality bonds provide yields of 7%, in which case the value of your bond holding would have increased significantly.

At this point, the corporation that has issued your bonds decides that if they pay off all the bonds you own and issue new bonds at current rates, they can save 3% per year in interest payments, paying 7% in interest rather than 10%—and so they exercise a call provision that allows them to "call in" your bonds. You get back your investment plus, perhaps, an additional 5% premium over the face value—but the price of your bonds immediately drops down to the call redemption price in the open market as soon as the call is announced. In addition, you face the prospect of having to reinvest capital for which you were receiving 10% annual income with newly issued bonds paying just 7%. This is not the very worst of fates if you had purchased the bonds at face value at issue, but represents a very definite risk if you purchase bonds at prices above the call level in the secondary market after issue.

For this reason, many savvy bondholders seek information not only about a prospective bond's yield to maturity but also about its "yield to call date," which is usually less if the bond has a call provision.

Before purchasing any bond, especially if you are purchasing above face value, carefully verify the call provisions of that bond. You can do so through your broker, who should be able to readily provide this information.

Treasury Inflation-Protected Securities (TIPS)

In 1997, the U.S. Treasury introduced a new type of bond and note designed to provide to investors an investment guaranteed by the full faith and credit of the U.S. government to provide total income and return of principal (if held to maturity) that exceed the rate of inflation.

Although there are active secondary markets in TIPS, which can be readily purchased through brokerage houses, you may also buy these instruments (5-, 10-, and 20-year maturities) directly from the U.S. Treasury at no commission costs or mark-ups. These are issued periodically and are listed at www.Treasurydirect.gov, through which you can open an account with the U.S. Treasury.

Positive

The redemption or face value of TIPS, which are priced at $1,000 each at issuance, is increased or decreased every 6 months based on changes in the Consumer Price Index (CPI). For example, if you purchase a newly issued bond at $1,000 and at the next adjustment period the CPI is 2% higher than at the time of purchase, the face value of your bond increases from $1,000 to $1,020, 2% higher. If inflation over the next 6 months is an additional 3%, the face value of your bond rises to $1,050.60 (3% above $1,020).

Should there be deflation, the face value of your bond reduces accordingly. However, the face value of the bond can never decline to below $1,000, its initial purchase price. The government pledges to redeem the bond at maturity for at least its initial purchase price or at the compounded rates of inflation during its life, whichever is greater.

In addition, the interest rate you receive is adjusted to reflect the rising face value of the bond. For example, if the bond is issued with an interest payment of 2% annually, (1% every 6 months), the interest for the first 6 months is $10 (1% of $1,000 face value). If the value of the bond were to rise to $1,020 as a result of price adjustment to reflect 2% inflation, the interest for the second 6 months would rise to $10.20 (1% of $1,020). This probably does not seem like very much stated this way, but the annual compounding of face value and of the rate of income payments becomes more significant as time passes.

Total rates of return for 10-year TIPS in mid-2005 were in the area of 5% per year—roughly 3.5% as an inflation adjustment to the bond's value, 1.5% per year cash interest payout. Although it is possible for the value of bonds to decline in a deflationary climate (consumer prices falling), this is an unusual situation; after all, prices generally advance over the years rather than deflate.

Whereas market prices of TIPS may fluctuate on a short-term basis, their inflation protection tends to make them more stable in value than bonds without this protection—and, of course, at maturity their adjusted face value is repaid in full. All in all, TIPS represent a very safe investment, guaranteed against loss over the long term and at least reasonably predictable in their expected return.

Negative

Nothing, however, is perfect. There are disadvantages to TIPS. For one, yields available from TIPS are usually at least somewhat less than yields available from other 10-year U.S. government notes—a price you pay for the inflation protection, which is probably not all that significant given the benefits.

For another, and this is more serious, investors outside of tax-sheltered accounts, such as IRAs and other qualified shelters, are liable for income taxes based on increases in the face value of bonds based on inflation adjustments, although there is actually no cash flowing through to them. For example, if a bond purchased at $1,000 is revalued at $1,030 over its first year to reflect a 3% rate of inflation, you must pay income taxes on that $30 increase in face value in addition to taxes on the cash interest paid by the bond—an obvious disadvantage because you have no access to the capital appreciation resulting from the inflation adjustment until the bond is sold.

Good as they are, TIPS are a much better investment when they are held under the auspices of some sort of tax-protected structure. *They are not as desirable when held within a taxable structure.*

Zero-Coupon Bonds

Zero-coupon bonds—issued by the federal government, municipalities, and corporations—are generally long-term bonds that pay no interest while they are maturing but rather, like Treasury bills, pay at maturity a full redemption face value for bonds that are originally sold at a deep discount. The differential between the discount purchase price and the full redemption price represents the income received by the bondholder. Inasmuch as zero-coupon bonds are long term in nature, investors have to put up only a fraction of the bond's redemption price at original purchase.

Such bonds may be created as zero-coupon bonds by their issuers or may have been originally structured as interest-paying bonds, in which case their interest payments have been "stripped" by a bond dealer, the bond then resold as a zero-coupon instrument.

Zero-coupon bonds have some particular appeals to both conservative income investors and to speculators. Long-term zero-coupon bonds, purchased at a favorable juncture, can prove to be fine holdings in retirement accounts. However, risks can be high if you are forced to redeem prior to maturity and if the issuer is somewhat less than absolutely creditworthy.

Positive

Zero-coupon bonds allow conservative investors to put up relatively small amounts of initial capital for the purchase of long-term debt instruments whose long-term returns, if held to maturity, are quite predictable.

These are particularly favorable instruments to purchase at a time when interest rates are peaking and likely to turn down. For one, the leverage inherent in zero-coupon bonds, which sell at large discounts from their face value, allows for the purchase of larger numbers of bonds with relatively small amounts of capital. Investors who do not require a current income flow receive a lot of bang for their buck.

Apart from the capital gain potentials inherent in this use of leverage, investors in zero-coupon bonds do not have to deal with the reinvestment of interest payments during periods of declining interest rates. Zero-coupon bonds rise in price as they approach maturity, reflecting the fact that they will be paid back at par or face value at maturity. This rise in the value of zero-coupon bonds as time passes represents the form in which the zero-coupon bondholder receives ongoing growth in his original investment.

Long-term zero-coupon bonds are quite volatile, responding with broad price movement to variations in the general interest rate climate. This volatility may not be significant to bondholders who plan to hold until maturity, but is an element to consider if you plan on shorter-term holding periods. (Active bond traders often prefer to invest in zero-coupon bonds because of their volatility, which provides opportunity for profit but also entails risk.)

Negative

A major disadvantage to zero-coupon bondholders lies with the tax treatment of these vehicles. Investors have to pay annual taxes on the amount of interest that would have been earned if their bonds were structured as interest-paying bonds rather than as zero-coupon bonds. These bonds are probably best held in tax-sheltered portfolios rather than as currently taxable assets.

Another disadvantage lies with risks associated with default of such instruments. Federally issued zero-coupon bonds are almost certainly safe enough, but corporations and municipalities do occasionally default. Whereas interest-paying bonds are returning portions of your original investment with each passing interest payment, with zero-coupon bonds it may be an all-or-nothing situation, and in a total default you might lose your entire investment. In any event, before purchasing zero-coupon debt, be certain that you will not be requiring ongoing interest income from the investment. The purchase of zero-coupon bonds should be restricted to only the most creditworthy of issuers.

And as a third disadvantage, there is always the risk of these long-term bonds being called, redeemed by the issuer, prior to their expiration. You will receive a prorated percentage of the face value of these bonds (and a potential income tax complication should you have to sort out with the IRS the accuracy of tax calculations that you have been making along the way).

Municipal Bonds: Winning the Tax Game

A municipal bond is a bond issued by a state, city, or county for general financing or to finance specific projects such as highways, stadiums, hospitals, dormitories, and schools.

The major advantage to the bondholder lies with the fact that the income provided by municipal bonds (munis) is generally exempt from federal income taxes and usually from income taxes of the issuing entity and the state in which it is located. For example, the interest paid by a municipal bond issued by the city of New York would be "triple tax free" to a resident of New York City—no taxes due to the city, state, or federal government. However, the interest from a muni issued by New Jersey and owned by a New York City resident would be tax free only in regard to federal taxation. The bondholder would still be subject to income taxes due to the state (New York) and to New York City.

As a result of their interest being tax sheltered in this manner, municipal bonds tend to pay less interest than bonds of similar credit rating and maturity. However, as a general rule, given their favorable tax consequences, municipal bonds generally provide higher after-tax returns than comparable taxable bonds and usually represent excellent alternatives to other bonds of similar maturity and quality.

If you purchase such bonds through a broker, the firm should be able to provide you with the taxable equivalent return provided by their offerings.

Caveat

Although municipal bonds have had a fine record insofar as safety is concerned, and although they provide superior after-tax returns compared to taxable bonds, they may not be suitable for investors who anticipate possible reductions in their earnings, and a resultant decline in their tax obligations, in the relatively near future.

If such declines do occur, the benefits of the tax shelter involved with munis reduce. Investors in such a situation might be better off with their capital placed in a higher-paying taxable instrument.

Municipal bonds can be divided into two categories, as follows:

- **General-obligation bonds.** These bonds are backed by the full taxing power and creditworthiness of the issuer in the same manner that U.S. Treasury bonds are backed by the full faith and credit of the U.S. government. This does not guarantee their solvency; however, if they are issued by a well-financed community and have a high credit rating, credit risks associated with their purchase should be minimal.

- **Revenue bonds.** These bonds are issued to finance specific civic operations—the building of highways, hospitals, college facilities, stadiums, and the like—and are supported by the revenues generated by these operations, not necessarily by the total municipality or state. There would appear to be greater risks associated with revenue bonds than with general-obligation bonds should anticipated income not meet expectations, although, in general, risks in the tax exempt area have not been high.

Investors should secure credit ratings by Standard & Poor's or Moody's before making investments.

Suitability for Retirement Accounts

Munis are not really suited for retirement accounts because there are no tax benefits in such a structure to offset the disadvantages of the lower yields provided by these instruments. As with other bonds, the longer the term to maturity, the higher the yield. As with other bonds, maturities in the range of between 5 and 10 years probably represent the best balance between risk and return.

Municipal Bond Mutual Funds and Trusts
Viable Alternatives to Individual Bonds

There are no particular disadvantages to municipal bonds as opposed to other bonds. In fact, my impression has been that the vast majority of municipal bondholders are quite satisfied with this form of investment, which usually provides steady, predictable, and tax-sheltered income. Risks can be reduced by the use of bond ladders.

However, municipal bonds—unlike U.S Treasury issues—do have credit risk as well as risks associated with changing interest rates, so portfolios should be as broadly diversified as possible, even if this results in some tax disadvantage should you not be able to totally diversify within your state. Moreover, although munis are generally quite liquid, their purchase and sale do involve commission and bid-asked spreads, so there are costs involved in establishing portfolios.

Investors with insufficient capital to establish broad portfolios or who do not want to become involved with complex portfolios of investment positions will find ample choice among the many open-end and closed-end mutual funds and trusts that manage and offer investment portfolios of both nationwide and state-restricted (to eliminate state taxes) municipal bonds. For example (not a specific recommendation), Nuveen Investments (www.nuveen.com) sponsors municipal bond funds whose holdings are state specific for many states.

Current Yield vs. SEC Yield

Bond mutual funds of all types are now required to provide to investors yield information in two areas: current yield and SEC yield. The current yield is the interest return secured by investors as an annual percentage of the current value of their mutual fund shares. It does not take into account any gains or losses that may be involved in the bond holdings of the fund on a total return to maturity basis. The SEC yield represents the income return to investors with adjustments that allow for the fund's holdings lying above or below face value, with resultant gains or losses at maturity.

High-Yield Bonds and Bond Funds

These are generally long-term bonds (usually issued by corporations) that have less-than-investment-grade ratings. Their appeal lies with their high yields, which tend to run approximately 2% to 5% above yields available from long-term Treasury bonds. (If long-term treasuries are yielding 6%, high-yield corporate bonds will tend to yield between 8% and 11%.)

Because of credit risks involved with high-yielding lower-quality bonds, they are probably best held within portfolios of high-yield mutual funds that generally maintain broadly diversified portfolios of such holdings. Prices of such mutual funds are fairly volatile during periods of economic uncertainty, so high-yield bond funds should be purchased only by investors who can assume the risks involved.

Interestingly, price fluctuations of high-yield bond funds appear to be more influenced by the ups and downs of the NASDAQ Composite (where smaller, higher-risk companies are listed) than by general levels of interest rates. High-yield bond funds often decline in harmony with declines in the NASDAQ Composite Index and rise in price during periods of strength in this stock market sector. This is understandable in view of the fact that bond defaults in this area are higher when the economy and the stock markets are declining than when economic conditions are favorable.

Individual high-yield bonds are often relatively illiquid (a disadvantage), whereas high-yield bond funds are quite liquid (although many now charge redemption fees, usually about 1% of assets, to investors who sell within 90 days or so of purchase). Most investors are likely to be better off investing in high-yield bonds via the mutual fund route rather than directly.

Trading Tip

Chapter 5, "Securing Junk Bond Yields at Treasury Bond Risk," includes a simple but quite effective way to time purchases and sales of high-yield bond mutual funds, a method that, historically, has removed much of the risk associated with these instruments, thereby increasing their attractiveness as investments.

You can use another strategy to identify favorable periods for the purchase of high-yield bond funds as well as periods during which associated risks are likely to increase. This strategy uses the relationship between yields of high-yield bonds and long-term Treasury bonds.

On average, high-yield bond funds provide yields that are approximately 3% to 4% higher than those provided by long-term Treasury bonds. When yield spreads lie in this area (3% to 4%), high-yield bond mutual funds tend to show average performance for this sector.

Best Time to Buy

During periods of economic weakness (which result in high investor pessimism), high-yield bond funds have provided yields that have been as much as 9% or more higher than yields available from long-term Treasury instruments, such as the 10-year note. During such periods, investors tend to emphasize safety rather than maximum return, so demand for the safety of U.S. Treasury issues increases, whereas the demand for more-speculative high-yield instruments decreases. Periods of pessimism are often the best periods during which to accumulate investments. Historically, high-yield bond funds have often been fine investments when their yields have surpassed the yields available from 10-year U.S. Treasury notes by 6% to 8% or more.

As stock market bear markets are winding down, well-timed purchases can be very rewarding in this sector.

Best Time to Sell

Conversely, during periods of economic strength (often accompanied by generally low interest rates in the credit markets), yield spreads between high-yield bonds and long-term U.S. Treasury issues tend to narrow. Bond investors, who are generally more optimistic regarding the economy and willing to take extra risks for extra yield, tend to actively purchase (thereby bidding up) high-yield bonds to secure acceptable interest rate returns. Such periods of high investor optimism and complacency are often good periods during which to liquidate high-yield bonds. (Remember the media indicator.) Historically, high-yield bond funds as a group have tended to lie in dangerous territory when their yields are less than 3% higher than yields available from 10-year Treasury notes.

Historical Examples

Yield spreads between 10-year Treasury notes and corporate high-yield bonds narrowed to below 2% as early as 1984, by which time the high-yield bond market had already risen considerably from the lows to which it had declined during the 1980–1982 period. The high-yield bond market did rise further to a peak in 1987, but the largest part of the price advance was already complete by mid-1984.

High-yield bond prices declined sharply between 1987 and mid-1990, the yield spread finally peaking in mid-1990 when high-yield bonds provided interest returns approximately 9% to 10% higher than those of 10-year Treasury notes. The peak in the width of the spread coincided with lows in high-yield bond prices (an excellent time to buy).

High spreads reappeared between 2001 and 2002, which again turned out to be an excellent period in which to accumulate high-yield bonds.

Fearless Forecast

Spreads in yield between high-yield bonds and 10-year Treasury notes have narrowed as this is being written, September 2005, to approximately 3.5%, suggesting that the high-yield bond market is unlikely to show significant upside progress in the years immediately ahead.

Figure 4-2 shows historical patterns of yield spreads.

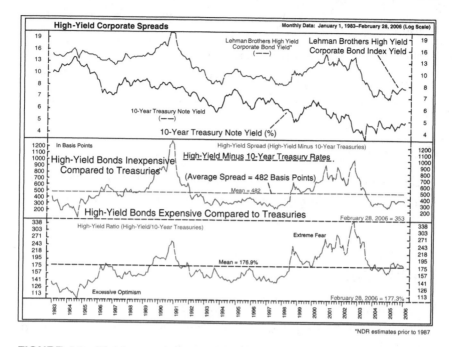

FIGURE 4-2   Yield spreads between high-yield bonds and 10-year Treasury bonds, 1983–2005

The average spread between yields provided by high-yield bonds and 10-year Treasury bonds was 4.84% between 1983 and 2005. Peaks in this spread in the area above 8.5% took place during 1990 and again during the bear market of 2000–2002, both excellent periods in which to accumulate high-yield bond funds for long-term investment, although bullish indications during 2000 and 2001 were somewhat premature.

(Source: Ned Davis Research, Inc.)

The Wall Street Journal, in the "Markets" section, publishes yield comparisons. For example, on September 7, 2005, 10+ year Treasury issues were providing interest yields of 4.34% while high-yield corporate bonds were yielding 7.65%. The yield spread of 3.31% was below average, indicating no better than a neutral outlook for high-yield bonds.

Positive

Higher rates of return provide speculative appeal for this investment sector, which is most suited for active investors who are able and willing to assume extra risk for higher potential return.

Negative

Higher risks, relatively low liquidity for individual bonds, and redemption fees charged by an increasing number of bond funds.

Summing Up

For maximum safety, emphasize short maturities, the highest credit ratings, current interest flow, money-market and Treasury bills, bond ladders, and the broadest diversification.

For maximum potential return, emphasize longer maturities, lower investment-grade credit quality, deferred income flow (zero-coupon bonds), and high-yield bonds. Maintain high levels of diversification.

For a balance between risk and return, emphasize intermediate maturities, a largely investment-grade portfolio, high-grade municipal bonds, Treasury inflation-protected securities, and bond ladders. Maintain high levels of diversification.

For further information, check out the many Web sites that provide excellent discussions of the topics discussed in this chapter as well as specific information related to investment opportunities and management companies. The following sites are recommended, but this list is far from exhaustive:

- www.teenanalyst.com

    Diverse articles regarding bonds, general investment, mutual funds, and the economy. Not detailed, but a good introduction.

- http://apps.nasd.com/investor_Information/smart bonds/
  000100.asp

  A long and excellent series of articles relating to issues and concepts involved with income investment. Highly recommended
  as a thorough introduction to the subject.

- www.investopedia.com

  Diverse and excellent articles about many areas of investing,
  including various forms of income investing.

An Internet search for any of the topics discussed in this chapter
will produce a variety of useful information.

We now move along to Chapter 5, in which you will learn some
specific and excellent strategies for market timing and for investing in
a very special type of mutual fund.

5

SECURING JUNK BOND YIELDS AT TREASURY BOND RISK

High-yield bond funds (funds that invest in bonds of less-than-investment-grade quality, BB, B, and even C and sometimes below) have had their good years, their super years, but also their dismal years. High-yield bonds have yielded as much as 10% more than Treasury bonds, although usually the spread runs between 3% and 5%. During favorable economic climates, capital often flows into high-yield bonds because of their yield advantage. For the most part, this has worked out well for investors.

On balance, long-term returns from high-yield bond funds—which generally maintain well-diversified portfolios of such instruments because of their risks—have outstripped the performance of bond funds that invest in higher-grade debt instruments. However, to the extent that long-term returns favor the high-yield funds, their outperformance definitely comes at a price. Often, the price movement of the typical high-yield bond correlates more to the price movement of the NASDAQ Composite Index than to changes in prevailing interest rates (which generally govern the price movement of higher-grade bonds). This is because default represents the greatest risk to high-yield bonds. Risks of default tend to be the greatest during weak economic periods, periods during which stocks tend to decline. For example, during the 2000–2002 bear market, as many as 10% of high-yield bonds held by high-yield bond funds defaulted, well above the usual annual rate of 2% to 3%.

Overall, investments made in high-yield bond funds have produced quite adequate rates of return, although at some considerable risk.

Figure 5-1 illustrates the pattern of total return movement of a typical high-yield bond fund.

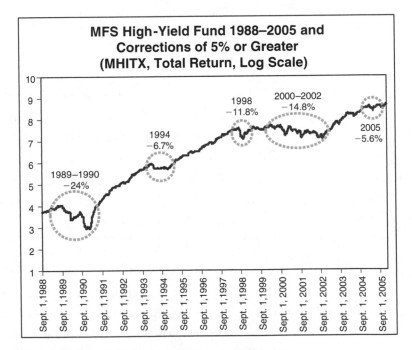

FIGURE 5-1   The MFS High-Yield Fund, 1988–2005

The MFS High-Yield Fund has produced adequate rates of return over the full period, 1988–2005, but has, along the way, seen drawdowns of as high as 24%, more than three times the average annual return of 7.6%. The periods between 1988 and 1990, 1993 and 1994, the year 1998, and the period between 2000 and 2002 were particularly difficult for high-yield bond fund investors.

As you can see in this figure, although the total compound rate of return of the MFS High-Yield Bond Fund (7.6% between 1988 and 2005) was acceptable compared to the usual rates of interest income over the years, risk/return relationships would have been much stronger if periods such as 1988–1990, 1998, and 2000–2002 could have been avoided, or if the damage done to this fund during those years might have been ameliorated.

Mission Impossible: Keeping the Gain without the Pain

Based on past performance at least, the mission (keeping the gain without the pain) has proven quite possible. A timing model that may be applied to high-yield bond funds—variants of which my firm has used in real-time investment for many years—seems to fit the needs of high-yield investors quite well. I will let you judge that for yourself when we examine the track record.

The good news is that the use of this timing model, the 1.25/0.50 timing model, has been well documented and appears to provide benefit (if not necessarily to all, then certainly to most high-yield bond funds) in comparison to buy and hold strategies.

The bad news is that as an investor you will have to take a few minutes each week to maintain the timing model, and will then have to call your mutual fund(s) to transact every time that signals are produced. The procedures involved in this model may seem just a bit complicated at first, but when you get the idea, you will find them quit straightforward.

The 1.25/0.50 Timing Model

The 1.25/0.50 timing model falls into the class of what market technicians refer to as "market-reversal timing systems." Market-reversal timing systems are designed to operate in the following manner and under the following assumptions:

- The stock and bond markets sometimes advance by considerable amounts before changing direction (reversing).

- The greatest amount of money is made by remaining in these markets for as long as their prices are trending upward (and by moving into cash positions when uptrends appear to have ended).

- The strategy is then to remain out of these markets, avoiding loss, until the period of downtrend has come to an end, at which time the timing model is expected to provide a signal to reenter the markets.

Signals

Reversal timing systems are based on the premise that when a market, or in this case a bond fund, has moved by a certain amount in a direction opposite a trend in motion, the presumption can be made that that the trend is no longer in effect and that a reversal in trend is taking place.

For example, the 1.25/0.50 timing model presumes that if high-yield bonds have been in a downtrend, and then rise in price by 1.25% from a low price level, the downtrend has come to an end (a buy signal).

The model also presumes that if high-yield bond funds have been advancing in prices, a decline of 0.50% in the prices of such funds from their most recent high level indicates that there are good chances of ongoing decline (a sell signal).

It is unrealistic to expect every signal to prove profitable. Sometimes buy signals fail, and markets that seemed ready to reverse from down to up fail and resume their declines. When this occurs (and failures definitely do occur) the strategy is to quickly acknowledge and to act on your recognition that the entry seems to be failing and to retreat again to the safety of cash.

Sometimes your timing model will generate "sell" signals, for which there is no downside follow through in the price action of the markets you are tracking. When the timing model recognizes this failure and alerts you, the strategy is to quickly acknowledge the resumption of upside trends in your investment and to immediately reenter the market.

As a general rule, only approximately 50% of signals generated are likely to prove accurate, but because you reverse course quickly when signals go awry, your losses as a result of false signals are likely to be moderate.

Conversely, those signals that prove accurate are often followed by extensive advances—in which you will participate—or extensive declines—which you are likely to essentially avoid.

It is important for the success of this investment plan for investors to follow *every* signal in a timely manner. There will be losers. There will be winners. History will be on your side.

You have had enough of an introduction. The time has come to cut to the chase.

Timing Decisions

This is, again, a strategy for actively managing open-end high-yield bond fund portfolios that will require just a few minutes each week of your time, and that has, at least in the past, increased returns for almost all high-yield bond funds. Even more significant, increases in profitability have been accompanied by major reductions in drawdown and general risks associated with investing in the high-yield bond sector.

Although research results and track records in this discussion are hypothetical, based on research rather than actual trading, my personal favorable experiences in applying variants of the 1.25/0.50 timing model in actual accounts under management have not been hypothetical. No particular level of performance can be guaranteed for the future, of course, but I would be surprised if readers did not find the effort of applying the model to be justified by its results.

I'll go further. The following procedures may seem, at first, some-what complicated, but I have found, over nearly two decades of actual trading of high-yield bond funds, that methods such as you will learn have produced satisfactory rates of return, exceeding those normally associated with bond investment, at relatively low levels of risk and drawdown.

Future profitability, once again, cannot be ensured, but, if the past has any predictive value, I do believe that after you have learned and have begun to apply the procedures involved you will have acquired a technique that may be profitable for you for the rest of your life!

Tracking Total Return

The 1.25/0.50 timing model is based on procedures that take into account the total returns of high-yield bond funds. The total return of a bond fund is the net gain or loss created by a combination of the price movement of these instruments and the dividend flow that investors receive. For example, suppose that a high-yield bond fund paying 8% per year in interest dividends rises during a month from a price of 10.00 to a price of 10.10. What would be its total return for the month?

Well, the gain of 0.10 in price represents a 1% gain (based on a starting price of $10 per share), so the monthly rate of return based on price alone is 1%. However, if we divide the 8% or 80 cents per year annual interest payout by 12 (each month represents one twelfth of the annual period), we secure the result, 6.67 cents (or .67% of the share price of 10) additional return generated by the income derived from your holdings. The total return for the month, therefore, comes to 16.67 cents, 1.67% (more than either the capital gain profit or the income dividend taken separately).

Now suppose that instead of gaining 0.10 during the month, the fund's price lost 0.10, the price declining from 10.00 to 9.90. What would be the month's total return in that event? The dividend payout of 6.67 cents continues to be received, offset in this case by a 10 cent loss—the total change for the month, a loss of 3.33 cents or of 0.33%, just about one third of 1%. As you can see, the dividend payout does provide income that can cushion price declines.

The 1.25/0.50 timing model is designed to signal investors to hold positions in high-yield bond funds for as long as the total return from such positions remains favorable, rather than to encourage the liquidation of high-yielding positions because of relatively minor price declines. You will see how this works as we move into the rules of the timing model.

Rule 1: Timing

Trades are made on the first trading day of each week, based on the price levels of the last day of the preceding week. For example, during most weeks, you need to secure closing prices of the fund(s) you are trading and dividend streams after the close Friday, process the data prior to the close the following Monday, and execute your trades prior to the close of the markets during that Monday.

There may be some weeks when it will be apparent before the close on the last day of the week that buy or sell signals will be generated as a result of market action that day, in which case you may prefer not to wait until the first day of the next week to trade. On balance, it is usually preferable to trade on the actual days that signals are generated rather than the days after, but performance differences are likely to be quite minor.

Rule 2: Buy/Sell

You buy when the total return level of the fund(s) you are tracking rises by 1.25% from the lowest low that has existed since the most recent sell signal. You sell when the total return level of the fund(s) you are tracking declines by 0.50% from the most recent high since the onset of the most recent buy signal. There are no other buy/sell rules in this model.

The buy/sell rules are not complicated, but the process of calculating trigger points does take some time each week at first (much less when you become familiar with the required procedures).

Calculating Total Return Levels

You must secure the weekly closing prices of mutual funds that you are tracking. These should be available before the close of the first trading day of the subsequent week in *Barron's,* from your broker, from the fund, and elsewhere.

For most funds, you also need to keep track of occasional capital gain distributions (distributions to shareholders of profits created by the sales of assets that have been sold at a profit) as well as dividend (interest) distributions, which are generally made monthly.

The majority of open-end bond mutual funds adjust their daily net asset values, which are the same as their prices, to reflect income streams coming into them from their investments—this cash flow does represent additional assets—so their prices reflect total return, interest income plus changes in the value of their underlying holdings. Dividends are distributed, generally monthly, in the form of either cash or additional fund shares, depending on instructions from shareholders. At the time that these dividends are paid, the prices of many such funds are reduced by the amount of dividend payout to shareholders, which represents a decline of fund assets.

However, this drop in price does not represent in any way a loss to shareholders, who receive the value of the dividends either in cash or in additional shares.

Calculating Buy/Sell Levels for Funds with Prices That Are Reduced When Dividends Are Paid

1. On purchase of the fund, secure from the fund estimated dates and amounts of income/capital gain distributions.

2. When such distributions are made, the fund's price will be reduced by the amount of such distributions, in addition to whatever other price changes may take place as a result of changes in the value of the fund's holdings. You are likely to recognize distributions by larger than normal price changes in the fund on the days that distributions become effective (days of record).

3. If you are currently holding the fund, lower the sell stop by the amount of the dividend. If you are not holding the fund, lower the buy stop by the amount of the dividend. The fund family will alter the fund price.

4. You buy when the fund's price rises by 1.25% from the lowest low since the most recent sell signal. This level can be calculated by multiplying the lowest low price by 1.0125. For example, if the low price since the last sell has been 10.00, if you multiply (10.00 × 1.0125 = 10.125) you will secure your buy stop.

5. You sell when the fund's price declines by 0.5% from the highest high price achieved since the most recent buy signal. This level can be calculated by multiplying the highest high price by 0.995. For example, if the highest price since the last buy entry has been 10.00, if you multiply (10.00 × 0.995 = 9.95) you will secure your sell stop.

Example A

Example A illustrates a more or less typical series of weekly price movements for a hypothetical high-yield fund, and timing actions that resulted from signals generated by these price movements.

We presume that the hypothetical high-yield bond fund has been on a sell signal and that, on Week 1, it stood at the lowest price level since the most recent sell signal. We are going to look for a rise in total return of 1.25% from a low for a fresh buy and for a decline of 0.50% from the highest high since the last buy signal for a sell.

EXAMPLE A   Hypothetical High-Yield Bond Fund 1
Buy 1.25% Above Lows, Sell 0.50% Below Highs

Week	Net Asset Value (Price) (Includes Dividends)	Buy Level	Sell Level	Action
1	10.25	10.378[a]		Look for Buy
2	10.20	10.328[b]		Look for Buy
3	10.22	10.328[c]		Look for Buy
4	10.18	10.307[d]		Look for Buy
5	10.27	10.307[e]		Look for Buy
6	10.32 BUY!		10.268[f]	Look for Sell
7	10.28		10.268[g]	Look for Sell
8	10.31		10.268[h]	Look for Sell
9	10.34		10.288[i]	Look for Sell
10	10.40		10.348[j]	Look for Sell

Capital Gain Dividend of $1.25 Declared

Week	Net Asset Value (Price) (Includes Dividends)	Buy Level	Sell Level	Action
10 (modified)	9.15[k]		9.098[l]	Look for Sell
11	9.04 SELL!	9.153[m]		Look for Buy

a. Latest price, 10.25 + (1.25% of 10.25) or .128 = 10.378, the new buy stop.

b. The price has declined to a new low, so the buy stop is lowered. 10.20 + (1.25% of 10.20) = 10.3275, or 10.328.

c. The price has not fallen to a new low, so the buy stop remains unchanged.

d. The price has fallen to a new low, so the buy stop is lowered.

e. The price has not fallen to a new low, so the buy stop remains unchanged.

f. A buy signal has been generated! The new sell stop is 10.32 – (0.5% of 10.32), or .0516 = 10.268.

g. No new high has been made since the entry. Sell stop remains unchanged.

h. No new high has been made since the entry. Sell stop remains unchanged.

i. A new high has been made at 10.34. New sell stop is 10.34 – (.5% of 10.34) = 10.288.

j. A new high has been made. Raise sell stop to 10.40 – (.5% of 10.40) = 10.348.

k. A dividend of $1.25 has been declared. The price of "Hypothetical High Yield Fund," adjusted to reflect the dividend, is reduced by $1.25 from 10.40 to 9.15.

l. The sell stop is also adjusted down by $1.25, from 10.348 to 9.098.

m. A sell signal has been generated. The new buy stop is 9.04 + (1.25% of 9.04) = 9.153.

At the close of Week 10, hypothetical high-yield fund announces a capital gain distribution of $1.25 per share, to be distributed to recorded shareholders on that date. Inasmuch as this distribution comes from fund assets, the price of each share, 10.40, immediately declines by $1.25 to $9.15.

Adjustments in price, and in buy/sell levels, are required. The amount of the distribution, $1.25, is subtracted from the closing price that week and also from the price level required for a sell signal.

If the fund had been on a sell signal prior to the distribution, the fund's price would still have declined by $1.25 as a result of the dividend, and the buy stop would have been lowered by 1.25.

Reviewing the Procedure One Final Time

After you have entered into your fund, you place a trailing stop-loss order, 0.50% below the daily price, the level of which rises as new highs are made.

When a sell signal takes place, you enter a buy stop, which gets lowered as prices decline. Once again, sell stops are placed 0.50% below the most recent closing highs; buy stops are placed 1.25% above the most recent closing lows.

Price and signal adjustments are made to adjust for capital gain distributions in the manner shown. As a general rule, you must adjust daily fund prices, buy, and sell levels once each month as dividend payments are made and fund prices decline as a result. (You can obtain the amount of dividend payments made from your mutual funds, which generally pay at approximately the same time each month.)

Handling High-Yield Funds That Do Not Reflect Interest Income in Their Share Pricing

The majority of high-yield bond funds do include interest income in their daily pricing, the movement of which actually reflects the total return of such funds—changes in the values of the assets they hold, plus the income stream.

Some high-yield bond funds, however, do not include income accruals in their pricing. Income (as it comes into the fund) is collected and set aside in a separate holding area (credited to shareholders daily), but is not included in the fund share pricing. Such income distributions usually take place at monthly intervals in the form of additional fund shares or cash dividends, depending on shareholders' instructions.

Sell stop calculations that include undistributed income accruals while invested in such funds are quite complicated, so we can bypass any adjustments in price that might be made to allow for such accruals in establishing sell stops. However, adjustments can be made in levels of buy stops to reflect dividends that might be paid while investors happen to be uninvested in high-yield funds that do not adjust their prices to reflect dividend payouts. Therefore, timing models are at least partially based on total return; in this case they are based on the buy side rather than on price movement alone.

Here is a procedure that may be employed: Secure the scheduled monthly dividend payment from the mutual fund at the time of purchase and at the times it is determined each month thereafter. If you are currently invested in the fund, you do not have to make any adjustments based on dividends to maintain sell levels. Sell when the fund price, on a weekly closing basis, has fallen by 0.5% from its most recent weekly closing high price. If you are not invested in the fund, and the fund pays a dividend, lower the buy stop by the amount of dividend that has been declared. This recognizes the total return value of the dividend stream and makes it easier to re-enter the fund.

Example B

Example B presumes you are in a cash position awaiting a buy signal, 1.25% above the lowest low since you have been in cash, and that the price on Week #1 is the lowest price since the most recent sell signal.

EXAMPLE B   Hypothetical High-Yield Fund 2
Fund Does Not Lower Its Price When Dividends are Paid

Week	Price	Dividend Declared	Buy Price	Sell Price	Action
1	10.00	–	10.125^a		Look for Buy
2	9.90	–	10.024^b		Look for Buy
3	9.95	–	10.024^c		Look for Buy
4	9.94	.06	9.964^d		Look for Buy
5	9.98 BUY!	–		9.93^e	Look for Sell
6	9.97	–		9.93^f	Look for Sell
7	10.00	–		9.95^g	Look for Sell
8	10.03	.06		9.98^h	Look for Sell
9	9.97	–	10.095^i		Look for Buy

a. The buy stop price is 10.00 + (1.25% of 10.00), or 0.125 = 10.125.

b. The new buy stop is 9.90 + (1.25% of 9.90), or 0.124 = 10.024.

c. Because price has not fallen to a new low, the buy stop, 10.024, does not change.

d. There has been no new low. However, because a dividend of .06 has been paid, the buy stop is lowered by that amount. The former buy stop (10.024 – .06 = 9.964) becomes the new buy stop.

e. New sell stop = 9.98 – (.5% of 9.98) = 9.93.

f. Price has not risen to a new high, so the sell stop remains at 9.93.

g. Price has risen to a new high, so sell stop is raised from 9.93 to 9.95.

h. Price has risen to a new high again, so the sell stop is raised to 9.98, 10.03 – (.5% of 10.03), or 0.5 = 9.98. No adjustment is made for the dividend payout of .06.

i. A sell signal has been generated at a close of 9.97, below the sell stop of 9.98. The new buy stop is 9.97 + (1.25% of 9.97), or 0.125 = 10.095.

Performance of the 1.25/0.50 Timing Model

As a first step, consider Figure 5-2—a weekly chart of the Dryden
High-Yield Bond Fund, with buy and sell signals shown as rising and
falling arrows, respectively.

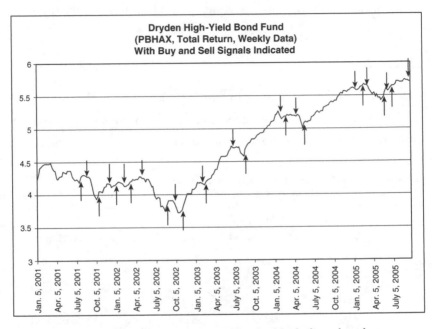

**FIGURE 5-2   Dryden High-Yield Bond Fund with timing signals,
2001–2005**

The performance of the timing model during this period was excellent.
Acting on signals produced by the model, investors would have participated fully in all advances while avoiding declines of the nature that
took place during the summers of 2001 and 2002 and the spring of
2005. (Chart based on hypothetical data.)

This chart illustrates the benefits of using timing models such as
the 1.25/0.50 timing model compared to buy and hold investment in
high-yield bond funds. Gains achieved via buy and hold strategies are
maintained. Drawdowns, as you can see, were considerably reduced,
in particular during the bear market period for the NASDAQ
Composite, 2001–2002.

These benefits are achieved without a large trading frequency—just 13 round-trip trades over a 4.5-year period, an average of 2.81 trades per year. Transaction costs and redemption fees, if any, are likely to be quite moderate.

We will move along now to Table 5-1, a tabular comparison of performance, buy and hold versus trading via close variants of the 1.25/0.50 timing model, for 15 different mutual funds over periods of as long as 17 years.

TABLE 5-1   Comparing Buy and Hold Strategies to Timing via a Close Variant of the 1.25/0.50 Timing Model, From Starting Dates Noted through August 24, 2005

Mutual Fund	Starting Date	Buy and Hold, Gain per Annum	Maximum Drawdown	Timing Model, Gain per Annum	Maximum Drawdown
Franklin AGE HY	9/01/1988	+8.17%	−23.92%	+10.63%	−3.35%
Blackrock HY	1/05/2001	+9.92	−11.87	+11.92	−1.94
Delaware Delchest.	9/01/1988	+5.82	−42.15	+10.15	−3.61
Fidelity Adv HI Ad	9/01/1988	+10.86	−31.84	+12.50	−6.54
Federated Hi Yield	9/01/1988	+7.99	−20.54	+9.23	−3.37
Janus HY	1/02/1996	+8.31	−10.70	+6.61	−2.06
MFS High Income	9/01/1988	+7.64	−23.91	+9.81	−3.80
Northern HY Fixed	2/18/1999	+5.62	−9.73	+6.63	−4.63
Northeast Invest.	9/01/1988	+8.63	−14.01	+8.95	−2.24
Oppenheimer HY	9/01/1988	+8.09	−17.58	+8.17	−5.72
Pimco HY	1/13/1997	+5.64	−13.26	+6.52	−4.78
Sun America HY	9/01/1988	+5.71	−31.86	+9.86	−3.67
SEI HY	1/13/1995	+7.78	−10.89	+7.03	−7.83
Pioneer HY	7/07/1998	+10.93	−17.88	+11.97	−3.93
W & R Adv High Inc	9/01/1988	+6.50	−25.18	+8.45	−4.65
Averages		**+7.84%**	**−20.35%**	**+9.23%**	**−4.14%**

These results are based on hypothetical research, not real-life trading. Moreover, they are based on a slightly different version of the 1.25/0.50 timing model that uses SEC yields rather than dividend distributions in its methodology. I do not believe that performance results have been significantly affected by modifications introduced in this book for purposes of simplifying the calculations required. Future performance cannot be ensured.

These calculations include dividends while in the high-yield bond funds but, for trading accounts, do not include money-market interest while in cash. Inasmuch as positions in high-yield bond funds were maintained for approximately 65% of the time on average, approximately 1% to 1.5% per year money-market interest earned the remaining 35% of the time would have provided additional return to trading accounts, bringing the total gain per annum for traded accounts to approximately 10.5%.

However, these calculations do not include transaction or redemption fees that might apply. You can minimize these by trading directly with the mutual fund family rather than via a brokerage house and if investments are confined to high-yield bond funds that do not charge redemption fees for shorter-term holding periods. (Verify arrangements regarding such with your brokerage or proposed mutual fund before you initiate positions.)

Comparing Results

High-yield bond funds purchased and sold on the basis of the 1.25/0.50 timing model well outperformed such funds held on a buy and hold basis, particularly insofar as risk/reward ratios are concerned. As you can see at the bottom of Table 5-1, high-yield bond funds traded based on signals generated by a close variant of the 1.25/0.50 timing model produced average annual gains of 9.23% compared to an average of 7.84% for the same funds held on a buy and hold basis. Inasmuch as a large proportion of the total return achieved from investment in high-yield bond funds derives from their interest payout, there are relatively few negative impacts arising from taxes created by trading activity.

Of even more significance, the average worst case drawdown (calculated monthly) for funds traded based on the timing model was only 4.14%, less than 45% of the average annual gain of these portfolios; whereas the average worst case drawdown (calculated daily) for funds held on a buy and hold basis came to 20.35%, nearly 2.6 times greater than the average annual gain of 7.74%. (If drawdowns for high-yield bond funds traded on the timing model were calculated daily, they would probably be somewhat higher than drawdowns recorded only at month end.)

Why High-Yield Bond Funds Relate So Well to This Type of Timing Model

As a general rule, investments of higher volatility benefit more from the application of effective timing models than investments of lower volatility, because timing models tend to produce greater reductions in risk for volatile investments than they do for less-volatile holdings.

High-yield bond funds are characterized by greater longer-term risks than higher-grade bond funds but actually tend to show more moderate price swings on a day-to-day basis, a favorable pattern because prices do not overshoot buy/sell signal levels to a large extent when such signals develop. (If a sell signal would take place if a fund were to decline to below a stop of 10.50, for example, you would be better off if the fund were stopped out at a price of 10.49 than because of a daily decline from 10.51 to 10.40. Remember, mutual funds can be sold only at the ends of days.)

By comparison, the Standard & Poor's 500 Index has had annual rates of return of approximately 11%, including dividends, but has seen drawdowns in recent years of as much as 45%, not including dividends. Although high-yield bonds are generally considered to be speculative investments that do, indeed, carry certain risks, on balance they have produced returns relatively close to returns achieved by stocks, with considerably less risk.

High-yield bond funds do not change much in price most days because on most days large portions of the bonds they hold do not trade at all, and are marked to the market as unchanged insofar as calculations of the funds' net asset values are concerned. By comparison, Treasury issues tend to be actively traded.

Summing Up

Overall, high-yield bond funds represent a sector of interest even on a buy and hold basis. Remember, however, that this sector has shown particularly favorable risk/reward relationships when investments are maintained with certain relatively simple but totally objective timing models that involve only relatively infrequent trading. The 1.25/0.50 timing model is that sort of timing model.

Highly Recommended

Place a certain portion of high-yield mutual funds in your investment portfolio to be traded on the 1.25/0.50 timing model. These positions are likely to produce an above-average income stream as well as certain amounts of capital gain, all the while retaining stability in its values. The high-yield components of your portfolio are also likely to help reduce the asset fluctuation in an otherwise all-stock portfolio.

You can find additional useful information on the numerous Web sites that provide performance data for high-yield bond funds. Morningstar, for example, assigns star ratings to funds that invest in high-yield bonds. Yahoo.Finance.com provides information on strongly performing high-yield bond funds over varying periods of time. MSN.Money.com provides similar information and commentary.

Higher-Grade Bonds and Bond Funds

My research staff has done considerable research into the market timing of investments in higher-grade bonds and bond mutual funds and has yet to find a timing technique that outperforms buy and hold strategies applied to these investment sectors in terms of total return.

Some techniques reduce price risk (that is, the risk of declining bond prices), but this risk reduction is by and large offset by the loss of income (which takes place when capital is removed from longer-term bond positions that pay higher rates of interest and placed into safe havens such as money-market funds that pay lower rates of interest). Transaction expenses would be a further drag on the performance of timing models in this regard.

Risks on a total return basis, at least historically, have been particularly low for investors who place capital into diversified higher-grade mutual fund and bond portfolios whose average maturities lie in the area of 7 years or less. There have been very few years in which losses accruing from such portfolios, after interest payments, have been at all significant.

Do not forget the technique of laddering investments in higher-grade bonds. This strategy is likely to outperform random purchases and sales over the long run.

We have not completed your arsenal of market-timing techniques. If timing does not add much to investing in short- to intermediate-term high-grade bonds, market-timing tools can certainly add considerably to returns from the stock market. We will be returning to timing models in subsequent chapters.

6

THE WONDERFUL WORLD OF EXCHANGE-TRADED FUNDS

Mutual funds remain arguably the most familiar of investment vehicles that provide to small and large investors alike the ability to assemble broadly diversified portfolios by way of single transactions in as few as one investment vehicle. Mutual funds also enable investors to invest in diverse groups of various bonds/stocks that represent limited- or single-sector portfolios of stocks segregated by capitalization (for example, small cap), geography (single- or multi-country companies), industry (for instance, health, energy), and other categories into which investments might be classified.

Occasional scandals aside, the industry as a whole has probably served investors well over the years, with some—definitely not all— mutual fund families providing excellent long-term returns at relatively low cost, expense, and risk.

Still, there are definite disadvantages to investing in mutual funds. For example, management fees, although reduced in recent years, represent a drag on the performance of the mutual fund industry. The majority of equity mutual funds have actually underperformed stock market indices against which their performance might be compared.

For another, there have been increasing trends in the industry toward greater restriction of fund liquidity. More and more mutual fund families are imposing redemption fees for assets held for 90 days or less, some requiring even longer minimum holding periods if redemption fees are to be avoided. Some mutual fund families restrict annual trading to just one or two round trips per year. It appears that even moderately active investors are no longer welcomed in the halls of Fidelity or at the gates of Vanguard.

Also, certain negative tax consequences are associated with many mutual funds for investors who invest with capital that is not tax sheltered. If you purchase a mutual fund and hold (even for years in some instances), certain portions of your profits may end up being taxed along the way even though you do not sell any shares of your fund(s). This comes about when mutual funds distribute to shareholders realized profits that accrue from the sale of certain assets by the funds that take place from time to time as portfolios are reallocated. These "capital gain distributions" are subject to federal and state income taxes for the year in which they have been distributed even though investors have not profitably sold any shares of the mutual fund itself.

Prices of funds that make such distribution decline to reflect reductions in net asset values that develop from the sale of assets, capital gains distributed to shareholders as a form of dividend (which may or may not be reinvested by shareholders in new shares at a new cost basis). As a general rule, most investors do reinvest such distributions in new fund shares, ending with the same total assets as before the distribution—but with an immediate tax bill for their trouble. For accurate tax reporting for the past and going forward, investors have to maintain records of such distributions and of the prices at which these distributions were reinvested into new fund shares.

In short, sometimes investors have to pay taxes on mutual fund profits that are not really profits at all.

> ### Tax Tip
>
> Most capital gain distributions are made during the month of December. Before buying into a new fund late in the year, call the fund to secure an estimate of the amount of capital gain distribution the fund anticipates and the date at which it is scheduled to take place. Avoid the distribution, if possible.

Enter the Exchange-Traded Funds (ETFs)

Various attempts have been made over the years to develop investment vehicles that would provide internal diversification, ready liquidity, and be tradable at low cost at any time of the market day with no restriction other than those created by the marketplace itself. For a while, baskets of stock—often hedged in one way or another against futures contracts—were popular, but the market crash of 1987 illuminated the pitfalls of this sort of strategy, which has since faded from favor.

Other attempts have involved instruments such as Index Participation Shares (IPS), Toronto Stock Exchange Index Participations (TIPS), and Supershares. There is no need for you to know more than these names, if that much. None of these vehicles survived for long.

Finally, in the early 1990s, a more-lasting instrument was developed: the SPDRS (Standard & Poor's Depository Receipts), usually referred to as "spiders," a unit trust that holds portfolios designed to replicate the Standard & Poor's 500 Index, whose composition can change as the composition of the Standard & Poor's 500 Index changes. Initial trading in SPDRs was moderate, but during the mid to late 1990s, a period in which the Standard & Poor's 500 Index rose sharply, interest and activity in these instruments increased dramatically.

Unlike mutual funds, and like stocks, SPDRs (and subsequent ETFs) are traded on various stock exchanges and over the counter, the vast majority of trades conducted between investors rather than between investors and the organizations or sponsors that create ETFs. Markets for an increasing percentage of ETFs have become quite liquid—liquid enough for active trading at fairly narrow spreads between bid prices (the price at which investors are offering to buy) and asked or offered prices (the price that current holders or short sellers are requesting to sell). Other ETFs feature somewhat less liquid markets but remain quite viable as investments for traders who prefer less frequency in their activity.

Over the years since the initiation of SPDRs, a host of ETFs have been introduced, including DIAMONDS (a unit-trust ETF designed to replicate the movement of the Dow Industrials); a NASDAQ 100 Index ETF (QQQQs), which grew to even larger popularity than the SPDRs during the heyday of NASDAQ speculation in 1998 and 1999; numerous sector SPDRs; and other sector ETFs. Certain ETFs replicate bond portfolios. In recent years, as foreign stock markets have been outperforming the U.S. stock market, ETFs that maintain portfolios of foreign stocks have been developed.

By the end 2005, there were ETFs available for just about every taste and speculative level of investor.

Pros and Cons of ETFs

ETFs are interesting investment vehicles, indeed, with many advantages over mutual funds and stocks of individual corporations. They are, however, not perfect investment instruments. We will first consider their more favorable attributes, then their less favorable, and finally some market-timing models that may be used to select and to trade ETFs with greater profitability than simple buy and hold strategies.

Pros

Diversification: Many Different Stocks in One Investment Vehicle

ETFs have many things in common with index mutual funds, funds whose portfolios are designed to replicate one or the other stock market index, including the weighting of its components, rather than designed to reflect the investment styles, selections, and prognostications of portfolio managers. Purchasers of SPDRs, Diamonds, and QQQQs are, in effect, purchasing these stock market indices in the same manner that investors in the excellent Vanguard Standard & Poor's 500 Index Fund purchase, in effect, "shares of the Standard & Poor's 500 Index."

No attempt is being made by the managers of index mutual funds—and index ETFs—to outperform the stock market, as represented by its various indices. Index mutual funds and index ETFs are designed to replicate the stock market at the lowest costs. There are no needs for expensive portfolio managers, for large portfolio turnovers, or for high investment expenses.

To the extent that large and broad portfolios are likely to be more predictable and less volatile in their price movements than individual stocks, index ETFs provide the benefits of ready diversification, high intra-day liquidity, marginability (they can be purchased on margin), price visibility throughout the day, and relatively low expenses in comparison to most mutual funds.

Lower Management Costs

ETFs are issued by an ever-increasing array of companies that then act as their managers and administrators. Such companies include, for example, Barclays Global Investors, Morgan Stanley, State Street Global Investors, mutual fund families (such as Fidelity, Vanguard, and Rydex), and many others that use various structures within which ETFs may be created.

These companies make their money by charging management fees to these ETFs in the way that closed-end management companies make their money by charging management fees for index funds.

As a general rule, the expenses for management fees borne by investors in ETFs are lower, sometimes considerably lower, than the management fees charged by traditional open-end (or for that matter, closed-end) mutual funds.

For example, the Barclay's Web site (www.ishares.com) notes that whereas the average annual expense ratio for large-blend open-end index funds is 0.69%, the expense ratio for the iShares S & P 500 Index Fund (an ETF) is only 0.09%. Expense ratios for foreign ETFs are higher, however, 0.35% for iShares MSCI EAFE and 0.75% for the iShares MSCI Emerging Markets ETF. By comparison, the average expense ratio for traditional mutual funds that invest in foreign equities was, during 2005, 1.07% for index funds and 1.81% for actively managed mutual funds that attempted to outperform their benchmark indices.

These differentials in management expense charges are not insignificant and can easily represent between 5% and 10% of annual returns to investors (a hidden tax on your investment, so to speak).

More-Favorable Tax Treatment

I have already alluded to the unfavorable tax treatment involved in the ownership of the traditional open-end mutual fund.

Capital gain distributions, which create tax liabilities, represent a very low percentage of assets of most ETFs. For example, Yahoo!Finance (go to www.yahoo.com, and then to Finance) reported that average capital gain distributions, August 2000 through August 2001, for a group of index mutual funds came to 5.87% of assets, whereas for a group of ETFs (same indices, same time period), the capital gain distributions averaged only 0.31%. Capital gain distributions for actively managed mutual funds, which have larger portfolio turnovers, are likely to be even higher.

These differentials are significant and represent a major advantage to ETFs as opposed to the typical open-end mutual fund.

Liquidity and Portfolio Visibility

ETFs can be traded throughout the day, and most trades occur between secondary shareholders rather than between shareholders and management (which can take place if the number of shares traded is large). Markets are generally, although not absolutely, fluid. There are disadvantages involved in this "liquidity benefit," which sometimes encourages emotionally based overtrading stimulated by intra-day short-term market fluctuations; by and large, however, it is generally a positive.

Mutual funds do not readily provide information regarding their individual stock holdings, which are released generally months after the fact as funds update their prospectuses. ETF management companies release the compositions of their funds relatively frequently because of the manner in which their portfolio compositions are exchanged and created in relationships to the baskets of stock represented in each ETF.

Asset Allocation and Portfolio Control

Inasmuch as open-end mutual funds have become increasingly restrictive of active investment strategies, it is more difficult for investors to rapidly shift capital from market sector to market sector as industry and other market sectors rise and fall in strength. There are no restrictions in this regard for ETFs, whose portfolios can be readily organized by industry sector, the balance of which can be changed readily at almost any time.

The repertoire of the ETF industry has become quite extensive, more so as time passes. Active traders and asset allocators have a broad field in which to play and, by and large, a rather liquid field.

Cons

Transaction Costs and Bid-Asked Spreads

Whereas it is true that mutual funds sometimes involve redemption fees, particularly if they are actively traded, they can, for the most part, be purchased and sold with no transaction costs. This is not necessarily the case, of course, for mutual funds purchased and sold via brokerage houses rather than directly with the fund.

ETFs involve brokerage commissions for purchase and for sale that are likely to be more significant as a percentage of assets for smaller than for larger accounts and transactions. Generally, no transaction costs apply when investors deal directly with mutual funds.

Bid-asked spreads, which have already been mentioned, are potentially a greater expense, particularly for certain ETFs. During the afternoon of October 13, 2005, the bid price for the SPDRs was 117.80; the asked price was 117.81. The difference was just one penny for a share priced at $117.80, or of just .0001 or just one hundredth of 1% per round-trip trade. (Bid-asked spreads for round-trip (buy and then sell) trades affect you only one way, not both ways.)

If you were to make 20 round-trip trades in SPDRs over a year, you would have an additional expense of twenty hundredths (two tenths) of 1% of the value of SPDRs, which would represent an increase in expenses associated with trading ETFs. Not too bad.

Spreads for QQQQs at the time were three hundredths of 1% per trade, which would have amounted to six tenths of 1% for 20 round-trip exchanges—a cost that, with commissions, would pretty much have offset the expense ratio advantages of this ETF compared with mutual funds.

Another ETF, the IJJ, represents the Standard & Poor's MidCap 400 Index, a fine ETF for investing in companies of medium capitalization. This ETF is not nearly as liquid as the QQQQs or SPDRs. At a price of approximately 65.12, this ETF was trading on October 13, 2005, at 65.07 bid / 65.18 asked, a spread of 11 cents or of seventeen hundredths of 1% per trade. If you were to trade 20 round trips per year, your additional expenses, from spreads alone, brokerage commissions apart, would come to 3.38%! Transaction expenses alone might well offset any other savings involved by being in ETFs rather than mutual funds and would, in any event, certainly argue against actively trading this ETF.

Moral of the Tale: Nuthin' for Nuthin'

It can be nice, indeed, to be able to trade into and out of ETFs as market conditions change, but the temptation to trade into and out of the stock market on every short-term market swing is likely to prove more costly than profitable. Before purchasing any ETF, check out prevailing bid-asked spreads to ascertain estimated trading costs. Create for yourself a table listing spreads of ETFs you are considering and calculate the amount of round-trip trades you can make without exceeding perhaps 1% to 1.50% total transaction expenses per year.

For example, if you trade in IJJs at a per-trade cost of seventeen hundredths of 1% for bid-asked slippage alone, you would not want to make more than eight round-trip transactions per year. (Seventeen hundredths of 1% times 8 trades = 1.36%. This does not include commission costs, which vary brokerage by brokerage and by the size of trade and which should be included in your total transaction calculations.)

Trades That Vary from Net Asset Value

As we know, mutual funds are always priced at their net asset value, although shareholders do sometimes have to pay entry/exit fees. We have seen that closed-end mutual funds may trade either above or below their net asset value, with premiums/discounts benefiting sometimes the buyer, sometimes the seller.

In a similar manner, ETFs sometimes trade slightly above or slightly below their net asset value. Spreads rarely reach the levels of spreads seen in closed-end funds because of arbitrage possibilities if spreads and net asset values diverge to a great degree. For example, suppose that an ETF sells for $40 per share while its underlying assets are worth $41. Savvy arbitrageurs could buy the ETF, simultaneously selling short $41 of underlying assets for every ETF purchased at 40. When the spread reverts to parity, both sides could be closed for a guaranteed 2.5% profit no matter which way the market moved. Larger holders might simply turn in the ETF shares for shares of the ETF's underlying holdings, which could be sold at net asset value.

Investors may and are likely to run into trouble if they have to sell ETFs into a market plunge (a circumstance that often results in sales made below net asset value) or if they join a stampede to buy during a rising market period (at which times purchases may be made above net asset value). Sometimes these deviations of ETFs from net asset value benefit investors, sometimes not. On balance, the fact that ETFs often trade away from their net asset value is probably a negative.

Other Caveats

We will be discussing specific ETFs in somewhat more detail as we go along. You should be aware that in many cases index-based ETFs, ETFs that are supposed to replicate one or the other market indices or sectors, actually are not structured to precisely replicate the index that they supposedly represent.

For example, certain market sectors may actually be represented by ETFs that hold in their baskets only a relatively small number of highly liquid stock issues of a certain index rather than by the full index. This limited representation may add to the volatility of such ETFs that are not as diversified as their supposed benchmark indices.

In addition, ETFs provide good indexing but no particular management panache. This is probably no disadvantage in most cases—index mutual funds do tend to outperform the majority of mutual funds. Still, every so often, outstanding mutual fund managers come along, managers that add a special "something" to their fund that results in superior performance.

ETFs may prove more predictable in their price action relative to the general stock market, but do not expect happy surprises or significant outperformance. The benefits of indexing do have their price.

A Closer Look at the ETF Universe

And a rapidly growing universe it is!

In 1995, there were two ETFs listed, with underlying assets of $1.1 billion. By 2004, there were 138 ETFs listed, with aggregate assets of $167 billion—still growing as I write. Once again, ETFs represent just about every area of the investment arena—from bonds to specific market sectors to broad market indices to foreign markets to commodity-related ETFs.

The following is just a limited sample of what is available.

Income ETFs

- **iShares Lehman TIPS Bond Fund (TLT).** Invests in Treasury inflation-protected securities

- **iShares GS$ InvesTop Corp Bond (LQD).** Invests in corporate bonds

Global Investment

- **IShares MSCI Emerging Markets Index (EEM).** Emerging market equity

- **Vanguard Emerging Markets VIPERS (VWO).** Emerging market equity

Domestic Market Indices

- **Diamond Series Trust I (DIA).** Designed to replicate the Dow Jones Industrials

- **SPDR 500 (SPY).** Designed to replicate the Standard & Poor's 500 Index

- **iShares Russell 1000 Growth (IWF).** Designed to replicate the Russell 1000 large-cap growth index

- **iShares Russell Microcap Index Fund (IWC).** Replicates the microcap market index

- **iShares Russell 2000 Value (IWN).** Replicates the small-cap value index

Specific Overseas Countries

- **iShares MSCI Brazil Index (EWZ).** Reflects the Brazilian stock market

- **iShares MSCI Mexico Index (EWW).** Reflects the Mexican stock market

- **iShares MSCI Pacific ex-Japan Index (EPP).** Pacific area, excluding Japan

- **iShares MSCI Sweden Index (EWD).** Reflects the Swedish stock market

Specific Industry Groups

- **Vanguard Financials VIPERs (VFH).** Financial services

- **HOLDrs Internet (HHH).** The Internet sector

- **iShares Dow Jones U.S. Basic Materials (IYM).** Basic materials (an inflation hedge)

- **iShares Comex Gold Trust (IAU).** Precious metals

- **iShares Cohen & Steers Realty Major (ICF).** Real estate

The ETF universe is broad, flexible, and encompasses virtually all market sectors that have led the stock market in recent years. (Actually, new ETFs are often created to reflect industry and geographical areas that have assumed market leadership in response to investor demand.)

Miscellanea

Most ETFs can be transacted in odd lots, in sizes not precisely equal to 100 shares. However, "HOLDrs" can be traded only in 100-share increments.

Fans of option-related strategies may purchase or sell puts and calls related to many ETFs, designated as "iShares."

For information about specific ETFs, check out www.price-data.com. This site provides listings, symbols, and descriptions of almost all current ETFs. You can also check out the "Money" section of MSN.com. You will find plenty of material. For example, the "Symbol Guides" direct you to a full roster of current ETFs. You can then secure more information about any ETF in which you might have interest by just clicking its symbols.

Creating Complete, Well-Diversified Portfolios

ETFs lend themselves well to the creation of well-diversified investment portfolios whose composition can then be readily altered as market conditions change. For example, strong industry groups during 2005 included energy-related stocks, utilities, emerging markets, sectors related to these, and health. As the year moved along, the energy and utilities sectors flamed out (October), giving way to large-capitalization growth stocks that assumed leadership as the year drew to a close. Emerging-market-related securities retreated in price during a market sell-off that took place during September and October, but quickly recovered.

Although not all (or even many) ETF investors can detect changes in leadership that take place soon enough or reliably enough to profitably rotate holdings on a short-term basis, the variety of ETFs available has been sufficient to provide many investment opportunities for ready and flexible ingress into the various market areas as strength develops.

Do mutual funds provide this flexibility? Yes and no. As we know, many funds charge redemption fees, entry commissions, and restrict trading. In addition, management fees, as previously noted, run higher for mutual funds than for ETFs.

Remember the Principles of Diversification

Some stock market traders have fine abilities to discern changes in market fashion and trend; they often enjoy and successfully deal with the challenges involved in the maintenance of relatively undiversified, actively traded portfolios, concentrated in what they hope will be the strongest of market sectors.

Most investors, however, will do better to maintain well-diversified portfolios, using various strategies described throughout this book to secure better-than-average performance from their holdings. Remember, diversification reduces risk and smoothes and generally improves investment performance.

Creating and Maintaining Your ETF-Based Portfolio

1. Become familiar with the universe of readily tradable ETFs.

   Learn their symbols, where they trade, what specifically are their underlying holdings, and what market sector(s) they represent. You will then be able to zero in on particular ETFs that represent market sectors in which you want to invest. You have already been given sources for this data. Our listing is hardly complete; there are many such sources.

2. Determine the mix of your diversified portfolio.

   Its composition should be diversified with relatively noncorrelated market sectors. We have seen examples. Six to ten market sectors should suffice. ETFs do provide bond equivalents to represent the income portion of your portfolio and, in particular, do provide access to many markets overseas.

3. Consider previously discussed strategies to overweight certain elements in your portfolio.

   Review the sections in which we considered procedures for the rebalancing of diversified portfolios at 6-month intervals to overweight portfolios with market sectors that are leading in performance while underweighting laggards.

My own research has indicated that ETFs can also be profitably maintained in portfolios based on more intermediate-term relative strength, in the way that we rebalance mutual fund portfolios. (In accordance with the principles and procedures you learned in Chapter 3, "Selecting Mutual Funds Most Likely to Succeed," investment positions are spread among funds that have been in the top 10% of performers and maintained until such funds drop from the first decile.) However, the benefits of using ETFs in this manner seem to be not quite as striking as when this sort of rotation is applied to mutual funds, because the performances of index-oriented mutual funds and ETFs tend to be more similar than performances of actively managed mutual funds.

As we have seen, investments made in ETFs as well as in mutual funds based upon leadership rankings for intermediate time periods tend to be quite positively productive. Research indicates that longer-term holding periods between reallocations may be used, too.

The premise is similar to premises that we have used before in the selection of mutual funds based on relative strength—that is, the premise that strength tends to indicate further strength and that it usually pays to follow market leadership for as long as leadership persists.

Large Cap vs. Small Cap

Sometimes the stock market favors larger-cap companies, and sometimes smaller-cap companies come to the fore. For example, smaller-cap companies outperformed larger-cap companies during the early 1980s but underperformed larger-cap companies between 1983 and 1988. Larger-cap companies took the lead again in 1994, and maintained this lead through 1998, when smaller-cap companies once again reasserted themselves.

As you will see, sometimes differentials in performance can be striking. The large-cap market sector can be represented on a total return basis by the Russell 1000 ETF (IWB). The smaller-cap sector may be represented by the Russell 2000 ETF (IWM).

You can achieve results superior to either area alone by just performing an end-of-year rebalance. On December 31 of each year, ascertain which of the two investment areas (large-cap blend [Russell 1000] and small-cap blend [Russell 2000]) has shown the larger total return for the year. Total return includes both price change and dividend payout.

Place your capital into the ETF that represents the sector that has led in performance over the previous 12 months and keep it there for at least the next full year. Sometimes, you will remain in a sector for just 1 year before rebalancing assets. At other times, you may maintain your positions for several years before a shift in relative strength takes place. That is all there is to it. Nothing more.

Here are the results of carrying forth this program from 1980 through October 31, 2005. You would have been invested in the Russell 2000 Index (small cap) as follows.

Model in Small Caps		Large Cap Total Return	Small Cap Total Return
From	**To**		
12/31/79	12/31/84	92.6%	111.5%
12/31/88	12/31/89	30.4	16.3
12/31/91	12/31/94	20.5	38.2
12/31/99	10/31/05 (open)	6.4	37.9

You would have been invested in the Russell 1000 (large cap) as follows.

Model in Large Caps		Large Cap Total Return	Small Cap Total Return
From	**To**		
12/31/84	12/31/88	88.2%	57.9%
12/31/89	12/31/91	27.4	17.6
12/31/94	12/31/99	244.2	116.4

Based on research conducted by Dr. Marvin Appel, Appel Asset Management Corporation, Great Neck, New York.

Overall Results

During this period, the Russell 2000 Index produced an annualized total return of 12.0% per year with a maximum drawdown of 36%. During this period, the Russell 1000 Index produced an annualized total return of 12.9% per year with a 45% drawdown.

The once-per-year switching strategy produced an average gain per year of 15.1% with a maximum drawdown of 35% (outperforming both market sectors with less risk than either).[1]

Comments

This strategy, in and of itself, does not produce dramatic improvement in investment return. Over the long run, however, differentials of more than 2% per year between the application of the switching strategy and buy and hold do add up. Risk reduction is only moderate—the model is invested 100% of the time in market areas that are relatively correlated. (It does not appear that more-frequent realignment of assets would significantly improve performance.)

The strategy provides favorable tax consequences, however. Inasmuch as all positions are held for at least 1 year, every capital gain profit receives favorable long-term tax treatment.

Figure 6-1 shows the results of the annual switching strategy, 1980–2005.

Combining Sector Selection with Market Timing for Improved Performance

Chapter 7, "A Three-Pronged Approach to Timing the Markets," and Chapter 8, "Time Cycles, Market Breadth, and Bottom-Finding Strategies," introduce you to certain fundamental, cyclical, and breadth indicators that have been designed for market-timing purposes to improve returns over those likely to be generated by buy and hold strategies alone.

---

[1] Based on research conducted by Dr. Marvin Appel, Appel Asset Management Corporation, Great Neck, New York.

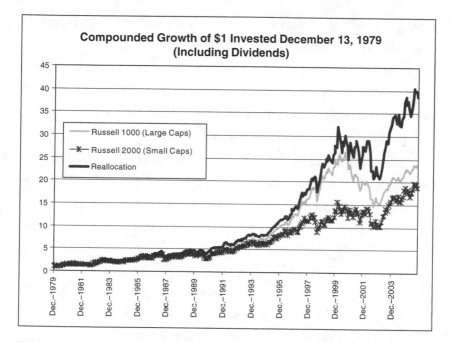

FIGURE 6-1   Switching between the Russell 1000 and Russell 2000 on an annual basis, depending on relative strength

The Russell 1000 and Russell 2000 moved pretty much in tandem between 1980 and the early 1990s, at which point the performance of these market sectors diverged more than it had in the past. The dark solid line reaching on the right side to the upper portion of the chart represents the final value of the reallocated portfolio, which far surpassed the value of either the Russell 1000 or Russell 2000 portfolio held alone. Annual rebalancing strategies have proven more useful since the early 1990s than previously.

Using ETFs as Hedges Against Inflation

Although a number of mutual funds invest in inflation-protective markets, ETFs definitely provide a broad variety of instruments that may be placed into portfolios as hedges against inflation. For ongoing income streams plus the maximum in safety, one might invest in the iShares Lehman TIPS Bond Fund (TIP). We have already discussed Treasury inflation-protected securities (TIPS) as an ultimate defense against inflation. TIPS, as bonds, are less susceptible to price decline during periods of rising interest rates because their rates of return generally rise during such periods.

Other inflation hedges include ETFs such as the iShares Goldman Sachs Natural Resource Index (IGE), the HOLDrs Oil Services (OIH), the Vanguard Materials VIPERS (VAW), and the iShares Dow Jones U.S. Basic Materials (IYM).

Interestingly, ETFs, like other areas of the stock market, tend to anticipate change rather than to follow change. For example, prices of energy stocks topped during 2005 in advance of the peak in oil prices, and ended their late-summer decline prior to oil prices reaching their lows later in that year.

Remember the media indicator. When the general media is almost unanimous in predicting an economic development, the odds are that the development will not take place. During 2005, for example, the general wisdom called for sharply rising interest rates. In fact, rates rose for a while during the late summer but did not particularly penetrate through their long-standing trading ranges before retreating in the fall. The inflationary pressures anticipated as a result of energy shortages and increases in short-term interest rates simply did not materialize and were therefore not reflected in the longer-term bond market.

It is probably not a bad idea, however, to maintain a certain proportion of your investments in inflation-protective investments. Given the developments of overseas economies, particularly the economies of China and India, price pressures for natural materials seem likely to be with us for some time to come. Ongoing positions in energy investments/utility stocks (many of which produce natural gas) may prove more than worthwhile.

However, such positions are probably best taken during periods of quiet, when prices are stable, rather than when inflation makes the headlines. Remember, smart money generally accumulates investments when they are *not* popular and certainly *before* they make the headlines.

Sample Portfolios

Here they are, three interesting portfolios of ETFs, representing a diverse array of industries, geographic locations, company size, volatility, risk, and current-income flow.

The Conservative Investor

This investor desires capital appreciation but places a high priority on capital preservation as well as income flow. Generally speaking, such an investor should organize a portfolio of below-average volatility, with relatively large holdings in income-producing investments. The following might well be a portfolio to meet those investment objectives:

- **10% SPDRS.** These ETFs, which mimic the price movement of the Standard & Poor's 500 Index, represent the most-established corporations in the United States. The Standard & Poor's 500 Index is less volatile than most market areas.

- **5% iShares Russell 2000 Value (IWN).** A representation in the small-capitalization value area.

- **10% iShares Cohen & Steers Realty Major (ICF).** Provides ongoing dividend payout as well as a participation in real estate investment. This sector tends to be relatively uncorrelated with most stocks, has usually been a good inflation hedge—ICF providing dividend yields in the area of 5% during 2005.

- **5% HOLDrs Utilities (UTH).** Utility issues provide dividend flow as well as protection against inflation because of their natural gas resources.

- **5% iShares MSCI EAFE Value Index Fund (EFV).** Value stocks from Europe, Australia, and the Far East.

- **5% iShares MSCI Pacific ex-Japan Idx (EPP).** Further geo-graphic diversification.

- **5% iShares Global Healthcare Sect (IXJ).** Industry as well as geographic diversification.

- **5% iShares S & P Global Financials Sect (IXG).** A foot into the financials, domestic as well as overseas.

- **10% SPDR Energy (XLE).** Energy and natural resources.

- **15% iShares Lehman 1–3 Yr Treasury Bond (SHY).** Just about as low risk an income investment as you can find.

- **15% iShares Lehman 7–10 Year Treasury Bond (IEF).** As long a bond maturity as most people need to have.

- **10% iShares Lehman TIPS Bond Fund (TIP).** Guaranteed income plus inflation protection.

Do not consider the preceding and following rosters specifically recommended ETFs but rather rosters that illustrate the form of diversification that may be achieved via the creation of balanced ETF portfolios. At such time as you might be ready to create and maintain a conservative portfolio of ETFs, you might review the selection of ETFs that represent the various industry and geographic areas and select from the best performing of such ETFs for your portfolio.

Review your selections periodically (not necessarily weekly or even monthly, but perhaps quarterly or semi-annually) to ascertain whether your holdings are showing at least average to above-average performance for their market sector (in which case, they should be maintained).

The preceding list also includes ETFs that represent the most conservative area of the portfolio: a 30% position in short- to inter-mediate-term U.S. government debt. Actually, many investors may prefer to invest in actual bonds rather than through ETFs or mutual funds; if limitations in capital preclude the establishment of diversified bond portfolios (because of the typical price of $1,000 per newly issued bond), however, ETFs may provide better opportunities for the establishment of diversified income positions.

It is also possible to create well-diversified portfolios by blending ETFs, open-end mutual funds, closed-end mutual funds, and actual bonds or stocks—taking the best from each asset category. This is the procedure I recommend.

The Moderate Investor

This investor is concerned about risk, but is able and willing to accept certain business risks to secure additional capital gain. Predictable current income is not necessarily a high priority, but long-term capital growth does rank high among this investor's objectives. The moderate investor can accept interim losses in his portfolio and, if need be, can absorb a certain amount of risk.

The conservative portfolio previously listed is, for the most part, suited for the moderate investor, too, but some changes might be made with the goal of increasing the profit potential of its mix.

We will delete the 10% investment in the iShares Lehman 1–3 Year Treasury Bonds (SHY) and replace this income holding with the following:

- **5% iShares Russell Microcap Index Fund (IWC).** Microcaps have their risks, but over the long run have tended to outperform larger companies.

- **5% iShares FTSE/Xinhua China 25 (FXI).** This ETF reflects the 25 most liquid and largest companies in China, providing a foothold into a rapidly growing economy with a group of stocks actually less volatile than the S & P 500 Index. China has its problems, but appears to warrant at least one holding. (The iShares MSCI South Korea Index (EWY) is an alternative.)

The Aggressive Investor

Such investors are mainly oriented toward the achievement of capital gain, with ongoing income a secondary consideration. Aggressive investors are able and willing to accept higher levels of risk for the opportunity to maximize rates of return. Whereas the conservative investor will probably want to maintain larger positions (30% to 40% of assets) in low-risk income-producing investments, and moderate investors will want to have at least a 20% position in such investments, aggressive investors may be willing to forego the safety of short- to intermediate-term bonds completely.

Inasmuch as I believe that every portfolio should have at least some income component, I recommend that even the most aggressive investor retain at least a 10% income position. In this case, we will forego the 10% position in the iShares Lehman Bond Fund and replace it with the following:

- **5% PowerShares Zacks Micro Cap (PZI).** A relatively new microcap-based ETF. (Verify its performance prior to taking actual positions.)

- **5% iShares MSCI Canada Index (EWC).** A country rich in natural resources, Canada has been showing strong economic growth. This position should probably be considered speculative in view of recent advances in the Canadian stock market, but it may prove to be a strong long-term holding.

Summing Up

Just one final admonition, if I may: *Although it is tempting when one or the other area of the stock market is "hot" to want to concentrate your assets into just one or two such areas, it is much safer to maintain diverse, uncorrelated investment portfolios of the type that I have laid out for you.*

Take your time. Check the Web sites. Check the financial news reports. Verify performance and particularly consistency of performance. Most investors should maintain at least 20% to 30% of their assets in income-producing positions for risk reduction.

That said, do not be afraid to think out of the box—to new markets, to new opportunities, to smaller-growth companies. ETFs are certainly not the only avenue of opportunity. However, they have, at least so far, been creatively managed, represent a broad array of investment possibility, have been sufficiently liquid for most purposes, and allow for shifting investments to meet shifting market climates.

In short, ETFs do, indeed, qualify as "opportunity investments."

7

A THREE-PRONGED
APPROACH TO TIMING
THE MARKETS

We have already discussed a number of stock market timing tools in previous chapters of this book. For example, we have reviewed the tendency of the stock market as a whole to perform best when the NASDAQ Composite leads the New York Stock Exchange in relative strength and during periods of interest rate decline. Public psychology has been explored, as has the best 6 months of the year to own stocks and the best and worst years of the 4-year presidential market cycle (Chapter 1, "The Myth of Buy and Hold").

I know of no stock market timing tools that are perfect in their performance. I know of several that are useful in tilting the odds in your favor—which is about all that an investor can reasonably expect.

The art (hardly a science) of stock market forecasting relies on the following two major approaches:

- **Fundamental.** The fundamental approach bases its predictions on assessments of the economic prospects for industries and companies: the world and local economies, prospects of sales, the influence of interest rate trends on the economy, anticipated levels of actual corporate profits, actual values of corporate assets, and the like.

- **Technical.** This second approach, generally referred to as technical as opposed to fundamental market analysis, studies the behavior of the stock market itself, basing predictions of future market action on past patterns of stock market movement.

An underlying assumption of the fundamental approach to market analysis is that the price levels of the total stock market in its aggregate as well as the price levels of shares of individual companies will tend to find their own levels at which they are neither undervalued nor overvalued. If basic measures of value can be assigned to stocks or to the stock market as a whole, stocks are most likely to advance when they are undervalued in price, most likely to decline if they have become overvalued. This is not to say that the stock market will react immediately when price and value become disjointed; it is to say, however, that low risk can be separated from high-risk periods if investors are aware of relationships that exist between the assessed value of company shares and the stock prices at which they happen to actually be trading.

Common Measures of Valuation

Experienced and expert market analysts may delve into the balance sheets, cash flows, sales trends, market share, and labor contracts of individual companies and of general industry conditions to determine future growth rates upon which to forecast future stock prices.

Experienced and expert market analysts may also delve into macro-economic trends—levels of interest rates, balance of trade figures, rates of inflation and economic growth, unemployment figures, and so forth to determine the general state of the national and international economies (which exert large influences on the fortunes of individual corporations).

However, as knowledgeable and as educated stock and economic analysts appear to be, they rarely agree in the conclusions that they draw from looking at the same data, data that is subject to subjective as well as objective observation. In fact, this may be as good a time as any to reflect again on the "media indicator"—when a consensus of forecasts becomes overwhelming in one direction or the other, it is likely to prove incorrect.

> Some basic fundamental indicators relating to the stock market do appear to improve the odds.

The above caveats notwithstanding, some basic, readily accessible fundamental indicators have proven useful in predicting stock market trends (again, if not with perfection, with results definitely better than chance).

Company Earnings: The Core Fundamental

What, actually, does an investor (as opposed to a short-term trader) buy when he buys shares of a company? He may be seeking immediate income (dividends), perhaps with some capital growth should the company, hopefully, prosper. His emphasis might be on long-term capital growth as increasing corporate profits become reflected in higher share prices, less on immediate dividend income.

Either way, corporate profits—often referred to as earnings—are key to the ongoing prospects of any company. Steady earnings produce stable and steady dividend payouts. Rising earnings produce either rising value of corporate assets or ultimately increasing dividend payouts over the years. Companies referred to as "growth companies" often pay minimal dividends for many years, preferring to reinvest current profits, or what are hoped to be future profits, in corporate growth. Companies whose shares are described as "value stocks" are companies that already enjoy favorable profit margins, have high levels of "book value" (net assets above obligations such as debt, including company property and cash), and that are more likely to be paying dividends.

The key concept is that shareholders are buying present earnings or future earnings when they buy company shares. If earnings growth declines to below expectations, company shares are likely to decline; if earnings growth exceeds expectations, company shares are likely to rise in price. The concept applies to the general stock market as a whole as well as to individual companies.

The Long-Term Correlation Between Corporate Earnings and Changes in Stock Prices

Corporate profits are usually expressed as earnings per share of stock that has been issued by a company. So, if a company has 1 million shares outstanding, and has total profits of $10 million, the profit that might be attributed to each share of stock is $10 ($10 million profit divided by 1 million shares). The next step in calculating earnings per share is to divide the $10 in profit attributed to each share into the price of each share. Suppose that each share of stock in our model company is priced at $100. The shareholder has to pay $100 per share, and each such share is allocated $10 in earnings. The cost to each shareholder for every dollar of profit is $10 ($100 cost per share divided by $10 in profit). This relationship between share price and earnings per share is called the price/earnings ratio (in this case, 10). Each share is selling at 10 times earnings.

Investors are likely to be willing to pay more for shares of companies whose earnings are rising rapidly, less for companies whose earnings are flat or declining; more during periods of optimism, less during periods of pessimism; more when interest rates are low (meaning less competition from bond investment), less when interest rates are high (which adversely affects corporate profit because companies have to pay more interest for their credit needs and which also encourages investment in high-yielding bonds compared to relatively lower-yielding stocks).

Relationships between earning trends and the price movement of the stock market are not precise over the short term but are actually quite consistent over the long term. Long-term trends in earnings and in stock price movement are highly correlated. Figure 7-1 shows the relationships involved.

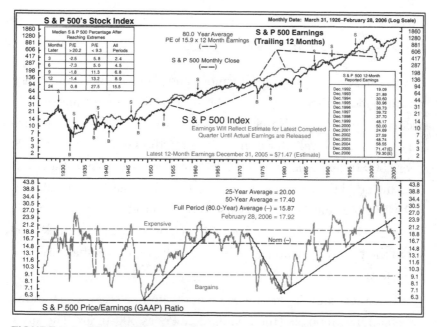

FIGURE 7-1 **The relationship of price movement of the stock market and earnings, 1927–2005**

The rates of earnings growth and growth in the Standard & Poor's 500 Index have been consistently equal over the long-term. However, there are times that earnings growth runs ahead of growth in the stock market (favorable buying opportunities) and periods when stock price movement runs ahead of earnings (riskier periods in which to invest).

Source: Ned Davis Research, Inc.

Let's review Figure 7-1 carefully. One line on the upper scale represents the aggregate earnings for shares of the stocks in the Standard & Poor's 500 Index. The other line represents the monthly close of the Standard & Poor's 500 Index. If you have trouble separating the one from the other, the lower scale of the chart, which reflects the ratio of earnings to price (earnings/S & P 500 Index) should be of help.

Opportunity Investing Strategy 1

Use price/earnings patterns to locate the best times to enter the stock market.

Price/Earnings Patterns

As you can see, sometimes prices move ahead of earnings. Sometimes earnings move ahead of prices. The best buying opportunities have occurred during periods that earnings growth (dotted line in Figure 7-1) have moved well above the price growth line of the Standard & Poor's 500 Index (solid line). Periods that were favorable by these criteria included the starts of major long-term bull markets that started in 1942, 1949, and 1974. The early 1980s, considered by many to be the beginning of the best two back-to-back decades for the stock market in the twentieth century, were marked by very favorable earnings/ price level relationships.

These relationships are reflected in the bottom scale, which shows price/earnings ratios for the Standard & Poor's 500 Index. The stock market has been favorably situated, historically, when price/earnings relationships have declined to 9.3 or below (that is, when investors have paid no more than $9.30 per share of the Standard & Poor's 500 Index for every $1 in corporate per-share profit). Such buying opportunities are shown on the upper scale, marked by B with rising arrows.

Remember, stocks advance most of the time. If you look at the chart, however, you can see how favorably stocks have performed during the months and years immediately following buy signals generated by low price/earnings ratios. Yes, sometimes stocks are, indeed, bargains.

Riskier Periods

Conversely, the stock market has tended to produce minimal profit, on balance, during periods that prices have advanced ahead of profits. Periods in which this has taken place include the late 1920s just before the great crash, the mid-1960s to the mid-1970s, and the mid-1990s into the early 2000s.

The great speculative bull market that developed between 1990 and early 2000, and especially between 1995 and early 2000, actually took place, for the most part, during periods in which price/earnings relationships were essentially negative because prices had been rising for years at higher rates than earnings. This period of heavy speculation in stocks finally culminated in the worst stock market decline in decades. Price levels of major market indices such as the Standard & Poor's 500 Index had not yet recovered by the spring of 2006 to levels seen early in 2000 in spite of rapidly rising earnings between 2002 and 2005, which did, however, result in more normalized relationships between market levels and company profits.

Stocks have, historically, been expensive and the stock market on treacherous ground when price/earnings ratios have risen to above 20.2, but that normally dangerous level was well penetrated during the late-1990s, price/earnings ratios reaching a high of 46 in early 2000 before stocks finally succumbed. By the end of 2005, price/earnings ratios had declined to just under 19, relatively high but not quite in the total-high-risk zone.

Some Relevant Statistics

- The average price/earnings ratio for the 25-year period ending in November 2005 was 19.9. Investors, on average, paid $19.90 for every single dollar of corporate profit.

- The 50-year average price/earnings ratio was 17.38. The average since 1925 was 15.87. Investors, by and large, have been willing to pay more for stocks as the years have passed.

- Investors who purchased stocks between the mid-1920s and the end of 2005 at times when the price/earnings ratio for the Standard & Poor's 500 Index rose to 20.2 or higher showed net losses for the following 12 months with gains of just 0.8% for 24-month holding periods.

- Investors who purchased stocks when price/earnings ratios fell to 9.3 or below enjoyed average price gains of 13.2% over the next 12 months and gains of 27.5% over the next 24 months.

By comparison, the Standard & Poor's 500 Index, during this period, showed average gains of 9.0% over all 12-month periods and 15.6% rates of return over all 24-month periods.

Although correlations have not been absolute, it does appear quite clear that investments in stocks made when prices have been low in relationship to earnings have done considerably better than investments made when price/earnings relationships have indicated that stocks were relatively expensive.

Investment Strategy Based on Price/Earnings Ratios

Emphasize buy strategies when price/earnings ratios fall to very low levels, in the past below 9.3. Become increasingly cautious when price/earnings ratios rise above 20, particularly if interest rates are rising and high.

This buy-caution procedure has proven generally useful in the identification of major-term buying junctures and major-term areas of increasing risk. However, corporate earnings do not exist in an economic vacuum. The bond market does provide an area for investment that at times is competitive with stocks and can exert its own influence on the general economic climate.

Using Bond Yields to Know When to Buy Stocks

The stock market generally performs best during periods of rising bond prices and declining interest rates and worst when interest rates advance and bond prices decline. In part, these relationships occur because rising interest rates tend to exert negative impacts on business. Mortgage rates rise, which adversely affects the real estate market and home construction. Higher interest rates involve higher margin costs for stock traders, lowering profits and trading activity. Businesses and consumers alike have to pay more for credit, reducing economic activity and investment.

There is another reason why rising rates exert a negative effect on stock prices, a simple and logical reason: Why buy stocks when bonds may be providing greater rates of return? It has not always been the case historically, but in recent decades, bonds usually pay more in interest than the cash dividend payouts of stocks, generally because bonds provide less opportunity for large capital gain and long-term growth than stocks. Stock investors invest for capital growth, for dividend income, or for a combination of these. Bond investors turn to bonds for predictable rates of income flow, safety, and a predictable time (date of maturity) at which their investments will close out at predictable values.

At certain times, bonds, providing above-average income in relationship to the growth rates of stocks, appear undervalued in comparison to stocks and attract investor capital from the stock market. At times, stocks appear to be undervalued relative to bonds, representing good value. Astute capital invests in the area that seems to provide the best opportunity at any given time.

Earnings Yield

The earnings yield represents the return to investors in corporations that is represented by the ratio of corporate profit to the aggregate market value of the shares of stock outstanding. A portion of this profit may, in part, be distributed as income. Most, if not all, of earnings may be reinvested in the corporations, increasing their book values, business capacity, and general ability to grow, a form of return to shareholders even if this return does not take the form of regular cash distribution.

To calculate earnings yield, first divide the profit per share into the cost of each share to secure the price/earnings ratio. For example, suppose that a company earns $2 for every share of stock, which stock is priced at $40 per share. Inasmuch as shareholders have to spend $40 for each share of stock to secure $2 worth of profit, the price/earnings ratio of that company's shares is 20 times earnings, or 20. The cost per share of every dollar of profit is $20.

We can calculate that if an investor receives one twentieth of his share cost back in earnings each year, it will take 20 years for him to recoup his initial investment, based on the earnings return alone. If we divide $2 (earnings) by $40 (price of shares), we secure the earnings yield, 0.05, or 5%. (Of course, many companies provide returns in the way of cash dividends in addition to the earnings yield.)

Naturally enough, the higher the earnings yield, the better, particularly for investors in companies that pay minimal cash dividends. Total return from share ownership includes both earnings yield and cash dividends.

Opportunity Investing Strategy 2

Buy stocks when they are cheap relative to bonds.

Given the above, it is not surprising that stocks tend to achieve their best gains when they are undervalued in comparison to bonds based on relative yields, and show the least gains when they are over-valued in comparison to bonds based on the relationships of stock earning yields to bond income yields.

Figure 7-2 illustrates this concept and suggests an objective measurement that can help you determine when stocks are undervalued, relatively inexpensive, and in good buying position. You can use the measurements to determine when risks are roughly average for stocks and when risk levels are high.

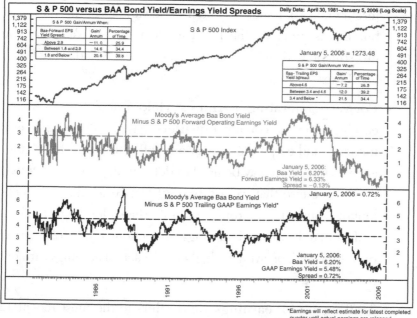

FIGURE 7-2   Moody's average Baa bond yield versus S & P 500 Index yields, 1981–2005

The greater the bond yield in comparison to earnings yield, the greater the risks and the lower the rates of gain of the stock market. Very bullish conditions for stocks have existed between 35% and 40% of the time since 1981. Neutral conditions have existed for approximately the same periods. Bearish conditions, based on this indicator, have existed approximately 26% of the time, during which periods the stock market has shown, on balance, net loss.

Figure 7-2 is quite revealing, but also involves a number of new concepts. You may have to take some time to follow along with the discussion, but there are likely to be worthwhile long-term benefits when you set this indicator to work for you, which should take just a few minutes each week.

Let's start with some definitions:

- **Moody's Baa bond rating,** roughly equivalent to a rating of BBB by Standard & Poor's, represents the lowest grade of bond that may be considered of investment quality. Yields from different grades of bonds may be used in variants of this indicator, but Baa is probably the bond grade most equivalent to the investment grade of the average stock in the Standard & Poor's 500 Index.

- **Forward operating earnings yield** refers to anticipated earnings over the coming 4 quarters, based on various analyst forecasts and corporate projections (often referred to as guidance). This figure may be used in determining stock valuations on the premise that we are trying to place a value on stocks looking ahead in time rather than looking behind. Unfortunately, forward earnings projections tend to be rather optimistic and, on average, higher than actual earnings turn out to be.

- **Trailing GAAP earnings yield** refers to the most recent 12 months of already reported earnings, stated in accordance with full accounting principles and procedures.

Inasmuch as forward earnings tend to be higher than trailing earnings, slightly different parameters will be used in our bond yield/earnings yield valuation model depending on which earnings set is used. With parameter adjustments applied, little variation seems to exist in inferences that may be drawn from the use of forward earnings versus trailing earnings.

Finding the Data You Need

You can find trailing price/earnings ratios and earnings yields, calculated weekly, in the *Barron's Financial Weekly*, in the "Market Laboratory" section.

You can find forward earnings projections by doing an Internet search for that topic. Different analysts make different projections, so no fixed number may be considered definitive.

You can find Moody's bond yields by rating for the Baa-rated category of bonds at www.federalreserve.gov/releases/H15/data.htm. If you scroll down the site, you will find the section with Moody's bond yields, including the yields of AAA bonds (which you may also want to secure).

The upper scale is a price chart of the Standard & Poor's 500 Index, dating back to 1981. This indicator, with its present parameters, was not operative prior to 1980. So, going forward, investors should remain alert to changes in the character of the data used—a factor in many stock market indicators whose parameters change over the years. For example, prior to 1980, stocks frequently provided yields greater than bonds, which was not the case starting in 1980.

The second scale shows the Moody's average Baa bond yield minus the S & P 500 forward operating earnings yield. On December 21, 2005, for example, the yield from Baa bonds stood at 6.33%; the forward earnings yield of the S & P 500 Index stood at 6.38%. Bond yields were actually slightly lower than the earnings yields available from stocks. Given the greater growth potential of stocks, earnings yields were, at the time, relatively high compared to bond yields (with stocks valued favorably on a comparative basis). The spread was –0.05 (6.33 Baa bond yield minus 6.38 forward stock earnings yield).

The chart is divided into three segments, based on research carried forth by the Ned Davis Research Corporation:

- It has, in the past, been very bullish when Moody's Baa bond yields have been no greater than 1.8% above forward earnings yields of the Standard & Poor's 500 Index. Bullish relationships existed 39.7% of the time between 1981 and 2005, during which periods stocks advanced at a rate of 20.6% per year, the rate of gain while invested. (If bond yields were 7.0% and stock yields were 5.2%, the differential would be +1.8%.)

- Conditions have been relatively favorable when Moody's Baa bond yields have lain between 1.8% and 2.9% greater than the forward earnings yields of the Standard & Poor's 500 Index. These conditions existed 34.4% of the time between 1981 and 2005, during which periods the Standard & Poor's 500 Index advanced at a rate of 14.6% per year, the rate of gain while invested.

Special Observation

If you study Figure 7-2 carefully, you can see that on many occasions stocks have advanced as rapidly when relative yields stood in the middle zone as when they stood in the most bullish area. However, failures of the stock market to advance rapidly during 1981 and 1982 and again in 2002 (for a short while) did downgrade the performance of this zone.

- Stocks have shown net losses on balance during periods that Moody's Baa bond yields have been more than 2.9% higher than forward earnings yields of the Standard & Poor's 500 Index. There have actually been long periods of time during which stocks have advanced when such conditions, bond yields high relative to stock yields, have been in effect (for example, many months during 1987, 1991, and during 1999). However, the market crash of 1987 occurred when this negative condition pertained (as did the major portion of the 2000–2002 bear market). Bond yields exceeded forward earnings yields from stocks by more than 2.9% during 25.9% of the time between 1981 and 2005, during which periods stocks declined on average at a rate of 11% per year.

The data reflected in Figure 7-2 clearly indicates that the best times to own stocks are during those periods when bond yields are equal to or just moderately above forward earnings projections for the Standard & Poor's 500 Index. Investors should use favorable periods to accumulate stock positions, with plans to reduce positions gradually as the stock market moves from lower-risk to higher-risk positions.

Trailing Earnings vs. Forward Earnings

The lower portion of Figure 7-2 makes use of the previously discussed concepts, but uses earnings yields based on already reported rather than forward projected earnings. The indicator seems more stable when actual reported earnings are used in the various calculations rather than anticipated (forward) earnings; however, changes in the performance of the indicator, although present, do not appear significant between these alternatives.

- The most bullish area for investing occurs when the Moody's Baa Bond Yield is greater than the S & P 500 reported earnings yield by no more than 3.4%. This condition took place 34.3% of the time between 1981 and 2005, during which periods the Standard & Poor's 500 Index advanced at a rate of 21.5% per annum. (This does not represent the total amount of annual gain recorded by stocks but rather the rate of gain while invested.)

- Stocks still showed above-average performance during periods when the Moody's Baa bond yield was between 3.4% and 4.6% greater than the reported earnings yield of the Standard & Poor's 500 Index. This condition existed 39.2% of the time between 1981 and 2005, during which periods the Standard & Poor's 500 Index advanced at the rate of 12% per year, somewhat above its average rate of growth during the period.

- Stocks showed a net loss during periods when the Moody's Baa bond yield was more than 4.6% higher than the reported earnings yield of the Standard & Poor's 500 Index. These conditions occurred 26.5% of the time between 1981 and 2005, during which periods the Standard & Poor's 500 Index declined, on average, at a rate of 7.2% per annum.

- There have been periods when stocks continued to advance in spite of bearish spreads between the yields of bonds and the earnings yields of stocks—for example, during the late 1990s—but risks have definitely tended to be higher when bond yields surpassed earnings yields by greater-than-average amounts.

Indicator Implications

As mentioned previously, rates of return from the stock market increase considerably, while risks diminish considerably, during periods when stocks are undervalued based on reported as well as forward earnings yields. These are favorable periods during which to purchase and hold equities.

This indicator can be maintained in just a few minutes each week. Can you afford *not* to make use of it?

I first encountered this indicator among the many technical and fundamental indicators described on the Web site of Ned Davis Research, Inc. (www.ndr.com), a highly regarded company used by many institutional and large private investors. The results shown in Figure 7-2 are reproduced here courtesy of NDR.

In reviewing the conclusions presented by Ned Davis Research, Inc., my own staff research has found the following:

- Test results essentially confirmed the results suggested in Figure 7-2. Any differences were moderate, insignificant in terms of the basic concepts involved, and very possibly attributable to differences in data sources.

- The parameters that have been presented were not applicable to periods prior to 1980. This raises some prospective issues going forward, too, so users of this indicator should, again, be alert to changes in the significance of parameters. My staff will be reviewing the periods between 1934 and 1980 to determine whether we can develop further insight into the issue.

- The use of the bond yield/earnings yield indicator appears to *provide very significant benefits in terms of risk reduction*. If you had been in stocks between 1981 and 2005 at all times except when the bond yield/reported earnings indicator lay in its most bearish position (above 4.6%), your maximum quarterly drawdown would have been limited to 11.7%, based on the Standard & Poor's Index, which declined by more than 44% during the 2000–2003 bear market.

We move along now to briefly review a variant of the bond yield/earnings yield indicator, a variant that reflects on the relationships between bond yields and stock earnings yields in a somewhat different manner.

Bond Yield: Earnings Yield Comparisons Using Aaa Bond Yields

Figure 7-3 compares the yield of Moody's Aaa (high investment grade) bonds to the earnings yields of the Standard & Poor's 500 Index (darker line). Prior to the early 1960s, stocks provided higher earnings yields than bond yields, but by the early 1970s bonds typically provided higher income yields. For the 45-year period between 1960 and 2005, Aaa bond yields were, on average, 1.3% higher than earnings yields of the Standard & Poor's 500 Index.

During three major periods between 1960 and 2005, stock earning yields were clearly higher than interest income yields from Aaa bonds. The first developed during the early 1960s, generally a positive period for stocks. Bond yields overtook stock yields in the very late 1960s, this reversal of strength reflected first in the bear market of 1969 through mid-1970 and again during 1972 and 1973, the onset of another bear market.

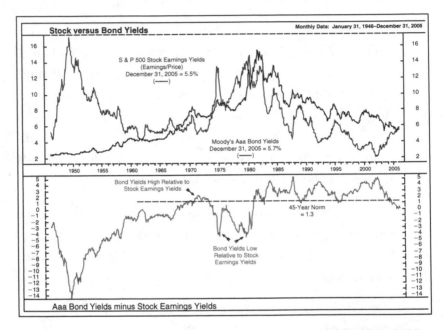

FIGURE 7-3   Aaa bond yields minus stock earnings yields, 1945–2005

Stocks provided clearly higher yields than bonds until the late 1960s, when bonds began to produce higher interest payouts than stock earning yields. Since 1980, it has been more usual for bonds to provide higher yields than stocks.

Stocks Bullish 1974–1980

The bear market of 1974—a very severe bear market—produced a significant and major buying opportunity for stocks as bond yields declined to areas well below those of stock earning yields. It was not surprising that stocks rose steadily (with one interruption, in 1977) between 1974 and mid-1980. Stocks were simply better valued than bonds during this period.

From that point forward, bond yields remained relatively high compared to stock yields. However, there were dips in 1982, 1988, and 1995 in the bond yield/stock yield comparisons. Each of these dips, which you can see in Figure 7-3, marked significant stock market buying opportunities.

A Significant Buying Opportunity?

Stock earnings yields did overtake AAA bond yields during 2005, indicating that stocks, at the time, were clearly undervalued compared to high-grade bonds. This relationship would appear to have represented a significant long-term buying opportunity.

Given the general parameters of this indicator for the most recent 25 years, it appeared at the time that stocks had become relatively inexpensive compared to bonds at the end of 2005 and that the stock market might be readying for a serious advance, possibly starting sometime in 2006. Readers may decide for themselves in the future whether this was a prescient conclusion.

Ten-Year Treasury Bond Yields vs. Earning Yields

Yields from the popular 10-year Treasury bond tend to lie close in level to earning yields of the Standard & Poor's 500 Index. Between 1974 and 2005, the yield from the treasuries averaged 1.1% above the earning yields of the Standard & Poor's 500 Index. Figure 7-4 shows the relationships.

Treasury bond/stock yield differentials have tended to reflect the same patterns that we have seen with Baa and Aaa corporate bonds. It has been bullish when bond yields were less than 1.1% above stock earning yields, bearish when the bond/stock differentials rose above 2.0%.

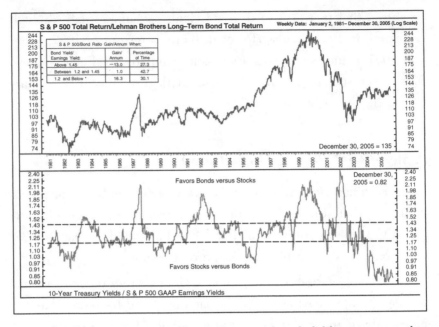

FIGURE 7-4   Comparisons, 10-year Treasury bond yields versus earning yields of the Standard & Poor's 500 Index, 1981–2005

Ten-year Treasury bonds generally provide somewhat higher yields than the earning yields of the Standard & Poor's 500 Index. The stock market has generally been favorably situated when trailing earning yields from stocks have risen above the interest yields available from 10-year Treasury bonds.

The favorable periods (1974–1981, 1982–1983, 1989–1990, 1995, late 1998, 2001 [failure of indicator], 2003, and 2004–2005) may be seen in Figure 7-4.

Between 1980 and 2005, at the least, stocks have proven to be excellent investments, on balance, during periods that earning yields of the Standard & Poor's 500 Index have been higher than average in relationship to interest yields derived from various bonds presented as examples. Stocks have had less-favorable price action during periods that stock earning yields have been well below average in comparison to bond interest yields.

A number of examples have been provided. In addition, Michael Santoli, writing in *Barron's* (August 5, 2002), reported that since 1980 the average 1-year gain in the Standard & Poor's 500 Index was 31.7% following periods that earning yields from the Standard & Poor's 500 Index were 5% or more greater than yields of 10-year Treasury bonds. On the other hand, the Standard & Poor's 500 Index had declined by 8.7% on average during years following periods during which yields from 10-year Treasury bonds were 15% or more higher than earning yields of the Standard & Poor's 500 Index (based on research conducted by Ned Davis Research, Inc.).

This indicator, in its various manifestations, has certainly made some excellent market calls.

That said, issues regarding the valuation of stocks are quite complex, and bond yield/earning yield comparisons represent just one method, among many, that is used by economists and other students of the stock market to derive at least theoretical stock valuations. Sometimes, however, simple works as well as complicated: the KISS principle (keep it simple, stupid).

This is not necessarily an indicator that should be used as a stand-alone decision maker. Although bond yield/earning yield comparisons have rendered some excellent market calls, there have been premature buy signals over the years, periods during which stocks advanced although the stock market was overvalued, some interim losses, and some missed opportunities. That said, bond yield/earnings yield comparisons have produced many excellent signals, have provided advance warning of numerous serious market declines, and would, on balance, have been of considerable help to investors.

And so, just once more: *Buy stocks when they are undervalued compared to bonds. Sell stocks as they become increasingly overvalued compared to bonds.* You can phase into fully or near fully invested positions as relationships move into positive territory. You can phase out of fully invested positions as relationships move into negative territory.

Surprise! Buy Stocks When Earnings News Is Bad, Sell When Earnings News Is Best

Viewers of financial news programs are generally presented with upbeat earnings forecasts (which, as we have seen, generally exceed what actually takes place). Often these forecasts suggest that stock prices will rise in the future in accordance with the rosy projections being offered to the public. Trends in corporate earnings are usually expressed in the form of year-to-year earnings comparisons, the extent by which earnings have risen or declined from the previous year, or the extent by which earnings are anticipated to rise next year compared to the present year (expressed as a percentage change).

Actually, *the reverse generally turns out to be the case.* The best earnings gains on a year-to-year basis tend to accompany lackluster periods for stocks. Poorer, although not the very poorest, earnings year-to-year comparisons tend to be better news for stocks. Bear markets rarely begin during periods in which poor earnings reports predominate, although they may continue until the initial signs reveal some firming, if not strong improvements, in corporate profits. Figure 7-5 tells the story.

Actually, as you can see in Figure 7-5, the reverse is true.

The stock market, in its price movements, tends to discount future events—changing its direction of movement between 6 and 9 months prior to significant changes in the direction of the economy, not concurrently with such changes. Savvy investors look ahead. Less-savvy investors invest in accordance with the latest media blitz.

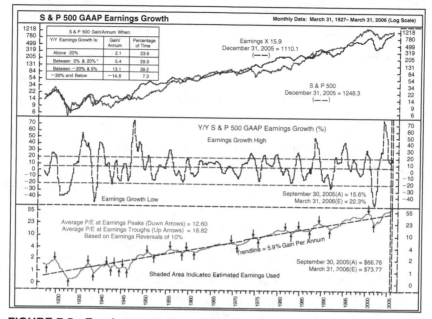

FIGURE 7-5   Earnings growth and stock price movement, 1928–2005

The stock market has had a tendency to perform best following periods when year-to-year earnings growth has been low, even somewhat negative. The very worst performance takes place on balance when year-to-year earnings growth is at its most negative levels, but the most positive performance for stocks takes place when earnings growth lies in a range between negative and slightly above neutral. Stocks do not perform particularly well when earnings growth lies at very high levels.

Source: Ned Davis Research, Inc.

Ned Davis Research reports the following relationships, 1928–2005.

Standard & Poor's 500 Gain per Annum When

Year-to-Year Earnings Growth Is	Annum	% of Time
Above 20%	2.1%	23.6
Between 5% and 20%	5.4	29.9
Between –20% and 5%	13.1	39.2
–20% and below	–14.8	7.3

There have been only a few periods during which earnings growth was as negative as –20%. Two of these took place during the great depression, during the 1930s. Stock prices, during this period, advanced sharply even before year-to-year changes in earnings turned positive, generally peaking while year-to-year earnings relationships appeared favorable.

Year-to-year earnings comparisons fell to below –20% for a brief time as 1991came to an end but quickly reversed, with stocks dipping briefly during the process and then turning up before year-to-year comparisons turned positive.

The final period during which year-to-year earnings comparisons declined to below –20% took place during the bear market of 2001–2002. This was accompanied by declines in the stock market, which this time did not really turn upward until year-to-year earnings comparisons improved to favorable.

Once again, do not become lulled into a sense of security just because the media is trumpeting news of very favorable year-to-year growth in corporate profits. The stock market is usually a safer buy just as declining trends in earnings are ameliorating, the best gains taking place in anticipation of further earnings growth rather than after such growth has taken place.

There are, of course, other indicators, beyond the scope of this book, designed to provide fair valuations of stocks. Readers interested in further exploration of this and related areas might want to search the Internet for "valuations of stocks." Many interesting Web sites provide articles, theoretical approaches to the subject, and a plethora of further information.

In the end, however, values are generally tied to profitability and to how long it takes investors to reclaim their investment capital. Price/earnings relationships probably provide the very most of what is required.

The key to successful investing is, again, to take positions when the odds favor success, when the general public is relatively pessimistic, and when stocks are priced at relatively favorable levels in terms of price/earnings relationships and in terms of stock payouts in relationships to other investments.

Let's move along now to Chapter 8, "Time Cycles, Market Breadth, and Bottom-Finding Strategies," which examines some useful tools to fine-tune your stock market entry and exit decisions.

8

TIME CYCLES, MARKET BREADTH, AND BOTTOM-FINDING STRATEGIES

We discussed in Chapter 7, "A Three-Pronged Approach to Timing the Markets," certain ways to determine whether stocks in general appear fundamentally undervalued, fairly valued, or overvalued and how your stock portfolios might be modified to remain in tune with stock market profit potentials indicated by whether stocks are cheap or expensive.

In this chapter, we explore certain market indicators that reflect the "true strength" of "market breadth," which is often more significant as a measure of the strength of the stock market than many of the more popularly followed stock market indices such as the Standard & Poor's 500 Index and the Dow Industrial Average.

Before we move along into these market-breadth indicators, we examine the tendency of stocks to rise and fall in certain rhythms that appear to be related to time, how you might identify the most significant rhythms, and how you can profitably take advantage of the patterns involved.

Market Cycles

For whatever the reason—possible explanations range from the influence of political events such as the 4-year cycle of presidential elections in the United States to possible influences resulting from interplanetary movements—the stock market does appear to rise and to fall with certain cyclical regularities, a phenomenon that occurs throughout nature in many varieties and forms. Cyclical phenomena include, of course, seasons, tides, phases of the moon, numerous changes in the human body, and more.

Again, for whatever the reason, stock prices appear to trace out patterns that demonstrate both short-term and longer-term regularity in their periodicity—not a regularity that can be counted on to the day, but definitely (at least in my opinion) a regularity that may be used to reinforce judgments made on the basis of various stock market indicators, such as the ones described in this chapter.

We will bypass shorter-term market cycles—the tendency of the stock market to find low points at 4- to 5-day intervals, 6- to 7-week intervals, and 20- to 22-week intervals, among other operative time cycles, and concentrate on the most significant of market cycles, the 4-year cycle, which has had a fine history of identifying major turning points in the price movements of the stock market.

Time cycles are measured from low point to low point in the stock market's perambulations, the time period that elapses between a key cyclical low point through the subsequent rise and then to the next subsequent significant cyclical low point. If general trends are bullish, stocks may spend more time rising during cyclical periods than declining. During neutral market periods, the periods of market advance tend to be about equal to the periods of market decline. During bearish periods, stocks spend more time in decline than advancing. In all cases, the lengths of cycles are measured from low point to low point.

Figure 8-1 shows the pattern of price movement associated with a typical stock market cycle. Figures 8-2 and 8-3 show the concepts involved with real-time histories of stock market price movements.

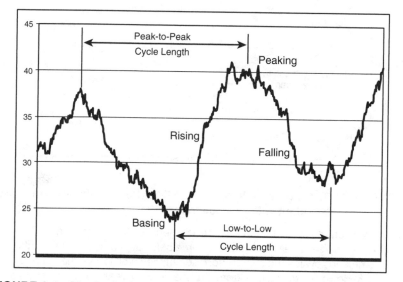

FIGURE 8-1 The typical stock market cycle

This chart shows the four phases of a typical stock market cycle, the nominal length of which is the period between the low points. During bullish market periods, stocks may spend more time advancing than declining, actually a fairly normal relationship. During neutral market periods, cycles tend to appear balanced, the rising and falling periods more or less equal. During bearish market periods, the falling area of the cycle may be lengthier than the rising period.

There are numerous sources of information regarding time cycles and their application to stock market investing. You may want to consult one of my other books, such as *Technical Analysis—Power Tools for the Active Investor* (Prentice-Hall, 2005), for further discussion. Resources on the Internet include www.investopedia.com, "Understanding Cycles, the Key to Market Timing" by Matt Blackman. There are numerous other sources of information which may be referenced by searching for "time cycles in the stock market." The subject is somewhat controversial—many analysts tend to discredit the general concept of time cycles—but is fascinating, and I do advise shorter-term traders and longer-term investors alike to pursue the subject.

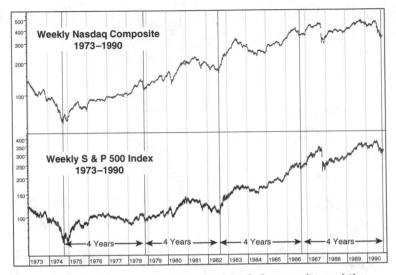

FIGURE 8-2   The 4-year cycle of the NASDAQ Composite and the Standard & Poor's 500 Index, 1973–1990

In this chart, cycle low areas are defined by the vertical lines. The 4-year cycle does not bottom precisely at 48-month intervals. Sometimes cycles run a little short, sometimes a bit longer than scheduled. However, deviations from the idealized 4-year period between major low points have not been greater than a few months, at most.

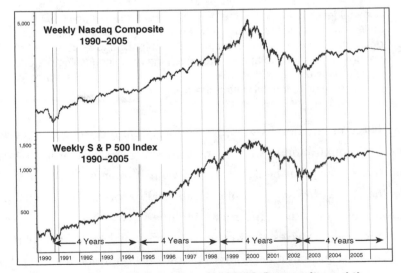

FIGURE 8-3   The 4-year cycle of the NASDAQ Composite and the Standard & Poor's 500 Index, 1990–2006

In this chart, the 4-year cycle marks bear market lows. As you can see, actual lows coincided with the cycle quite well. The next 4-year cyclical low was due to develop during the second half of 2006.

The Granddaddy of All Key Stock Market Cycles: The Four-Year (Presidential) Stock Market Cycle!

What, for stock market purposes, is the common attribute of the years 1962, 1966, 1970, 1974, 1978, 1982, 1986, 1990, 1994, 1998, and 2002?

Answer: These were all years, spaced at regular 4-year intervals, in which the stock market either completed a serious major decline prior to embarking on a new bull market or, at the least, completed clearly recognizable flat to declining intermediate- to long-term formations prior to resuming long-term uptrends.

In this case, pictures are worth a thousand words. Figures 8-2 and 8-3 illustrate the significant market turning points that took place between 1974 and 2005 at regular and consistent 4-year intervals. Not shown are the bear market low points that took place in 1962, 1966, and 1970—very much in conformity with the 4-year low-to-low market cycle illustrated in these charts. The next cyclical low is scheduled for 2006. Future readers will be able to judge the accuracy of this projection.

Review these charts again. What could it and would it have been worth to you as an investor to ignore the general bearishness that usually accompanies stock market low points and to have been accumulating stocks at the lows of 1970, 1974, 1982, and more recently, 2002? Not to mention the major low points in between.

All you have to do is to keep track of the time since the most recent 4-year cyclical low.

Check out confirming indicators—stock valuations, stock-bond comparisons, and breadth indicators that I discuss in this book. It is likely that these will all be in a favorable position shortly before, or at the time, that the 4-year stock market cycle is scheduled to reach a significant low point.

These are the best times to buy stocks!

As you can see on these charts of stock market history, if you had made stock purchases in the areas of the 4-year lows, you would have been able to enjoy at least 1 year of sharply rising stock prices, with a strong likelihood of a second fine year to follow. From that point on, as the cycle rolls over, the third and fourth years of the 4-year cycle tend to show less-predictable performance, requiring increased care on the part of investors. If you had entered the markets properly, however, you would have already secured more than your fair share of stock market return.

Confirming the Four-Year Cycle with Your Price/Earnings Ratio Indicator

This might be a good time to return to Figure 7-1, which shows the price/earnings ratio.

What can we see? We can see that at almost all of the 4-year interval cyclical bottom areas cited above, our various price/earnings, and "bond yield–stock yield" indicators stood in favorable or very favorable position and in no case no worse than in solidly neutral positions!

Price/earnings ratios were average at the lows of 1962; better than average in 1966 and 1970; and at positively bargain levels in 1974, 1978, and 1982. Ratios were average at the cyclical low of 1986, below average (favorable) in 1990, and 1994. Price/earnings ratios were above average (unfavorable) at the lows of 1998, and not particularly favorable at the lows of 2002. However, the "bond yield–stock earnings yield indicator," which is probably at least as significant as the price/earnings ratio indicator, was in very favorable position at the lows of 1990, 1994, 1998, and 2002 (as well as in 1982).

Have cyclical price-movement, fundamental indicator relationships been perfectly aligned? No. Would cycles have been of help in more closely identifying the best times to enter the stock market? I think so. Do you agree?

The Link Between the Four-Year Market Cycle and the Presidential Election Cycle

Whether by accident or by some form of political design (as many suspect), there have been close correlations between the 4-year stock market cycle and the presidential election cycle.

Basically, the stock market tends to initiate bull markets as the second half of the presidential term (for example, 1966, 1970, 1974, 1978, 1982) gets under way, rises strongly during its first year, continues to advance (albeit at a slower pace) during its second year (election year), shows much more moderate gains the third year of the 4-year cycle (first year of presidential terms), and tends to decline during the final year of the 4-year cycle, the second year of presidential terms.

Political cynics (realists?) tend to believe that stocks are reflecting various and sundry administrative tactics to make the economy look good in the months prior to reelection time, and that bad news that might adversely affect stock prices is saved for the second years of presidencies, at which times election stakes are relatively low.

This may, indeed, be the case, but may also not be the case. I have found that many foreign markets (for example, New Zealand) appear to fluctuate closely in conjunction with the 4-year market cycle of the U.S. stock market. Correlations have been close, indeed. Could it be that markets even as far away as New Zealand operate to the beat of the Wall Street drummer? Or could it be that there are cyclical forces at play here across the globe that we simply do not understand? I leave that to your conjecture, which is probably in this regard as good as my own.

Winning with Investments Based on the Presidential Election Cycle

Numerous articles and studies have been published detailing possible strategies for taking advantage of the presidential election cycle. *The Stock Trader's Almanac,* published annually, edited by Yale and Jeffrey Hirsch (Wiley & Co.), has been a pioneer for decades in studies of political and other investment cycles and tracks the presidential election cycle on a close basis with annual updates.

An interesting suggestion appears on the Web at http://pepperdine.edu/043/stocks.html: "Presidential Elections and Stock Market Cycles," by Marshall D. Nickles, Ed. D, on the site of the Grazadio Business Report, Vol. 7, No. 3, 2004.

Based on certain observations of historical price movements, the author suggests a strategy of buying the Standard & Poor's 500 Index on October 1 of the second year of presidential terms and holding positions through December 31 of election year (Strategy for Investor 1). The holding period for stocks would be 27 months. Stocks are sold at the close of election year, Investor 1 remaining in cash until the next entry, 21 months later.

A second investor buys stocks at the time Investor 1 closes out his positions (inaugural day) and holds positions through September 30 of the second year of the presidential term (Strategy 2). In short, the second investor buys when the first investor sells and sells when the first investor buys.

The theoretical results of the comparison—dividends and interest excluded—are shown in the following table.

Strategy 1 was profitable during every period, turning a $1,000 original investment into $72,701. No allowance is being made for taxes, expenses, interest while in cash, or dividends.

Strategy 2 was profitable in 7 of the 13 periods but ended with a loss of 36%, the original $1,000 investment declining to $643. No allowance is being made for taxes, expenses, interest while in cash, or dividends.

**Presidential Election Investing, 1952–2004
Starting Capital, $1,000***

Year of Election	Strategy 1	Strategy 2	Strategy 1 Cumulative Results	Strategy 2 Cumulative Results
1952	35%	22%	$1,350	$1,220
1956	45%	+8%	1,956	1,318
1960	16%	–2%	2,271	1,291
1964	52%	–9%	3,451	1,175
1968	39%	–19%	4,798	952
1972	40%	–47%	6,717	505
1976	70%	–4%	11,418	483
1980	32%	–12%	15,072	425
1984	37%	40%	20,649	595
1988	19%	11%	24,571	660
1992	38%	7%	33,909	707
1996	60%	42%	54,254	1,004
2000	34%	–36%	72,701	643

* Results are hypothetical.

Results are hypothetical and cannot be assumed to be representative of future results of this strategy.

I trust that the above study illustrates the power of the 4-year market cycle, coupled with the presidential cycle, which may influence or be the cause of the 4-year cycle or which may be the coincidental result of the 4-year cycle. We do not necessarily have to know what drives this significant cycle to benefit from recognizing its scheduled turning points and operating from the opportunities it presents.

Remember that risks in recent decades have been low during the first 2 years of the 4-year cycle, high during the last 21 months and particularly the final 12 months, give or take, of the 4-year cycle. As a general rule, you want to bias your thinking toward stock accumulation early in the 4-year cycle and also very late in the cycle as the stock market moves toward its final cyclical lows.

Market Breadth

Well, we have seen earnings, we have seen interest rates, we have seen market cycles—the time has come for everyone to hold their breadth . . . .

Yes, I did say "breadth," not "breath."

And what do we mean by the term *breadth* in relation to the stock market?

Market Breadth and Major Market Indices

Most investors are at least generally familiar with the popular market indices used to define the composition and strength of the stock market. The Standard & Poor's 500 Index, for example, is one such index. The NASDAQ Composite Index and the New York Stock Exchange Index are others. All of these are "capitalization weighted averages" of the stocks represented by these indices—500 for the Standard and Poor's Index, approximately 3,600 for both the NASDAQ Composite Index and the New York Stock Exchange Index.

Capitalization Weighted

One might think that daily readings of a popular indicator such as the Standard & Poor's 500 Index might be secured by simply adding up the closing share prices of the 500 domestic and foreign issues that comprise this index to secure the level of that index each day.

This, however, is not the case. The ongoing calculations of the levels of the Standard & Poor's 500 Index are actually quite complicated and refer to data from base periods for the Standard & Poor's 500 that date back to as long ago as 1941 to 1943.

A fuller discussion of the calculation processes involved is beyond the scope of this book. Should you be interested in more information, however, you can check out www.cftech.com/BrainBank/FINANCE/

SandPIndexCalc.html. At this Web site, you can find (as of January 2006) a lengthy and informative discussion of the maintenance of the Standard & Poor's 500 Index and requirements for company listings.

The main point that I want to make and that you should understand is that all stocks are *not* equal in the ongoing calculations of levels of the Standard & Poor's 500 Index. The index is "weighted by capitalization" so that the prices of the larger companies are given more weight in the calculation of the index than are the prices of small companies included in that index. The weighting is proportional to the total market capitalization of companies listed, which is the price of each share multiplied by the number of shares outstanding of each listed company.

This means that if only a relatively small number of the largest companies advance on a given day, the Standard & Poor's Index might be up for that day, even though most companies listed on that exchange show a decline. Conversely, if only a relatively small number of the largest companies decline on a given day, the Standard & Poor's 500 Index might decline, even though most companies represented in that index advance on a given day.

There may be many justifications for the weighting of the Standard & Poor's 500 Index in this manner. After all, the weighting does serve to emphasize the direction of price movement of the largest blocks of capital in the stock market, the capital that flows into and out of the largest, most liquid corporations. The Standard & Poor's 500 Index is the index primarily used by large pension funds and other institutions as their benchmark of performance. Such institutions are almost forced to invest in large, liquid, and well-established corporations that exert the greatest influence on the performance of the Standard & Poor's 500 Index.

That said, the weighting inherent in the Standard & Poor's 500 Index, and in the more broadly based New York Stock Exchange Index (which includes all 3,500+ stocks on the New York Stock Exchange) and in the NASDAQ Composite Index (which consists of more than 3,500 issues but whose index level has been largely determined by as few as 20 to 40 stocks at times) often results in erroneous perceptions by the public regarding what is actually taking place in the stock market.

For example, most investors date the start of the 2000–2002 bear market to the late winter of 2000, when both the NASDAQ Composite and the Standard & Poor's 500 indices reached their all-time highs before the major decline that followed.

However, many, many stocks had already begun major declines within their own bear markets, declines that had started during 1999 and even as early as 1998! The stock market as a whole did not advance into March 2000 when the nominal bull market peak occurred. Just about as many stocks had already fallen to new 52-week lows in price at the time that the most popular market indices were reaching their all-time highs as were rising to new peaks. The major market indices, which seemed so strong moving into this period, were actually being carried by small numbers of very visible, larger-capitalization, technology-oriented companies while the typical stock languished.

This was not an unusual occurrence. A similar pattern took place during 1972, when most stocks topped out during the early spring, while the Standard & Poor's 500 Index, carried by its largest components, advanced to new highs in January 1973. Note that whereas the Standard & Poor's 500 Index gained approximately 14% during 1972, the typical mutual fund advanced by only between 2% to 3% that year.

On the other hand, whereas the Standard & Poor's 500 Index did not establish its final lows until March and April 2003, the larger proportion of stocks actually started to rise in price during the final months of 2002, when the bear market ended for most issues.

The major point to consider here is that whereas the major market indices' price movement do often reflect the behavior of the typical stock, there are times when the major market indices do not reflect the behavior of the typical stock or the experience of most investors. Investors should be considering other market indicators as well as the Dow Industrials, the Standard & Poor's 500 Index, and the NASDAQ Composite Index when assessing the major trends of "the stock market." (Incidentally, the New York Stock Exchange Index, which, again, includes all 3,500+ issues on the New York Stock Exchange, but weighted by capitalization, is the index that seems the most to reflect gains and losses of the typical, broadly based mutual fund.)

Confirming Price Action of Major and Less-Major Market Indices with "Breadth" Indicators

Breadth indicators are indicators that reflect the percentages of stocks actually participating in market advances or actually incurring losses during market declines.

Among the measures of market breadth are the "advance-decline" relationships in the stock market on any given day. Advancing issues are stocks that rise each day in price. Declining issues are stocks that fall in price. Unchanged issues are stocks that do not change in price.

These ratios are often more significant than widely followed major market indices such as the Standard & Poor's 500 Index. For example, suppose that the Standard & Poor's 500 Index advances by one half of 1% on a given day. If 1,800 issues advance on the New York Stock Exchange that day, perhaps 1,350 declining, the plurality, advancing minus declining issues, would be +450 (1,800 − 1,350), indicating that most stocks did advance in conformity with the Standard & Poor's 500 Index, a good breadth confirmation of the rise in that index. It might be said that day that there was "broad" stock participation in the advance—a favorable sign for the stock market.

Conversely, suppose that, although the Standard & Poor's 500 Index gained one half of 1% on a given day, only 1,400 issues advanced in price, whereas 1,750 declined. This would constitute a day of "negative breadth," more stocks declining than advancing—the rise in the Standard & Poor's 500 Index is *not* confirmed by the action of the majority of listed stocks. This nonconfirmation would carry negative implications.

The same concepts would pertain on days that the Standard & Poor's 500 Index declines in price. If market breadth is negative on such days, it might be said that the action of the broad market confirms the negative action of the Standard & Poor's Index. If market breadth is positive even though the Standard & Poor's 500 Index declines in price, it might be said that there is a positive nonconfirmation or divergence between advancing market breadth and the declining, capitalization-weighted Standard & Poor's 500 Index. The typical stock has advanced in price even though the widely followed Standard & Poor's Index indicates a declining market, a nonconfirmation of decline in the Standard & Poor's, a reasonably favorable omen for stocks.

The most favorable market climates take place during periods when the price actions of the major market indices are generally favorable *and* when market breadth readings are favorable—more stocks advancing than declining. These "breadth-price" confirmations indicate that most market segments are participating in market advances. The odds improve that selections of stocks/mutual funds by investors will produce profit. During periods of negative breadth, more issues declining than advancing, the probabilities of selecting winning stocks decline, even if the Standard & Poor's 500 and other indices seem to be advancing.

The Advance-Decline Line

The advance-decline line is a cumulative total of daily advances minus declines that may be maintained on any and all popular exchanges such as the New York Stock Exchange and the NASDAQ Composite Index, including issues that trade within each market.

To maintain your own advance-decline line, start with any arbitrary number, say 10,000. If, on the first day, there are 1,500 issues advancing on the New York Stock Exchange and 1,200 declining, the day would show an advance-decline plurality of +300. You add that 300 to your starting level, 10,000, creating a new advance-decline line level of +10,300. If the next day shows 500 more issues advancing than declining, the advance-decline line rises to +10,800 (10,300 + 500). If there are 200 more declining issues than advancing issues on the day after (advances minus declines = –200), the next reading of the advance-decline line is +10,600 (10,800 – 200).

A Quick and Dirty Approach to Understanding Advance-Decline Data

As a general rule, it is bullish when

- New peaks in the major market indices are confirmed by concurrent or near-concurrent new peaks in the cumulative advance-decline line.

- The percentage of issues advancing in price over a 10-day period is more than 60% of the total number of issues either advancing or declining. The ratio, (advances/(advances + declines) is greater than 60%, if 10-day totals of both advances and declines are used. Such favorable market-breadth ratios do not occur all that frequently and usually carry bullish implications when they do occur.

- Market breadth remains positive or at least more or less neutral even if market indices do show some decline.

As a general rule, it is bearish when

- New peaks in the major market indices are not confirmed by new peaks in the advance-decline line for several months. Bull markets generally become gradually more selective as time passes, including fewer stocks. Breadth softening does not generally result in broadly based bear markets immediately but if breadth weakens for several months, bearish implications increase.

- There are patterns of continuing weakness in market breadth even as the price levels of major market indices maintain their advance.

Almost all newspapers with reasonably good coverage of the financial markets report daily advance-decline differentials for the major stock exchanges at the end of each day. *Barron's Financial Weekly* also provides weekly data. During the day, MSN and other Web sites report stock market data, including breadth information, on a streaming basis.

The New High–New Low Breadth Indicator—Including the Major Bull Market Confirming 28% Buy Signal!

Another group of breadth indicators are, in their own way, as effective as advance-decline breadth indicators and can produce significant market signals. These are breadth indicators designed around "new high–new low" readings related to major areas in which stocks trade.

Stocks that "make new highs" are stocks that have risen to their highest price of the past 52 weeks. Their price is at the highest level seen at any time over the past 52 weeks. Stocks that "fall to new lows" are stocks that have fallen to their lowest price of the most recent 52 weeks. Their price level is at the lowest level seen at any time over the past 52 weeks.

Bullish and Bearish Indications

The numbers of stocks that fall each day or week into these categories represent a breadth measurement in the way that advance-decline figures represent a breadth measurement. If weighted stock market indices are reaching new peaks, it is naturally a positive sign if broad sectors of the stock market participate in the advance, reflected in greater percentages of issues making new highs and in the presence of more issues making new highs than falling to new lows. The greater the positive disparity, new highs minus new lows, the better the stock market breadth, and the more bullish the implications.

Severe stock market declines are generally characterized by negative new high–new low breadth readings—more issues fall to new lows than rise to new highs. Often, there are contractions in the numbers of stocks falling to new lows even as market indices are declining to new low areas. This pattern is an early indication of an incipient upside reversal, telling us that even if stock market indices seem to be weakening, more and more stocks are finding support and are no longer declining. The number of issues falling to new lows declined during 2002, for example, even as major market indices continued to decline, suggesting a near end to the bear market.

New high–new lows data is not generally maintained as a cumulative line in the way that the advance-decline line is maintained. However, 10-day ratios of new highs minus new lows, or new highs divided by new lows, or new highs divided by the total of new highs plus new lows, can be usefully maintained.

A Quick Market-Breadth Bullish Indicator

The 10-day ratio of the number of issues making new highs divided by the sum of the number of issues making new highs and the number making new lows (NH/(NH + NL) often provides excellent bullish indications when the following takes place.

The 10-day average of daily ratios of issues making new highs to the total number of issues making either new highs or new lows climbs to above 90%.

If there are 150 new highs and 30 new lows on the New York Stock Exchange, the daily ratio—NH/(NH +NL)—would be 83.3% (150 new highs + 30 new lows = 180 NH + NL, so 150/180 = .833 or 83.3%).

For example, the 10-day average of daily ratios of new highs to the sum of new highs + new lows climbs from 88% to 91%, above the 90% level. (Average the daily ratios of the most recent 10 days, not the 10-day totals of new highs and new lows.)

When this happens, it is usually safe to remain invested until the 10-day average of daily ratios, NH/(NH + NL), declines to below 80% or, if you want to give the markets the benefit of the doubt, to below 70%.

The stock market does not necessarily decline following a decline in the 10-day ratio from above to below 70%, but can no longer be considered to be showing favorable new high–new low breadth readings.

Bottom-Finding Parameters

Serious intermediate (several month) stock market declines often result in 10-day averages of daily ratios of new highs to the sum of new highs + new lows declining to below 25%, sometimes even to below 15%.

As a general rule, stocks tend to be pretty sold out when readings in the 10-day ratio, NH/(NH + NL) decline to below 10% to 15%. Prepare to enter the stock market when you see readings at such low levels (referred to as very oversold), assuming new stock positions gradually as the 10-day ratio improves by 5% to 10% (for example, by rising from, say, 12% to between 17% and 22%).

Sometimes, entries will prove to be somewhat premature; for the most part, however, the stock markets tend to recover when extremely oversold levels have been reached and when daily ratios start to indicate improving new high–new low relationships. It is best to try to confirm this indicator with other market indicators, such as those related to cycles and price/earnings ratios previously discussed.

Significant Buying Pattern

The stock market prefers unanimity in market breadth readings.

Stock trends tend to be very positive when large percentages of issues are advancing compared to declining or when the numbers of stocks rising to new highs clearly surpass the numbers falling to new lows.

Surprisingly, or maybe not so surprisingly, periods during which breadth imbalances appear extremely negative—negative but still more or less unanimous, periods of general public and media panic— often turn out, in the end, to represent excellent "bottom-fishing" buying opportunities, particularly, again, if they conform well to the 4-year cycle. *Look for oversold conditions, accompanied by sharply rising trading volume, sudden market reversal from decline to advance, and sudden highly positive advance-decline pluralities. This form of highly emotional, high-volume, and sharp market reversal is referred to as a "selling climax."* Many bear markets and severe intermediate declines end with this form of stock market reversal.

Cautionary Conditions Indicated by New High–New Low Data

I mentioned a few paragraphs ago that the stock market prefers unanimity in breadth readings. If it is rising, it wants to see all ships rising with the tide. If it is falling, it may want to see climactic declines to indicate that the waterfall is approaching its bottom.

What the stock market does not like to see are climates in which large numbers of stocks are rising and large numbers of stocks are declining. Such periods indicate "split" stock markets, reasonably large numbers of issues carrying market indices upward while also reasonably large numbers of stocks are declining to new lows under cover of advancing market indices, propelled upward by just a portion rather than by large percentages of stocks.

Cautionary signals take place when, on a weekly basis (data in Barron's) the lesser of weekly new highs or weekly new lows is greater than 7% of the total number of issues traded on the New York Stock Exchange.

For example, suppose that in a given week, 3,500 issues trade on the New York Stock Exchange and that 280 issues advance in price that week and 180 decline.

Those 280 new highs represents 8% of 3,500 issues, so that criteria is met. However, 180 new lows represent only 5.1% of 3,500 issues, higher than we might like, but not yet sufficient to flash formal warning signals.

On another week, 280 of 3,500 issues traded (8%) reach new highs, but the number of issues falling to new lows is 265, or 7.6% of 3,500 issues traded. A market warning signal has been flashed! The lesser of new highs and new lows (265 new lows) is higher than 7% of issues traded.

The action of the stock market following such signals has been mixed. Sometimes advances resume; sometimes stocks drift for weeks and months following split market warning signals. Sometimes serious stock market declines follow shortly upon the generation of this form of warning signal.

Split market warning signals should probably not be taken as sell signals in and of themselves, but they are good indications of potential danger and serve well as yellow lights on the stock market roadway.

The 28% Major-Term New Highs Buy Signal

These do not occur often, but they have been 91.7% accurate in the past!

This will be the last of the stock market timing tools that I present in this chapter. The calculation of this timing trigger takes just a few moments each week, with signals occurring very, very infrequently. However, the implications of buy signals are so favorable that I, for one, consider this device well worth the tracking.

Here is all that has to be done. At the end of each week, check out the number of issues on the New York Stock Exchange that advanced to new highs in price during that week. Divide this number into the number of issues traded on the New York Stock Exchange. If the number of new highs is 0.28 (28%) of the total number of issues traded, this indicates very strong positive market breadth and creates a major-term buy signal that remains in effect for the next 52 weeks!

Here is a sample of the calculations involved.

Percents New Highs

Week Ending	S & P 500 Index	Issues Traded	New Highs	# of Issues Traded
5/16/2003	944.30	3535	599	16.9%
5/23/2003	933.22	3538	661	18.7%
5/30/2003	963.59	3543	797	22.5%
6/06/2003	**987.763**	**546**	**1097**	**30.9% *Buy!***

During the week ending June 6, 2003, 3,546 issues traded on the New York Stock Exchange, of which 1,097 (30.9%) of 3,546 made new highs, producing a major-term buy signal. (Weekly data required may be found in Barron's, among other sources.)

Here are the hypothetical performance results of this model, going back to 1943.

**Performance Results, 28% New Highs Timing Model, 1943–2004
Based on Standard & Poor's 500 Index**

28% Buy Date	Buy Level	52 Weeks Later	52 Weeks Later Price	Price Change	$10,000 Becomes
1/30/1943	10.47	1/29/1944	11.81	12.80%	$11,279.85
4/24/1948	15.76	4/23/1949	14.74	−6.47	10,549.81
7/30/1954	30.88	7/29/1955	43.52	40.93	14,868.12
7/25/1958	46.97	7/24/1959	59.65	27.00	18,881.91
5/5/1967	94.44	5/3/1968	98.66	4.47	19,725.64
6/7/1968	101.25	6/6/1969	102.12	0.84	19,891.21

**Performance Results, 28% New Highs Timing Model, 1943–2004
Based on Standard & Poor's 500 Index** *(continued)*

28% Buy Date	Buy Level	52 Weeks Later	52 Weeks Later Price	Price Change	$10,000 Becomes
1/22/1971	94.88	1/21/1972	103.65	9.24	21,729.80
3/14/1975	84.76	3/12/1976	100.86	18.99	25,857,33
10/8/1982	131.05	10/7/1983	170.80	30.33	33,700.36
5/24/1985	188.29	5/23/1986	241.35	28.18	43,197.10
7/11/1997	916.68	7/10/1998	1164.33	27.02	54,867.22
6/6/2003	987.76	6/4/2004	1122.51	13.64	62,352.30

The results are as follows:

- Eleven of 12 signals (91.7%) were accurate and proved profitable.

- The average gain per signal was +17.25%.

- The worst drawdown (intra-year) was a bit over 14% (1948–1949).

- The most recent six signals, since 1971, showed an average gain of 21.3%.

This seems to be one stock market indicator whose performance has been improving over the years rather than deteriorating. (Prior to 1971, the 30% level produced more accurate entry signals than the 28% level. Percentages of issues that make either new highs or new lows seem to have diminished in recent decades.)

The 28% new highs breadth indicator does not generate signals frequently but has, in the past at least, been extremely reliable. The model does have one interesting characteristic. Buy signals do not take place at the very starts of bull markets or of significant intermediate advances. They tend to occur 3 to 6 months into the move, thereby providing signals to investors who have not participated as yet, that there are still favorable opportunities in the stock market and that it is probably not too late to either take initial invested positions or to add to positions taken earlier. Figure 8-4 shows four "28% new high-breadth indicator" buy signals that took place between 1982 and mid 2006. All proved quite timely.

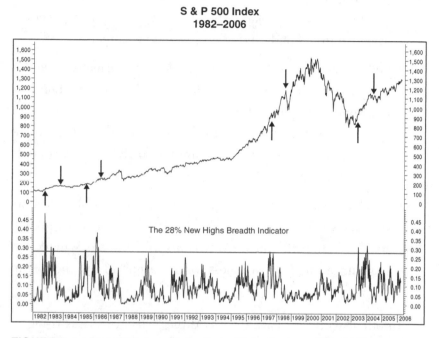

S & P 500 Index
1982–2006

FIGURE 8-4   The 28% new highs breadth indicator, 1982–2006

This chart shows buy signals generated by the 28% new highs breadth indicator, downward-pointing arrows indicating dates 52 weeks following buy signals, the nominal end to the entry signaled by the ability of weekly new highs to rise to as high as 28% of issues traded. As you can see, signals are not generated frequently, but have proven to be quite profitable since the early 1970s.

Such signals can be helpful inasmuch as considerable profits are lost by investors who are fearful of buying after they have missed the very starts of bull markets. Such investors often hold out and hold out as stocks rise in price, until they can bear it no longer, finally tending to enter too late. The 28% new highs indicator can help the cause a lot in that regard.

Summing Up

We have examined, in the last two chapters, the following:

- Some ways to determine whether stocks are relatively cheap or relatively expensive, based on historical parameters of levels of earnings and of the relationship of stock earnings to the income available from bonds and other income investments.

- Some ways to use stock market cycles to anticipate/recognize likely significant turning points for stocks based on certain regular long-term political and calendar cycles. Familiarity with cyclical patterns allows you to predict when market turns are likely to take place, and to prepare for portfolio readjustments based on changing patterns of stock valuation.

- You have been introduced to certain market-breadth indicators that allow you to confirm, from the action of the stock market itself, whether the most likely course for the stock market is ongoing strength or weakness, or a transition from the one to the other.

In other words, we have discussed the "why's of stocks rising or falling," the "when's of when major stock market reversals are most likely to take place" and the "what" of what stock market indicators confirm that the internal strength or weakness of the stock market is reflecting other market indicators.

I believe that value, time, and breadth measurements represent a fine trio in your investment arsenal. It is up to you now to make use of them!

9

CASHING IN ON THE REAL ESTATE BOOM— INVESTING IN REITs

Would an investment that has been profitable in 27 of the past 33 years be of interest? Would it be of more interest if it produced fine profit during those three awful bear market years for the stock market of 2000, 2001, and 2002 (as well as coming close to a breakeven during 1973, 1974, another highly unprofitable period for most stocks)?

And would it add to your interest if you knew that this investment had produced an annualized rate of return of 13.4% since 1971, including all the bad years as well as the good?

We examine the ebbs and flows of capital growth in the world of REITs (real estate investment trusts) a bit later on. REITs are a great counterbalance to the general behavior of stocks in general and well deserve to be a key element in your diversified portfolio.

REITs—Some Definitions

According to the U.S. Securities and Exchange Commission (SEC), "real estate investment trusts (REITs) are entities that invest in different kinds of real estate or real estate related assets, including shopping centers, office buildings, hotels and mortgages secured by real estate."

- **Equity REITs,** the most popular, invest in or own real estate of various types, producing profit from the rental income they collect from tenants.

- **Mortgage REITs** lend money to owners of real estate or to real estate developers. They also invest in financial instruments secured by mortgages on real estate.

- **Hybrid REITs** are a combination of equity and mortgage REITs.

We can see from just what REITs invest in that they represent an interesting diversification from the typical stock that represents companies that secure profits from financial services, manufacturing, raw materials, or other services. REITs make their money from real estate and from real estate operations. Real estate, over the long run, has been a consistent, if not always dramatic, investment winner. Americans have a strong cultural affinity to home and business ownership—and a related soft spot for real estate operations. (Home ownership increased during 2005 to 68.5% of American families, a new record.)

We return to the issue of REITs and diversification a little further on, but first a few words about the other major benefit of REITs.

REITs Provide Steady and High Rates of Ongoing Income

REITs, according to the Internal Revenue Code, are exempt from federal taxation of their profits as long as they pay out 90% of their taxable income to investors. Inasmuch as REITs do pay out at least 90% of their income, investors in REITs have secured large dividend payouts compared to the typical stock, often in the area of 8% to 9% per year, sometimes even more for REITs sold as part of closed-end REIT mutual funds which use leverage.

These large dividend payouts are a major attraction of REITs, which tend to be fairly stable in price compared to other stocks. Large dividends tend to stabilize the price of shares, and provide a source of profit to shareholders apart from advances in the price of shares alone. When you invest in real estate trusts you are, to a large extent, investing for ongoing, above-average income. Total returns to investors from real estate income trusts have come largely from dividend payouts, less from increases in the values of shares.

Caveat

There have been initiatives in Washington, D.C., to reduce or eliminate the taxes on dividends on the basis that corporations already pay taxes on profit and that taxes on shareholders based on dividend payout are, in effect, double taxation on the same profit—a tax on the corporation and then again on its shareholders when dividends are taxed.

Shareholders of REITs are not likely to benefit from legislation to this effect inasmuch as real estate trusts are not taxed on their profits because 90% of such profits are distributed to shareholders as dividends.

This caveat aside, REITs have in the past provided investors with relatively price-stable stockholdings that have provided well-above-average income streams. One might argue as to whether portfolios should have a 5%, 10%, or even 20% representation in REITs. This might depend on the general market climate at any given time or the significance of current income to individual investors. Less debatable is the past history of REITs as valuable elements in well-diversified investment portfolios.

Types of REITs

Real estate investment takes many forms. Some REITs invest in residential apartment houses, some in hotels, some in shopping centers, and some in commercial rental properties. Each has its appeal; each has its risks. Diversification is probably the best idea.

Investments may be made into individual REITs, traded like other stocks on the various exchanges. Open- and closed-end REIT mutual funds provide ready diversification. Closed-end funds are more volatile because of their use of leverage.

The majority of REIT mutual funds are actively managed. The Vanguard REIT Index Fund (VGSIX), however, is a passively managed REIT index fund, designed to replicate results of a broad REIT index, and has essentially succeeded in its objectives, showing an annualized rate of return of approximately 14.6% between its inception, May 1996, and November 2005.

Among fund families that sponsor more actively managed real estate mutual funds are the Kensington Investment Group, the Alpine Funds, and Cohen & Steers. You can search for REIT mutual funds at www.MSN.com. Look for "real estate mutual funds."

Closed-End REIT Mutual Funds

Closed-end REIT mutual funds generally provide higher dividend payouts than open-end mutual funds because of the leverage they use, but they also tend to be more volatile and carry more risk.

Venturesome investors, going into 2006, might have been interested in the Cohen & Steers Quality Income Realty Fund (RQI), a closed-end mutual fund that invests in real estate trusts. Late in 2005, the fund was paying approximately 8.5% in yield, and selling at a 13.75% discount from its net asset value, just about the largest discount in its history. Also of potential interest might have been the Neuberger Berman Real Estate Securities Income Fund (NRO). The fund was selling as 2005 was drawing to a close at a large 16.9% discount from its net asset value to provide a current yield of 8.4%.

Large discounts in income closed-end funds do not necessarily reflect favorably upon a fund's prospects. Sometimes they indicate that a reduction in dividend payout is looming or some other bad news. Still, discounts of 14% to 17% for high-income producers do have their appeal, particularly if yields are very high.

You can find rosters of closed-end real estate mutual funds at www.etfconnect.com, which provides a good deal of information on the many funds listed.

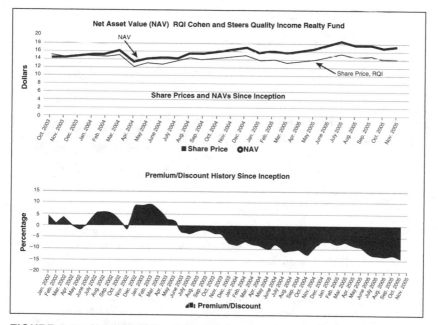

FIGURE 9-1   Cohen & Steers Quality Income Realty Fund (RQI)
Price of shares, net asset value, premium/discount
2003 (inception)–2005

Although net asset values of this fund's holdings advanced since its inception, the fund's price went from a premium (when the fund was first issued) to a discount of approximately 14% at a time that the fund was yielding approximately 8.5%. At these levels of discount and yield, the fund would have appeared to have considerable interest for income investors, although the leverage used by the fund did add a definite element of risk.

As you can see, the fund, when released as a new issue, sold at a premium. This is not unusual. Most closed-end funds are better off avoided as new issues because between 4% and 5% of new issue proceeds go to the underwriters, leaving shareholders with only 95 cents of every dollar for investment purposes, the fund, in effect, starting with a premium of 5%, give or take, over its net asset value after the underwriters are paid.

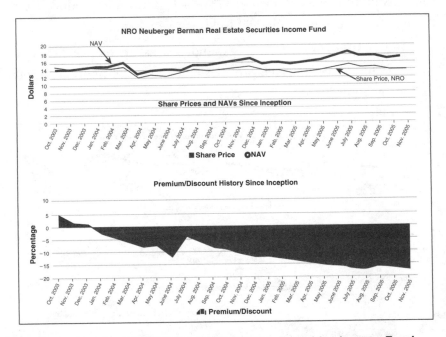

FIGURE 9-2   Neuberger Berman Real Estate Securities Income Fund (NRO). Price of shares, net asset value, premium/discount 2003 (inception)–2005

The Neuberger Berman Real Estate Securities Income Fund shows a similar pattern. As you can see, the fund's price at new issue was approximately 5% above its net asset value, but rapidly declined to a discount as underwriter support was withdrawn from the new issue. It rarely pays to buy any mutual fund as a new issue offering because initial pricing usually represents a premium over net asset value.

This fund, too, developed a good discount, more than 15%, as time passed, possibly as a result of investor expectations of rising interest rates and beliefs that the REIT sector had overshot its immediate potential and was likely to correct in its pricing.

> **Disclosure Note**
>
> The author, family, or clients of the author may hold positions in some of the mutual funds referenced or suggested in this book. There have been no payments of any sort made by the mutual fund families cited or by anyone else as compensation for the mention of any specific or general investment.

REIT ETFs

It should probably go without saying that the real estate arena has not been neglected by the exchange-traded funds (ETF) establishment.

ETFs that have been involved with real estate include the following:

- StreetTRACKS Wilshire REIT Fund (RWR)
- Vanguard REIT Index VIPERS (VNQ)
- IShares Dow Jones U.S. Real Estate (IYR)
- IShares Cohen & Steers Realty Majors (ICF)

REIT mutual funds, open and closed, and REIT ETFs sometimes reflect one or the other broad REIT indices and sometimes reflect more specific areas in which REITs invest—hotels, apartment houses, shopping centers, and the like. Unless you have a particular predilection for the one segment or the other, it is probably a good idea to diversify holdings within the REIT universe.

The Vanguard VIPERS involve low expense ratios—just over one tenth of 1% per annum. Unleveraged REIT ETFs produced an income flow of between 4% and 5% during most of 2005, roughly equivalent to yields available from 10-year U.S. Treasury notes. Total returns for the VIPERS, including increases in share price, were higher than that for REITS in general that year, in response to rising real estate prices in general.

Caveat

In many cases, yields from ETFs such as the Vanguard VIPERS include payments that partially represent a return of capital rather than returns to investors that accrue from operational profit. "Return of capital" means that the fund is paying to investors cash inflows to the fund that may accrue from the sale of assets, which in effect reduces the values of the underlying holdings of the ETF.

This is something to watch out for as well in closed-end mutual funds, which sometimes distribute "dividends" that are really payments to shareholders that derive from liquidated assets of their funds rather than from operating profits.

The moral: *If a dividend seems too good to be true, it is probably not a true dividend.*

If you are dealing via a full-service brokerage house, ask your account executive to check the true yield with his research department who should, properly, have made the analysis. If all else fails, call the fund offices to inquire (although with some funds, it can be difficult to find informed personnel who will speak with individual investors). One more alternative: Search the Web, listing the symbol or name of the ETF, mutual fund, or stock in which you are investing, followed by "yield" (for example, "Vanguard REIT VIPERS, dividend yield").

Dividend information is sometimes presented as a percentage return. If the percentage is laid out on a quarterly basis, multiply by four for the annual rate of return.

If the dividend is expressed as a dollar amount, multiply that by four and then divide by the current stock price to secure the annual rate of dividend return. (For example, stock is priced at $50 and pays 0.75 per quarter. Multiply .75 by 4. Result, $3. Divide $3 by 50 = .06 or 6% per year rate of return.)

Long-Term Performance of REITs

The popularity of REITs has had its peaks and troughs over the decades—as have the popularities of many other investments.

REITS, as an industry sector, have had some fairly broad swings in the price value of their shares. For example, on the downside, the NAREIT (National Association of Real Estate Trusts) Index of prices of all listed REIT shares fell from a little more than 100 to under 40 in the early 1970s, from near 120 to under 60 between 1987 and 1990, and from near 120 to below 80 during the late 1990s.

In a contrary vein, the price level of the NAREIT Index rose from below 40 to near 120 between 1974 and 1987, from below 60 to near 120 between 1990 and the late 1990s, and from below 80 to nearly 140 between 1999 and 2004.

Figure 9-3 shows the price movement of the NAREIT Index.

The Price Movement of the REIT Index Alone Does Not Tell the Full Story

REITs, unlike many technology-oriented stocks, are not purchased for price appreciation alone. Investments made in REITS are made for total return—a combination of price increase and dividend income. Dividends are significant to REITs. They add stability to the total return of these instruments and are a major component in the total returns achieved by long-term investors.

Figure 9-4 shows interest rates plotted against the total return of the NAREIT Index, 1972 through 2004.

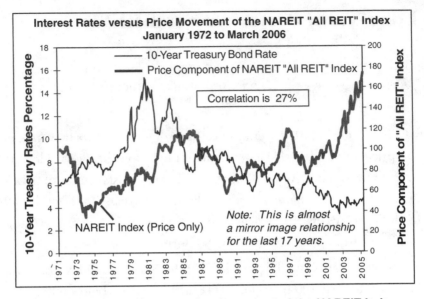

FIGURE 9-3   Interest rates vs. price movement of the NAREIT Index, January 1972 through September 2004

The prices of REIT shares have actually shown some fairly wide swings over the years. Declines in REIT prices coincided with general stock market weakness during the 1973–1974 period, but REITs remained firm during the bear markets of 1977 and 1981–1982. REITs underperformed the broad stock market during the second portion of the 1980s and again during the late 1990s, but actually advanced sharply during the bear market, 2000–2002.

There is a general, but not exact, correlation between the price movement of REITs and the general direction of interest rates—REITs generally performing best during periods that interest rates are declining. This correlation is by no means exact, however.

Source: www.Investopedia.com

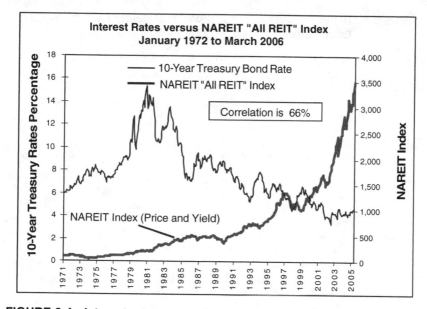

FIGURE 9-4 Interest rates vs. total returns achieved by the NAREIT Index, January 1972 through September 2004

The equity curve of "total return" has been much smoother than the equity curve of the price movement of the NAREIT Index alone—the combination of price and yield provides a much more positive picture of the results of investment in REITs than the pattern of price movement alone.

Stronger correlations exist between the performance of REITs and the direction of interest rates when the performance of REITs is measured by total return rather than just price movement. On a total return basis, REITs appear to clearly perform best during periods that interest rates decline, although correlations are not precise.

Source: www.investopedia.com

The National Association of Real Estate Investment Trusts (www.NAREIT.com) provides the following performance data, which encompasses the period ending June 30, 2004. Results between June 2004 and the end 2005 were rather consistent with the historical data shown.

TABLE 9-1   Historical Compound Annual Total Returns of the NAREIT Equity Index vs. Leading U.S. Benchmarks*

Year	NAREIT Equity	S & P 500	Russell 2000	NASDAQ Composite	Dow Jones Industrials
1-year	27.1	19.1	33.4	26.2	16.4
5-year	14.5	−2.2	6.6	−5.3	−1.0
10-year	12.1	11.8	10.9	11.2	11.2
15-year	11.6	11.3	10.4	10.9	10.2
20-year	12.3	13.5	11.1	11.3	11.7
25-year	13.6	13.6	12.6	11.4	10.6

° Results shown for the NASDAQ Composite and the Dow Industrials do not reflect dividends paid out to investors by companies within these indices. This has the effect of understating returns achieved by the NASDAQ and Dow indices, particularly the Dow.

The NAREIT Index did outperform the Standard and Poor's 500 Index during five of the six periods shown. For the 25-year period, the NAREIT Index showed a compound rate of return of 13.61% versus 13.56% for the S & P 500 Index.

REITs Have Provided Smoother and More Consistent Returns Than Most Other Stock Market Sectors!

The numbers in Table 9-1 speak for themselves.

REITs have provided the most persistent performance over the 5-year, 10-year, 15-year, 20-year, and 25-year periods. This result is probably consistent with the experience of most investors in their homes and with real estate in general. Rates of return achieved by most homeowners over periods of many years tend to be generally exaggerated because of the way that steady compounding works over periods of many years. (For example, a home purchased in 1966 for $52,000, valued in 2005 at $1.4 million, has achieved a compound rate of return of a little less than 10%, not all that much different from the total return from the stock market.)

However, the value of that home has rarely declined by as much as 10% in any given year, if that much.

Equity REITs tend to outperform mortgage and hybrid REITs.

The similarity in performance among the various market sectors is striking. Over the long run, there is relatively little difference in performance among various market areas—although smaller-capitalization companies do tend to show some advantage. REITs tend to be small to mid-sized companies, so some of their superior relative strength may have as much to do with their size as with their industry.

Dividend Payout by Type of REITs

Yields from all REITs in 2004 averaged roughly 5.5%, somewhat higher than 10-year Treasury bonds, clearly higher than the dividend yield provided by the Standard & Poor's 500 Index, which ran at less than 2%. However, REIT dividends are subject to full taxation, and not the lower scale for dividends that applies to most corporate payouts.

Diversified, residential, health-care, and office REITs tend to provide the highest income streams. Industrial, hotel, and retail REITs pay somewhat less, implying that investment in these areas has a larger capital growth objective.

The fact that REITs provide higher income flows than 10-year Treasury issues argues in their favor as the income instrument of choice. However, there are obviously greater risks (as well as potential rewards) associated with REITs. REITs should probably represent a reasonably significant portion of almost any diversified portfolio, not just because of their high yields. The price movements of REITs are relatively noncorrelated with the price movements of other stock market sectors; REITs frequently advance when other areas of the stock market are falling (for example, 2000–2002) and sometimes decline when other areas of the stock market are rising (for example, 1997–1999).

Timing Your Entries and Exits

Although REITs tend to be among the more stable of investments, particularly when measures are made of total return rather than just price movement, they are subject to the same excesses in temporary investment demand, to scandals similar to other forms of investment, to periods of pessimism, and to investor neglect.

Long-term investors may retain REITs, along with other sectors, of diversified long-term portfolios on pretty much of a buy and hold basis, trusting that the principles of diversification will produce the steady growth that is hoped for from such portfolios.

Nonetheless, the relationship between the direction of REIT prices and the direction of interest rates suggests that among the best times to purchase REITs are those times that interest rates are peaking and just beginning to decline from high levels. Interest rates, particularly long-term bond rates, are subject to market conditions that cannot necessarily be controlled by the Federal Reserve Board. That said, the Federal Reserve frequently indicates the direction in which it wants interest rates to move and steps that it is taking and plans to take to ensure that short-term rates, at the least, follow the course it desires. Federal Reserve Board announcements are widely publicized in the financial press and in financial news channels on television.

Links Between REITs and Interest Rates

As previously mentioned, REIT prices tend to advance during periods when interest rates decline, and REIT prices tend to decline during periods when interest rates advance. This is understandable when we consider two factors. First, REITs are purchased by investors largely for their yield. If interest rates are high, REITs have to compete with short-term Treasury notes, short-term corporate bonds, and even money-market funds at times when these instruments are providing their maximum returns. REIT yields are worth less in a climate of high and rising yields available to investors. Conversely, the unavailability of high income return from competing investments during low interest rate climates (for example, 2002–2004) adds a value premium to the high levels of dividend distributed by REITs to shareholders.

Second, low interest rates also translate into lower expenses for many REIT operators, who then pay lower mortgage costs, lower borrowing costs to develop shopping centers, and lower costs for building hotels. Rising interest rates add expenses to REIT operation, which may or may not be readily recoverable through price increases.

REIT prices were extremely strong during the 2000–2002 bear market and thereafter into 2005 when price action softened, but did not collapse. Many factors supported the REIT industry at this time. For one, a general real estate boom took hold, in part a response to capital leaving the stock market. This boom was also supported by a steady progression of steps taken by the Fed during 2001 and 2002 to reduce interest rates to support both the economy and the stock market. Low mortgage rates, a worldwide inflation in real estate, and the simple rise in home prices taking place—all encouraged speculation in REITs.

Your mission? Track interest rates during periods that interest rates advance. Look for signs that the Fed is preparing to or has already begun to step in to support the bond and stock markets by lowering rates. The Fed generally signals its intentions, which are closely followed in the financial press and news media. Periods during which the Federal Reserve Board shifts from tighter money policies to easing of credit are likely to be excellent periods in which to accumulate high dividend paying REITs.

For Long-Term Investment, Track the Major Channel of the REIT Sector

Figure 9-5 shows the long-term price movement of the NAREIT Price Index and three excellent major buying junctures that took place between 1972 and 1999.

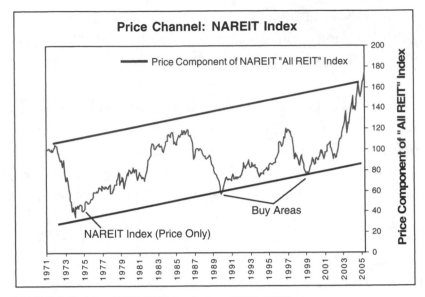

FIGURE 9-5   The NAREIT Price Index, 1972–2004

You have seen this chart before, but this time I have removed the interest rate line and have drawn in a major channel within which price levels of the NAREIT Index have fluctuated over the years. Significant
buying junctures have taken place as the index has approached the
lower boundary of this major channel. Risks have been high as the
upper boundary of the channel has been approached.

Use the major trading channel for long-term market timing (see
Figure 9-5). Studies of price movements of industry groups and the
stock (and other) markets in general often reveal certain channels
within which prices advance and decline, along with certain cyclical
rhythms that mark major and less major price fluctuation.

If you believe that these channels have some credence (as I do),
it follows that if you want to "buy low and sell high" you should find
charts that reveal such channels to be of help. Some stock charts are
regular in their movement, some not. Charts of income-oriented
investments tend to be more regular in their movements from channel lows to channel highs and back. Charts of bond prices often show
these characteristics. So do charts of REITs.

You do *not* need to try to pinpoint exact buying junctures or to
secure the absolute lows of any price downswing. It should be quite

sufficient for your purposes just to begin your process of accumulating REIT investments as the lower boundaries of the major channel are being approached, especially if interest rate news seems to be confirming this action. If you are able to create your REIT portfolio in the area of the lower channel boundary, so much the better. You may find yourself well positioned for years to come.

Conversely, if all goes well, you may want to close down some positions at least as the upper boundary of the major channel is approached, although you may choose to retain some holdings for income and to maintain portfolio diversification.

Unfavorable Implications

The real estate market in the United States is remaining fairly firm as I write late in 2005, but with REIT prices approaching the upper boundary of their long-term trading channel, and with interest rates no longer in decline, the immediate prospects (at the time of this writing) for the sector appear more guarded than they have been for some years.

Declines that set in at this time may provide investors better opportunities to accumulate longer-term REIT positions, at higher yields than have been recently available.

Selecting the Best Apartments in the REIT Apartment Building

Technical Tactics

1. If you are trading in REIT mutual funds, look for funds with the lowest expense ratios, best long-term performance record, the lowest entry/exit loads, and the most consistent management.

2. Rank the universe of funds that are available to you following the screen above by their performance over the past 6 months to 1 year. Make your purchases from those funds that are leading in relative strength.

3. You may have available to you long-term charts, which can help you locate where in the major cycle your potential selections lie. The odds, however, are that most of the industry's components will be moving more or less in tandem.

Fundamental Strategies

Harry Domash, writing for MSN.Money ("How to Screen for Top REITs," December 3, 2005; www.MSN.com), suggests the following criteria for the selection of REITs for investor portfolios.

Minimum Dividend Yield

Inasmuch as REIT dividend payouts are not favorably treated from a tax standpoint, the minimum acceptable annual dividend return for nonsheltered accounts should be 3.7%. This level may be lowered if holdings are being maintained in a tax-sheltered account.

A strong case may be made, I believe, for setting a higher level of dividend payout, starting at a minimum at the level of yields provided by 10-year Treasury bonds, which stood at approximately 4.5% in December 2005. With the average yield for nonleveraged REITs in the area of 5.5%, give or take, there would have to be some pretty favorable indications to accept anything less. Leveraged closed-end REIT mutual funds were producing yields of 8.25% or more, but such vehicles obviously carried higher levels of risk.

Dividends Should Show a History of Consistent Growth

Individual REITs should have shown a history of rising dividend payout. Rising dividends produce greater income for you and also support the potentials for your stock or mutual funds rising in price. Look for funds or individual companies that show a 5-year history of dividend growth greater than at least 4% per year.

Avoid REIT Companies Rated as "Sells" by Wall Street Analysts

Inasmuch as Wall Street analysts tend to be overly optimistic, "sell" recommendations are rarely made regarding stocks, so that when a "sell" warning does exist, some really bad news may lie ahead. Investors are advised to avoid REITs rated as sells. In Mr. Domash's experience, those rated a "hold" tend to do as well as those rated "buy."

This is obviously something of a subjective criteria since ratings are likely to vary from analyst to analyst and from brokerage firm to brokerage firm. To be on the safe side, it is probably best to try to secure multiple opinions prior to taking positions, and to adapt the conservative position that even one sell rating is taken as sufficient to look elsewhere.

Earnings per Share Growth Estimated to Be at Least 5% for the Coming 5 Years

In this case, investors will have to rely on various sources of industry analysis. Brokerage houses often provide analyst projections (available at sites such as MSN, too). Forward growth of even greater than 5% per annum would be more desirable, of course, but REITs tend not to show high rates of growth.

This is pretty much the rate of earnings growth that would be required to produce annual increases in dividends of 4%, inasmuch as at least 90% of earnings have to be channeled to investors as dividends. In this case, we are assuming that past earnings and dividend growth can be and is being forecast by experts familiar with the industry to continue into the future—which may or may not be a valid assumption.

Taken all in all, the above would appear to be sensible criteria to use as confirmation of REIT selections made on the basis of past performance and management continuity.

Further Information

REITs that provide dividend reinvestment and stock purchase plans are known as DRIPs.

Investors who do not need to draw upon dividend income for living expenses may find it usefully convenient to invest in REITs that offer DRIPs, dividend reinvestment plans by which your dividends are not paid in cash but rather in additional shares of company stock. This saves investors transaction costs, bid-asked spreads, and the inconvenience of re-investing possibly small amounts of capital distributed as dividends.

You can find a fairly large roster of REITs of various natures that provide such plans at www.investinreits.com, in the "Ways to Invest" area.

The same Web site carries a fairly large roster of REIT open-end mutual fund families and specific REIT mutual funds.

You can use this roster as a starting place, checking the Web sites of each fund family that sponsors REITs for further information as to past performance, current structure, investment philosophy, expenses, and the like.

Summing Up

- The universe of REITs represents a form of investment that provides higher-than-average current yield, and relative stability in terms of consistent levels of total return.

- Inasmuch as the price movement of REITs tends to be fairly independent of the general price movements of most other segments of the stock market, REITs represent a viable segment of diversified stock portfolios.

- Research has indicated that the addition of REITs to stock portfolios tends to reduce risk while showing no impediment to the achievement of profit.

- REITs may be purchased in the form of shares of individual real estate investment trusts, REIT mutual funds (open/closed-end), and ETFs. Closed-end REIT mutual funds provide the highest yields as a result of the use of leverage but are also the most volatile and risky.

- Although REITs may be maintained on any ongoing basis in diversified stock portfolios, new positions are best taken when 1) charts suggest that price declines have reached the lower boundaries of longer term trading channels and/or 2) there are indications that interest rates, recently rising, appear poised for a secular period of decline. Check news regarding plans of the Federal Reserve Board for indications as to the Fed's plans for raising or lowering rates. Check out the bond markets, particularly the price action of the 10-year Treasury bond, to see whether you can detect significant reversals in interest rate trends from higher rates toward lower rates.

- In selecting individual REITs in which to invest, concentrate on trusts that have been showing rising dividends that anticipate future earnings and dividend growth, and that show consistency in management life and performance. Holdings should be diversified.

Let's move along now to an investment area of opportunity that appears to be showing outstanding current performance as well as outstanding potential: the world of overseas investment.

10

OPPORTUNITIES ABROAD—INVESTING FROM BRAZIL TO BRITAIN

Definite changes (as a matter of fact, *very* definite changes) have been taking place among and between the economies of the world. Although the United States remains, to this day, the most desired depository for international capital, the dollar still the standard international currency, it can no longer be said that the United States clearly leads the world in economic power, prospects, profit, and growth potential.

Although the U.S. economy did seem healthy enough as 2005 drew to a close—corporate profits high, unemployment low, prices stable—its manufacturing sector was reeling from the outsourcing of both manufacturing and technological activity. The rate of growth of the economies of China and nations such as South Korea and India appeared to be clearly surpassing the rate of growth of the U.S. economy—particularly insofar as manufacturing for export was concerned.

Corporate profit did remain high among U.S. corporations, a good deal of this profit deriving from operations abroad. In this case, what was good for Nike (whose sneakers were manufactured abroad) was not necessarily good for General Motors (teetering on the edge of bankruptcy) or even for Intel (which was threatening to move its manufacturing operations overseas to join various textile and other manufacturing facilities which had already abandoned U.S. shores).

Issues connected with outsourcing aside, there have always been significant areas outside of the United States that have provided opportunity for sophisticated investment. The U.S. markets represent approximately 28% of the number of different stocks worldwide. Approximately 58% of companies with market capitalizations (value of all shares of those companies) of greater than $100 million are located outside of the United States compared to the 42% that are located within the United States.

The United States is certainly well represented among the globe's investment opportunities, but it does not have a total monopoly in this area—not by any means.

Emerging Markets

The United States retains a high degree of political stability, a high level of military capability, the most sophisticated and liquid of financial markets, and an excellent transportation network. These are significant qualifications, all to the good.

Less to the good, in terms of international competitiveness, are high labor costs, sluggishness in management responses to international competition (Why and how did America manage to lose its camera, film, electronics, television, clothing, textile, and now potentially, its automobile manufacturing industries to nations overseas?), and an educational system that has been badly lagging both India and

China, for example, in its output of professions such as engineering and whose students have begun to fall behind the students of other nations in achievement. (In one recent year, the United States graduated 16,000 students of engineering. In the same year, India graduated 80,000, and China graduated 200,000.)

Does the U.S. stock market remain competitive with the stock markets of other nations? By and large, yes. Does the U.S. stock market retain the more or less absolute competitive edge that existed for decades, particularly between the conclusion of World War II and the end of the twentieth century? By and large, no.

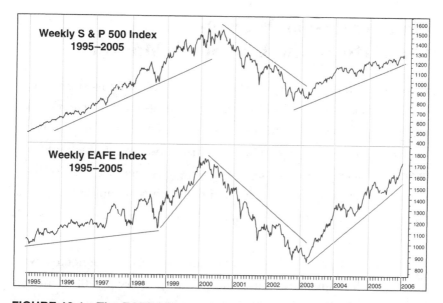

FIGURE 10-1   The EAFE Index and the Standard & Poor's 500 Index, 1995–2005

These charts show the Europe, Australia, and Far East (EAFE) market, representing generally well-established overseas stock markets, and on the lower scale, the Standard & Poor's 500 Index, representative of the U.S. stock market. Between 1995 and 2005, although there were periods when this was not the case, longer-term trends favored the U.S. stock market in comparison to markets overseas. Since the start of 2003, however, markets overseas have been leading the United States in performance, particularly certain emerging markets that are not represented in the EAFE Index.

The U.S. stock market remains competitive with old world markets such as those in many (not all) areas of Europe. It has not remained consistently competitive in recent years with the stock markets of nations such as China, Brazil, Mexico, India, South Korea, Canada, Australia, and South Africa, all of whose stock markets have begun to either outperform our own or, at the least, to represent at any given time serious alternatives to the U.S. stock market.

Figure 10-1 provides some indication of changes in relative strength that have taken place in recent years.

Many Overseas Markets Outperform the U.S. Stock Market

It would probably be an overstatement to say that investors should maintain all or even most of their investment assets in overseas stocks, mutual funds, or exchange-traded funds (ETFs). It would probably not be an overstatement to suggest that most investors should use overseas stocks on an ongoing basis as at least one segment of their diversified investment portfolios and that investors should be alert at all times to special investment opportunities as they develop in stock and bond markets overseas.

Table 10-1 shows investment results for ETFs connected with developed foreign markets for the period January 1, 2005 through November 25, 2005. Table 10-2 shows investment results connected with emerging foreign markets for the same period.

The U.S.-based equity markets ranked just about in the middle of developed-country stock markets in performance during 2005, well below the performance of some of the better-performing emerging-country stock markets.

In evaluating these tables, keep in mind that the performance results shown reflect only a single 11-month period and that the performances of the strongest emerging-market funds during 2005 are unlikely to prove typical in the years ahead.

TABLE 10-1   Developed Foreign Markets ETFs
January 1, 2005 through November 25, 2005

Symbol	ETF	Country	Percent Change
EWC	iShares MSCI	Canada	24.1%
EWO	iShares MSCI	Austria	15.9
EWA	iShares MSCI	Australia	14.3
EWL	iShares MSCI	Switzerland	10.7
EWN	iShares MSCI	Netherlands	6.4
EWQ	iShares MSCI	France	6.1
SPY	**S & P Depository Receipts**	**USA**	**5.2**
EWD	iShares MSCI	Sweden	4.2
EWG	iShares MSCI	Germany	4.1
EWK	iShares MSCI	Belgium	3.3
EWU	iShares MSCI	United Kingdom	3.3
EWP	iShares MSCI	Spain	2.9
EWI	iShares MSCI	Italy	−1.1

TABLE 10-2   Emerging-Market ETFs
January 1, 2005 through November 25, 2005*

Symbol	ETF	Country	Percent Change
EWZ	iShares MSCI	Brazil	+53.1%
EWY	iShares MSCI	South Korea	+39.8
EWW	iShares MSCI	Mexico	+38.5
EZA	iShares MSCI	South Africa	+16.6
EWS	iShares MSCI	Singapore	+9.3
SPY	S & P Depository Receipts	United States	+5.2
EWM	iShares MSCI	Malaysia	0
EWT	iShares MSCI	Taiwan	−2.8

° Single-country mutual funds associated with mainland China showed gains for the period mainly ranging between 5% and 9%.

The following inferences, however, may be made from these tables.

- There are definite opportunities for investors alert to changing economic and stock price trends across the globe.

- Opportunities (as well as risk) are probably greater in emerging-country bourses than in the markets of more developed countries where companies are larger, where stocks have larger capitalization, and where it may take more capital to create significant price movement in equities on their exchanges.

- The emergence of ETFs has provided to investors liquid and visible instruments through which they can participate in markets worldwide—something that had not been available in past years.

Long-Term Results Reflect the Potential in Foreign Stocks

Barron's Financial Weekly ("There's More Offshore," by Leslie P. Norton, February 27, 2006) reported that during 2005, American investors placed $156 billion into global and international funds compared to $102 billion in domestic funds, the first time in more than a decade that global and international funds attracted more capital than domestic mutual funds.

The same article reported that for the 30 years ending in December 2005, foreign markets had risen by 9.3% versus 8.9% for the United States markets. For the 35-year period prior to the end of December 2005, foreign stocks had returned 8.9% per year versus 7.3% for domestic stocks. (Calculations are by Morgan Stanley.)

These tabulations certainly do support the idea of diversifying your equity positions to include foreign issues.

Participating in the Growth of Overseas Stocks

Americans may invest in overseas stocks via direct ownership of "ordinaries" (actual foreign shares denominated in their local currencies), via American Depository Receipts (ADRs), via ownership of open-end mutual funds that invest in specific regions or specific countries overseas, via ownership of global mutual funds whose portfolios include both U.S. and foreign shares, via ownership of closed-end mutual funds that invest in markets abroad, and via the ownership of ETFs that represent foreign markets.

American Depository Receipts

ADRs, available since 1927, are stocks that trade in the United States (prices specified in U.S. dollars), and that represent shares in foreign corporations. ADRs, traded on U.S. stock markets, are sponsored in the United States by domestic banks or brokerage houses.

ADRs were introduced to provide to American investors a ready means to purchase stocks issued abroad that represent overseas companies. They are created by banks/brokerage houses that purchase blocks of shares of foreign companies, which shares are then reissued as ADRs. Each ADR represents a certain number of shares of the foreign company, the ratios set by the issuing bank or brokerage.

Most ADRs are priced between $10 and $100, and may represent less than one or more than one share of a foreign company, depending on the value of those shares in their home countries. ADRs provide to U.S. investors the ability to invest in overseas companies without having to deal with currency conversions, duties, and overseas market transactions.

The downsides to this form of investment include the often lesser visibility of specific foreign companies in the United States compared to domestic companies. Liquidity may be more limited in ADRs than in the shares of comparable domestic issues. In addition, the pricing includes a certain mark-up that is being taken by the banks or brokerages that sponsor and package these issues.

Potential investors in ADRs should consider the following, which, to a certain extent, represent issues associated with all investments in overseas securities:

- **Stability of the governments involved**

  A major support to the U.S. stock markets, and a major reason for its attractiveness to foreign investors, is the stability of the U.S. government and the commitment our country has to the free market, capitalist-oriented way of life. When considering the purchase of any foreign security, via the ADR route or otherwise, investors should consider the stability of the government(s) involved as well as the attitudes of those governments toward business, the free market structure, the Western world, and to the financial obligations of their country.

  The Chinese government today, for example, is hardly the Chinese government of the 1960s (or even the1970s and 1980s for that matter). India appears to be welcoming American economic involvement, but is Pakistan, given the anti-American sentiments of large blocs of its population, as reliable a potential economic partner?

- **Currency risks**

  As a general rule, foreign stocks tend to perform better relative to American stocks during periods that their currencies show greater strength than the U.S. dollar. They tend to lose ground relative to U.S. stocks when their respective currencies are weaker or losing ground to the U.S. dollar. Relationships are neither fixed nor absolute, but definitely do seem to exist in these regards.

  Inasmuch as most ADRs, as well as holdings of international mutual funds, reflect holdings denominated in the currencies of the country in which overseas corporations exist, the value of their shares may rise or decline based on changes in the relative values of those countries' currencies and the value of the U.S. dollar. Again, foreign company shares are likely to benefit if the value of foreign currencies increase compared to the dollar. Foreign country stock shares will be handicapped in terms of their performance for U.S. investors if our currency gains ground against the currencies of their countries.

These relationships are not limited to investment in ADRs. As a general rule, international mutual funds perform best when currencies overseas are stronger than ours but are under some handicap if and when the reverse is true.

• Risks of inflation

Although there are periods of strong inflation in the United States, inflationary pressures have been, by and large, better contained here than in many places abroad.

Emerging-market countries often incur periods of high economic volatility, including periods of widely fluctuating economic performance. For example, countries such as Thailand and Vietnam encountered serious economic issues during the early 1990s.

Inflation within a country weakens its currency relative to other currencies, indirectly weakening the value of shares of local companies as well in overseas markets.

• The usual risks of stock and bond ownership . . . plus

Investment overseas involves the usual risks associated with investments in domestic equities and bonds. However, most investors have more ready access to information concerning our domestic economy than they have regarding economic conditions and trends overseas.

Moreover, many overseas stock markets, particularly those associated with emerging nations and economies, have been considerably more volatile than our own. For example, Russia funds led the emerging markets in 1997, gaining 98%, but then lost 85% in 1999, leaving investors with a loss of more than 70%

over the 2-year period. Korea-based funds lost 70% in 1997, gained 99% in 1998, and then declined sharply once more during 1999 and 2000 (source: www.atozinvestments.com).

Although temptations to concentrate investments in one or the other "hot" country may be strong, it is, in fact, more important to maintain policies of broad diversification when investing overseas than when investing within the United States.

- **Investing in "ordinary" or foreign-based common shares**

  It is possible to purchase shares of foreign companies, denominated in their own currencies, either through certain U.S. brokerage firms or through overseas brokerage firms. Ownership of such shares allows shareholders to participate to some extent in the companies involved (for example, via shareholder meetings) and may provide shares at better prices than investors can secure via indirect purchase, such as ownership of mutual fund shares.

  Most investors, however, are probably better off finding other avenues for investment overseas and will not be all that interested in the currency relationships, potential currency involvements, and tax issues that may arise from the direct ownership of foreign securities.

  The direct purchase of foreign ordinaries may be of interest to certain investors who already have interests abroad, but probably of not too much benefit to the typical investor.

  Readers who would like further information regarding investment in overseas ordinaries may visit www.foreignstocks.com.

Although ADRs and other individual investment options carry some potential, the majority of domestic investors are likely to be better off investing abroad via various investment vehicles that provide professional management, built-in diversification, and ready liquidity compared to actual shares of foreign corporations.

In this regard, the typical investor might want to consider ETFs that represent ownership of foreign country stocks and bonds.

Overseas-Based ETFs vs. Open-Ended International Mutual Funds

We have already observed that ETFs are much like index mutual funds except for their ability to be traded during the day rather than only at the closing net asset value of each day, that trades are generally made between shareholders and not between shareholders and the sponsoring funds, and that exact pricing is set between buyer and seller in the market rather than precisely at net asset value (the total value of the holdings signified by each ETF).

Although actual prices of ETFs are sometimes somewhat above or somewhat below the actual value of their asset holdings, premiums and discounts generally remain relatively small because of market mechanisms that allow large ETF holders to exchange their shares for an equivalent portfolio of the holdings represented by those shares.

In other words, just to refresh, suppose that an ETF represented 10 different foreign stocks whose actual share value totaled $40 per ETF share. If the ETF were to trade at a substantial discount, say at $35 per share, a 12.5% discount from its net asset value of $40, a large investor could buy the ETF (minimum 50,000 shares for this purpose) and tender it for shares of stocks that it represents, in effect securing $40 worth of underlying shares for the $35 price that was paid for the ETF. Inasmuch as these shares could then be sold at their net asset value in the open market, it would be unlikely for market forces to allow an ETF to fall in price to such a discount, which would not be unusually large for a closed-end mutual fund.

The ability of ETFs to remain close in price to their net asset value, if not absolutely priced at their net asset value, does represent an advantage compared to closed-end mutual funds, if possibly a slight disadvantage compared to open-end mutual funds. Other advantages include the following:

- **Ready diversification**

  Compared to the purchase of ADRs or of actual shares of foreign corporations, ETFs provide in one transaction the purchase of a diversified group of overseas companies. The number of options in this regard is large and has been increasing. Investors can select ETFs that represent broad geographic regions or specific countries, for example.

- **Visible and flexible markets**

  You can place limit orders, stop orders, market orders, and such for ETFs that provide foreign-investment choices that are typically available for trading on the stock exchanges and over the counter. You can establish what you are willing to pay to open a position with ETFs, whereas when you purchase a typical open-end mutual fund you do not know the price you will pay until after you make the purchase.

  This may or may not be an advantage for most in the end, but it is possible to purchase ETFs on margin, to sell ETFs short, and in some cases to buy and sell put and call options related to ETFs for hedging/speculative purposes. (Puts are options that allow the option holder to *sell* shares of a stipulated security at a stipulated price until a stipulated time. The buyer of the put pays a charge or premium to the seller of the put for these rights. *Call* options entitle the owner of the call the right to buy a stipulated security at a stipulated price until a stipulated time. The call buyer pays to the call seller a premium for these rights.)

  You can look to www.optionsmart.com, among other Web sites, for more detailed descriptions of option hedging and speculative strategies that may be used with put and call options.

The various strategies that may be used with options frequently sound better in theory than they actually perform in a real world (because the real word includes commissions, bid-asked spreads, thin markets, and such). Still, basic hedge strategies often do have their place in portfolio management.

- **Liquidity issues**

  Although buyers of ETFs can establish terms under which they will make purchases, there are no assurances that desired selling prices can be realized. Be prepared sometimes for poor fills resulting from wide bid-asked spreads if you want to urgently sell. *This can be a definite disadvantage to investing in international markets via ETFs, especially if trading volume in your holdings is low.*

  The underlying holdings of ETFs are more frequently released to the public than are the holdings of open-end mutual funds. Investors who want to remain familiar with what is going into their investments have better opportunity to do so.

- **Favorable tax treatment**

  Open-end mutual funds often sell their holdings in ways that produce capital gains, which are passed along to their shareholders and which are taxable. ETFs, on the other hand, frequently redeem in shares to large redeeming shareholders, not in cash, which process does not create taxable profits to other shareholders. One plus for the ETFs.

- **Low expense ratios**

  As we know, ETFs generally involve lower expense ratios than the typical mutual fund. This is probably even more the case for ETFs that invest in overseas stocks in comparison to mutual funds that invest in overseas markets than for other market sectors. The majority of international-oriented ETFs charge less than 1% per year in expense ratios, approximately one half the level of most international open- or closed-end mutual funds.

Passive Management: Boon or Bane?

ETFs are basically index funds, even if it is not always clear which index each of them essentially represents. To the extent that they are index funds, they will tend to alter their portfolios less frequently than actively managed mutual funds, will tend to be more fully invested at any given time, and will tend to provide more predictable, if not necessarily better, performance than actively managed mutual funds.

Index funds are passively managed—their portfolio managers do not aim to outperform the stock market but rather to replicate in performance one or the other stock market segment or index. They usually come close; but because of expenses, trading spreads, and other costs, most fall a little short of actually matching their benchmarks—even the reputed and reputable Vanguard S & P 500 Index Fund.

Actively managed mutual funds generally involve more in the way of operating costs for investors, more in the way of management fees, may be in cash at the wrong times and may even be in the right stocks at the wrong times. Actively managed funds may underperform their benchmark indices by considerable amounts, but if management is strong may have the capacity to outperform their benchmarks, sometimes even substantially.

Are greater predictability and lower expense ratios sufficient advantages to offset the benefits provided by broadly based open-end mutual funds, which may or may not but at least have the potential to provide particularly astute management? This is a real question.

Summing up, the winner is . . . Let's call it a draw. ETFs do have those benefits associated with daily, even intra-day liquidity, low expense ratios, and the absence of redemption fees and trading restrictions.

Open-end mutual funds do offer, in many cases, the benefits of active management and the association of many international mutual funds with large mutual fund management families and the support such families can provide.

Consider both ETFs and the variety of open-end mutual funds that are available for your overseas portfolio in your search for overseas diversification. Both present ample opportunity.

Closed-End Overseas Mutual Funds

The structure and advantages (and disadvantages) of closed-end mutual funds, which were discussed in Chapter 5, "Securing Junk Bond Yields at Treasury Bond Risk," pertain to the suitability of closed-end mutual funds for investment in markets overseas, too.

The Closed-End Mutual Fund Association (CEFA) reported in the spring of 2005 that there were 660 closed-end mutual funds, with total assets of approximately $200 billion, of which approximately one third was invested in equities of one form or another.

Of the 660 closed-end funds, 44 concentrated their investments in markets overseas, investing among them just about $10 billion in this area. The number of international closed-end mutual funds may not be large, but they do include some of the fastest growing regions in the world.

Among the roster of closed-end international equity funds are the following:

- Asia Tigers Fund (GRR)

- Asia Pacific Fund (APB)

- Aberdeen Australia Eq Fund (IAF)

- Brazil Fund (BZF)

- Canadian World (T.CWF)

- Chile Fund (CH)

- China Fund (CHN)

- Europe Fund (EF)

- First Israel Fund (ISL)

- France Growth Fund (FRF)

- Germany Fund (GER)

- India Fund (IFN)

- Indonesia Fund (IF)

- Turkish Invest. (TKF)

- Taiwan Fund (TWN)

This is only a partial listing. Closed-end funds representing Mexico, Spain, Latin America, Japan, Eastern Europe, and Switzerland, for example, are also available for investors.

You can find more listings and information regarding closed-end overseas funds at www.closed-endfunds.com.

Pros

On the positive side, closed-end funds that invest overseas provide for intra-day, unlimited trading, unlike open-end mutual international funds, which often impose restrictions on the frequency with which their shares may be traded and/or redemption fees for shares held less than certain designated periods.

Closed-end funds also provide opportunity to invest in specific and relatively narrow geographic areas rather than in broader general regions. The roster above, for example, includes funds that invest in specific countries such as Turkey, Indonesia, Israel, and Chile. Such funds may use managers with specific expertise in their respective geographic specialties.

Cons

Unfortunately, this flexibility comes at a price.

Closed-end mutual funds tend to be aggressive in their portfolio management, using leverage, trading frequently—in the process incurring high expenses. Expense ratios for closed-end international funds are generally considerably higher than expense ratios for open-end mutual funds. These higher expense ratios, coupled with relatively thin markets and often wide bid-asked spreads, frequently more than offset the benefits of intra-day liquidity and additional area selection opportunities inherent in the closed-end arena.

Premium-discount relationships among closed-end mutual funds tend to be erratic and potentially troublesome to the unwary investor. For example, consider Figure 10-2, which illustrates the China Fund (CHN), a closed-end mutual fund that specializes in investments in Chinese stocks.

The fund has a history of periodically rising to high price levels that represent significant premiums above the actual net asset value of their shares. For example, during 1993, shares of the fund sold, at one point, at levels 40% above the net asset value of its shares. During 2003, share values advanced to levels more than 50% above the net asset value of these shares.

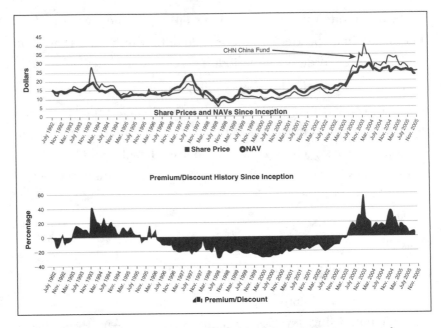

FIGURE 10-2   The China Fund (CHN), historical performance and premium-discount relationships, 1992–2004

This chart shows two periods (1993–1994 and 2003–2004) when market optimism and speculative buying pushed the market price of the China Fund to more than 40% over its net asset value. These periods, during which the China Fund sold at extremely high premiums above its net asset value, proved to be extremely difficult periods for investors, who sustained serious loss as the markets adjusted the prices of the fund to more normal relationships to net asset value.

Conversely, shares of the China Fund sold at discounts of more than 25% below the net asset value of its holdings during 1998 and again during 2000. Such discounts represented excellent value for shares of the China Fund, which ultimately enjoyed a strong market advance.

Playing the Premium-Discount Game Once More

Inasmuch as it is more normal for a closed-end mutual fund to trade at a discount from net asset value than to trade at a premium above its net asset value, the ability to trade at a premium may carry more near-term significance than the tendency of closed-end mutual funds to trade below the net asset value of their shares.

Closed-end funds tend to trade at large premiums only after considerable advances in price have already taken place, during periods of very high speculative, bullish interest in the sectors represented by the funds in question. These have, historically, been dangerous periods for such funds. Most investors are better off awaiting the development of discounts before stepping into the fray.

Conversely, savvy investors often take the advantage of periods of pessimism, reflected in deep discounts in the price of shares from net asset value. We are not simply looking for a discount—*we are looking for discounts that are well above average for that particular closed-end fund and for a cross-section of other mutual funds that invest in the same areas.*

Review Figure 10-2 once again. Observe the periods during which the China Fund sold at very high premiums. Notice how quickly prices of the China Fund declined when the public's ardor cooled a bit, even though changes were much more moderate in the net asset value of shares of that fund. Observe those periods when prices fell to such low levels that they represented serious discounts from net asset value, such periods, again, proving to be excellent buying opportunities for the China Fund.

Similar price premium-discount fluctuations are common in many international closed-end mutual funds, particularly those associated with emerging and developing nations that are not as broadly represented in the open-end as in the closed-end mutual fund communities. If you cannot buy at favorable discounts, better not to buy at all, or to invest via routes other than closed-end mutual funds.

Forgive the repetition. This is an important point: *Premium-discount relationships in closed-end international funds represent special opportunities that present themselves from time to time, but on balance, investors in overseas areas are likely to achieve more consistent performance investing via ETFs or open-end mutual funds.*

When to Invest in Overseas Equity Mutual Funds and ETFs

Overseas equity mutual funds should be represented in almost all diversified equity portfolios. They are likely to show their best performances when the following conditions exist:

- Interest rates across the economic globe should be declining.

- Foreign currencies should be showing strength greater than our own.

- The U.S. stock market is showing strength of its own.

This last point may seem a little counterintuitive. Why buy into stock markets overseas when the U.S. stock market is performing well?

Actually, certain definite correlations exist between the price action of foreign markets and the price action of the U.S. stock market. Days in which our stock market shows strong gains are likely to be followed by advances the next trading session in markets overseas, and particularly in the European stock markets.

Until regulatory agencies stepped in during 2003 and 2004, a favorite strategy for short-term international traders was to purchase European mutual funds at the close of trading on days that the U.S. stock market showed above-average gain. Markets in Europe were already closed by the time our markets closed, so you would be making purchases of their stocks as of their last closing price, which was set before the American markets established their final strong closing levels. The odds were high, with the American markets strong, that markets overseas would advance in price the next day, allowing traders to make low-risk one-day scalping trades.

Regulations have been put into place to prevent speculators from continuing to take advantage of day-to-day correlations between the U.S. and foreign markets via the scalping of open-end mutual funds. There are no restrictions, however, on closed-end mutual fund trading.

As a general rule, your holdings in overseas stocks will almost certainly perform best when the U.S. stock market is strong. Act accordingly.

Which International Funds to Buy

Investors are likely to do well if they follow the procedures for selecting strong mutual funds set out in Chapter 2, "Putting Together a Winning Portfolio." Track a universe of overseas mutual funds. Invest in those funds that rank highly in performance for the previous quarter. Hold positions until your funds drop out of the top 10% in performance. Replace them with overseas funds that have just entered into the top 10%.

You can mix international mutual funds with domestic mutual funds for this purpose so that overseas funds will occupy larger portions of your portfolio during periods that they are leading in strength. However, for purposes of diversification, you may want to reserve a portion of your portfolio for holdings in overseas funds that can be ranked within their own universe.

International Areas That Correlate Most Closely with the U.S. Stock Market

Stock markets of the following countries closely correlate with and tend to rise and fall in tandem with the U.S. stock market:

- Canada
- France
- Germany
- Italy
- Spain
- Switzerland
- United Kingdom

Stock markets of the following countries correlate with the U.S. stock market, but the correlations are not as strong as those in the group above:

- Argentina
- Brazil
- India
- Korea
- Singapore
- Taiwan

The price action of the following countries has been essentially independent of the price action of stocks in the United States:

- Austria
- Japan
- Russia
- Thailand
- Turkey

This summary, based on a study published by Morgan Stanley, covers the period October 2002 through October 2005. Relationships do shift over time.

Beware the "Buying Climax"!

Caveat! It sometimes happens that *advances within any market sector escalate into a sort of parabolic blow-off*, prices at the end surging almost vertically, to levels well above reasonable value.

Examples: Gold at $800 per ounce in 1980, the NASDAQ Composite at above 5000 in 2000, the Standard & Poor's 500 Index selling at near 50 times earnings at the same time, the China Fund selling at 50% above net asset value per share.

Parabolic blow-offs generally end in reversal spikes, prices declining as rapidly as they advanced, not to recover for months to come, often even years. Unfortunately, relative-strength measurements provide little warning of this sort of price reversal inasmuch as strength persists, even increases, until the very price highs of speculative advances are reached. The pattern involved—vertical rise, extremely high trading volume, *including broad public participation and wide media coverage,* sharp reversal in a spike-like pattern—is referred to as a "buying climax." It is a bearish formation with evil implications.

The defensive strategy is this: *Maintain perspective.* If you are having too much fun with your invested position, assume that the fun is coming to an end. If a great many people seem to be having the same fun at the same time, become especially ready to move toward the exits.

Lighten up positions during periods of strength. If just about everyone you know seems to be having the same fun and the media is turning out article after article and advertisement after advertisement about how to invest in the one hot arena or the other, assume that the fun is shortly coming to an end.

And finally, when mutual fund families begin to create new mutual funds to satisfy investor hunger for this or that emerging investment sector, including overseas mutual funds, assume that at least some of the fun being generated by these sectors is likely to be coming to an end.

It can be difficult to take profits and to close out positions during these periods of popular delusion, in part because investors at such times really hate to think of the party coming to an end, hate to give up the joy of seeing profits mount day by day. Once again, *maintain perspective.*

This advice relates to just about all investments—not just investments in stock markets overseas.

Investing in International Bond Mutual Funds for Income and for Currency Protection/Speculation

It is possible, of course, to invest overseas in income instruments directly, or via investment vehicles such as open-end and closed-end international bond or income funds of one sort or another.

Most investors are likely to find it easier and less expensive to invest in overseas bonds by way of mutual funds, although very large investors may prefer the direct purchase of bonds, which does eliminate the mutual fund middleman management fees. Whereas it is often preferable for U.S. bond investors to invest directly in bonds, overseas bonds are neither as liquid nor as visible to most investors as are mutual funds that specialize in this area, as well as in the currency relationships that influence risks and returns that derive from overseas income investing.

Open-End International Mutual Fund Investment

There are many open-end mutual funds that invest in overseas income funds or in global income funds (which represent a blend of U.S. and overseas income instruments). Funds of this nature are sponsored by mutual fund management companies such as Oppenheimer, MainStay, Templeton, Evergreen, Loomis Sayles, and Merrill Lynch, for example.

International bond funds often tend to divide into two camps: bond funds that emphasize price and credit stability, and bond funds that seek maximum yield and potential capital appreciation. The former usually invests in bonds issued within countries with developed economies and by companies or governments with high credit ratings. Yields may or may not be higher than yields from U.S.-based bond funds of similar credit quality.

Higher-Quality International Bond Funds

The 12-month yield of the Evergreen International Bond Fund I at the end 2005 was just 4.6%, roughly equivalent to the yield of the 10-year U.S. Treasury note. The four largest country holdings for this fund at the time were France, Sweden, the United Kingdom, and the United States. Eight of the top ten positions were issued in Europe; the other two were issued in Australia and the United States.

The Loomis Sayles Global Bond Institutional Fund's portfolio included U.S. bonds as its largest holding (36.3%), Germany and the United Kingdom next in line. Government-backed debt issues occupied 51.5% of its portfolio, with the average bond in the portfolio rated AA, very high. This fund provided a 12-month yield of only 3.0% at the end 2005.

Lower-Quality International Bond Funds

In contrast, the Morgan Stanley Institutional Emerging Markets Debt A fund had an average bond quality of just BB (below investment grade) in its portfolio, providing a 12-month yield of 6.0%. The three countries with the largest representation in its mix of debt at the end of 2005 were Mexico, Russia, and Brazil—a typical mix for emerging bond funds at the time. The extra yield did have its temptations for investors, who should also have been aware of the historical risks of this fund, which had declined by nearly 40% in value during 1998 and by more than 20% during 2002. (On the other hand, the fund advanced by nearly 30% during 2003, so risks sometimes do have offsetting rewards.)

Closed-End Bond Funds

The Morgan Stanley Emerging Market Debt Fund (symbol, MSD) is probably representative of the typical closed-end international fund that uses leverage in its operations to hype up yield. In December of 2005, this fund sold at a discount of 5.52% below its net asset value per share ($10.45 price versus $11.06 net asset value). The fund provided a dividend of 7.93% to investors, readily surpassing the yield of the funds above. As we might expect, more than 64% of this fund's holdings were below investment quality, the entire portfolio averaging a quality of B, well below BBB (which represents the lowest grade considered to be investment quality).

The discount for this fund was rather low for its category at the time. Closed-end bond funds of this nature tend to be highly volatile, susceptible to broad price swings occasioned by change in the general levels of interest rates (as rates rise, fund prices drop), to changes in currency relationships (stronger dollar equals weaker overseas income funds), and to international developments. The top-ten holdings of this fund included positions in government debt issued by Russia, Brazil, the Philippines, and Bolivia—not necessarily among the most stable governments in the world.

Balancing the Risks and the Potential Reward

Investments in higher-quality international bond funds may be made by more conservative investors as a form of ongoing diversification and hedge against debasement of the U.S. dollar, for additional income at times when overseas bond markets are providing higher yields than our own, and as investments in economies outside of the United States for diversification.

The best times to buy high-grade overseas income funds are when long-term interest rates appear to be peaking and getting ready to turn down and/or when the U.S. dollar appears to have peaked and appears to be initiating a downtrend.

Lower-grade overseas income funds—usually associated with emerging markets—represent a reasonable alternative to investment in emerging market stock funds when you anticipate strength in the particular countries involved. For example, if you anticipate ongoing growth in the Mexican economy, as an alternative to investing in the volatile Mexican stock market, you might want to invest in mutual funds that hold large positions in Mexican bonds. This may reduce the capital gain potentials of your investment but is likely to produce a steady income flow, and perhaps capital gain, too, as the economic community develops faith in and upgrades the quality rating of Mexican bonds. Risks, in addition, are likely to be reduced as the Mexican economy develops.

Closed-end bond funds carry special risks associated with their use of leverage, as well as with the frequently more speculative nature of their income holdings. For the very most part, foreign govern-ments do fulfill their debt obligations, but the fact is that Brazil and the Philippines do not issue debt of the quality of the United Kingdom and the United States. Taken all in all, many international closed-end bond funds provide higher potentials for return than safer income vehicles but at considerably higher levels of risk.

Such funds are suitable mainly for aggressive investors who are able to follow credit and currency markets closely and who are will-ing to take their chances on often difficult-to-make trading decisions. Rewards that may be derived from correct assessments of currency and interest rate trends are potentially exciting but, because risk lev-els are high, do not invest in amounts greater than you can afford.

Currency Relationships and Overseas Bond Valuations

I have mentioned the connections between currency trends and the valuations of international bond funds but have not as yet described how these connections work.

Let's suppose that you have $10,000 in U.S. money and want to purchase U.K. bonds denominated in British pounds, which at the time can be exchanged for American dollars at the rate of $1.50 for £1. You can convert your $10,000 into £6,667. If each bond costs £1,000, you will be able to purchase 6.67 United Kingdom bonds for your $10,000.

Now, let's presume that the value of the British pound rose to a price of $2 for every £1, and with everything else equal, you decide to cash in. You can sell your 6.67 bonds and receive back £6,667, your original purchase price denominated in the British pound. However, when you convert the £6,667 back into U.S, dollars at $2 per pound, you receive $13,340—a profit of 33.4% (rounded) based on your original investment in U.S. dollars, although the actual value of the bonds did not appreciate in their currency of issue.

We can easily see now that if the pound declined in value from $1.50 per pound to just $1 per pound, you would lose money if everything else remained the same. The bonds might in rise in value in terms of their currency of issue but show a loss when the sales proceeds are converted back into U.S. dollars.

Currency relationships are significant when it comes to overseas investments. If you are able to properly time this aspect of international operations, you will, indeed, have a large head start on your investments.

Ongoing Currency Diversification Is a Useful Strategy in and of Itself

Americans are not as generally familiar with dealing with currency relationships as Europeans, whose countries are smaller and in closer proximity.

Active currency trading may be conducted via the futures markets, based on numerous strategies involving comparative evaluations of economies, on highly technical short- and longer-term trading tools, and involves considerable leverage and high risk—best left to specialists in these areas.

American investors can reduce some of the risks created by the weakening of the dollar in comparison to other currencies by setting aside capital for the purchase of investments such as overseas bond funds denominated in foreign currencies. As we have seen, it is possible to invest in high-grade debt issued within a variety of large and developed economies, which considerably reduces both credit and currency risks.

Theoretically, foreign capital is expected to flow where the greatest interest is paid. For various reasons, however, foreign purchases of U.S. Treasury bills and notes has remained high, even when domestic interest rates have been quite low. The majority of U.S. Treasury issues are held by individual foreign investors and by foreign governments, in part as a quid pro quo for our providing goods manufactured overseas ready access to U.S. consumers.

Your Best Approaches to Overseas Opportunities

There are many opportunities and avenues for investment overseas. This has not always been the case. As we move into the twenty-first century, however, it seems more and more likely that economic strength will spread from the older, European- and U.S-based economies as well as Japan and Korea to newly emerging nations in South America, Europe, Asia, and perhaps even Africa.

Investments abroad should represent a meaningful portion of your diversified portfolios on an ongoing basis, increased during periods of public disinterest in markets overseas, reduced in areas that become the focus of heavy speculation.

Three Final, Fearless Forecasts

Expect above average long-term growth from Canada, New Zealand, and Australia.

China's economy and its share of world manufacturing capacity have been growing rapidly, but growth is not the same as profitability. Expect periodic shakedowns in China-based investments. Take your positions during such shakedowns, not during periods of high optimism.

More steady growth is likely to take place in countries that provide the raw materials and commodities required by countries such as China and Japan for their manufacturing activities. Canada appears to have grown considerably in economic stature because it is a major provider of materials such as lumber, oil, and coal, among other materials to countries such as China. In addition, Canada has a stable, democratic government and is large geographically with a small population. Canada does appear to have significant potential for investments, which, nonetheless, should be made with some care in view of recent gains.

New Zealand, a country approximately the size of England (in geographic terms), but with only approximately four million inhabitants, has been a major provider of wool, meat, and lumber to other nations around the world, particularly in the Far East. Its currency was quite strong in relationship to the U.S. dollar until mid-2005, when relationships reversed as the dollar strengthened. Although New Zealand short-term government bonds have generally provided higher yields than equivalent U.S. government debt, there are currency risks involved, and the purchase of actual New Zealand debt can be complicated, especially for small investors. This is a stable nation with a commodity-based economy that seems capable of fine long-term growth.

Australia is still another country with a large land mass in relation to its population, a stable government, and sizeable natural resources—a major supplier of various resource materials and commodities to other nations.

Investments in New Zealand and Australian stocks may be made indirectly via purchase of the ETF iShares Pacific ex-Japan Index Fund (symbol, EPP). This fund invests in companies of Australia, Singapore, Hong Kong, and New Zealand. EPP initiated operations in October 2001, and in its first four years of operation produced an annualized rate of return of 22.5% per year (certainly an auspicious beginning for a new ETF). But to participate in the Australian and smaller New Zealand portion, you do have to accept the rest.

I have already suggested www.etfconnect.com as a resource for ETFs and closed-end mutual funds. The site provides excellent coverage of ETFs and closed-end funds that invest overseas, too, including the breakdown of their portfolios. New ETFs are being introduced at a rapid rate. Check this Web site for up-to-date information.

Let's move along now to investments in the United States that involve commodities and other vehicles that may be used to maintain and grow the true value of your assets, this time during periods of inflation.

11

How to Get the Most from Closed-End Mutual Funds

When the term *mutual fund* is used, most people think of funds such as Fidelity Magellan or the Vanguard Standard & Poor's 500 Index Fund, or of other funds structured in the same manner. These are "open-end" mutual funds (also simply referred to as mutual funds), one of three classes of investment companies. The other two classes are closed-end funds and unit investment trusts. These three classes of investment companies have much in common, but they also have their differences, which we will examine before we move along further.

Open-End Mutual Funds

Open-end mutual funds are operated by investment companies that raise money from shareholders, which money is then invested in various ways according to the written investment objectives and strategies of the fund that appear in the fund's prospectus.

Proceeds from shares sold to the public are invested (for example, in stocks, bonds, money market vehicles, and other investments consistent with the investment policies of each fund). Investors in open-end funds receive shares of the fund, indirectly owning shares of the assets in which the funds have invested.

For the most part, portfolios of open-end mutual funds are *actively managed* by portfolio managers who seek to "beat the market" with various investment strategies involving market timing and/or stock and industry selection. Portfolios change over time, more or less frequently depending on the investment style of the manager(s).

Subject to fees and penalties that may be imposed by fund managements, shareholders are free to redeem (sell) their shares back to the investment company, at the close of almost any stock market trading day. The price shareholders receive is equal to the "net asset value" per share, calculated daily by the fund, which divides the total assets of the fund by the total number of shares of the fund that are outstanding. Shares are sold to new buyers, also at net asset value, so that all buyers and all sellers of a given fund on any given day essentially pay and receive the same price. (In some cases, transaction or other fees may apply.)

For the most part, open-end mutual funds, which do not have a fixed number of shares, can create shares to meet net buying demand and retire shares when redemptions exceed new purchases. Transactions in shares of open-end mutual funds are almost always made between shareholders and the fund itself, although it is possible for shareholders to sell shares to each other.

Key points:

- Open-end funds (mutual funds) do not have a fixed number of shares. Shares can be created to supply new shareholders or removed from the fund when they are redeemed and sold back to the fund.

- Transactions in shares almost always take place between shareholders and the management company at a common price for both. It is possible for shareholders to sell shares to each other, but this form of transaction may have to be approved by the sponsoring company.

- Although open-end funds may be purchased or sold during the day prior to market close, prices are established after the close of market trading each day and are determined by the calculation of the net asset value of each share. The per-share net asset value is determined by dividing the total value of the assets held by the fund by the total number of shares outstanding.

- Management of the portfolios of open-end mutual funds is usually active. Fund managers make serious attempts to outperform buy and hold strategies related to investment in the stock market.

Open-end mutual funds are the most popular form of investment company and include most funds managed by firms such as Fidelity, T. Rowe Price, Vanguard, and others.

Unit Investment Trusts

Unit investment trusts (UITs) are SEC-registered companies that purchase and maintain fixed portfolios of income-producing securities that are packaged in the unit trust, shares of which are sold to investors.

Whereas mutual funds are actively managed and generally have no fixed date of expiration, UITs are generally designed to maintain fixed portfolios and to terminate at fixed expiration dates, at which time assets are liquidated and proceeds divided among shareholders. Dividends and capital gains that accrue along the way are passed along to shareholders, who have the option of using such proceeds for reinvestment in additional shares of the trust.

UIT shares may be traded in secondary markets (trades made between shareholder and buyer at negotiated prices which may or may not be precisely equal to net asset value per share). In addition, the investment companies that create and manage unit trusts are obligated to buy back shares from investors at net asset value, if requested. Many UIT companies maintain secondary markets for their vehicles to facilitate liquidity.

Key points:

- Portfolios of UITs are unmanaged and fixed for the life of the trust.

- Trading in such funds, after shares have been issued, may take place between shareholders and the sponsoring investment company, generally at net asset value.

- Secondary trading of UITs may also take place at prices negotiated between buyer and seller and not necessarily at net asset value per share.

The structure of UITs is quite popular among investors in tax-exempt bonds. Companies such as Nuveen, for example, market such trusts, specializing in portfolios of tax-exempt bonds that invest in issues of single states. Such trusts allow for interest to be exempt from both state and federal taxes to residents of the state in whose bonds the trusts invests.

Many investors are also attracted to UITs because management expenses are lower in these vehicles because they do not use active management strategies.

Closed-End Funds

Closed-end funds are similar to open-end mutual funds in many ways. For example, their portfolios are actively managed in accordance with fund objectives. In fact, as a general rule, closed-end funds tend to be more aggressively managed than the typical open-end fund and are more likely to make use of leverage to secure higher rates of return, albeit at higher levels of risk.

Closed-end funds are, in one regard, more like stocks than they are like open-end mutual funds in that a fixed number of their shares are issued as initial public offerings (IPOs), after which time shares are purchased and sold between shareholders and buyers on various stock exchanges or over the counter (not redeemed to or purchased from the fund itself).

The prices of shares purchased and sold after the initial offering are determined by the forces of the marketplace and may be higher (at a premium) or lower (at a discount) than the net asset value per share. Trading may take place during the market day, not only at market close.

Key points:

- The number of shares that are issued by closed-end funds is fixed.

- Trading takes place between buyer and seller at negotiated prices, not necessarily at net asset value.

- Trading takes place throughout the market trading day at various exchanges.

Although the closed-end fund universe is considerably smaller than the open-end fund universe, the difference in structure between these two types of funds often provides special opportunities to investors who track the closed-end fund marketplace.

Closed-End vs. Open-End Mutual Funds

Whereas open-end mutual funds (mutual funds) usually create and offer shares for sale on a continuous basis, closed-end fund companies, at the inception of these funds, stipulate a fixed number of shares, which are offered by the fund to the public in initial public offerings.

When investors buy and sell shares of mutual funds, they buy from the mutual fund and sell to the mutual fund. Shares for purchase and sale (redemption) are priced at net asset value, which represents the proportion of actual fund assets represented by each share (plus or minus any entry or exit commissions or fees). When closed-end mutual funds issue their shares, they are not obligated to redeem such shares, the number of which remains constant. The prices of shares of closed-end funds are negotiated between buyers and sellers and may be higher than the net asset value represented by those shares (premium) or lower than the net asset value (discount).

Purchases and sales of open-end mutual funds may be made during the trading day but are priced after close of market trading, when net asset values are calculated. All buyers and sellers transact at net asset value. Closed-end funds may be traded throughout the entire market day, with prices negotiated for each transaction between buyer and seller.

How to Buy $1 Worth of Stock or Bonds for Only 85 Cents!

Closed-end mutual funds, which trade on exchanges such as the New York Stock Exchange or the over-the-counter markets, come in a broad variety of shapes and sizes. You can invest in numerous overseas stock and bond markets ranging from Brazil to Asia to Malaysia, India, Germany, and just about everywhere in between by way of closed-end mutual funds. You can also, of course, invest in domestic stock and income markets.

Once again, after the initial offering is complete, you can buy shares of closed-end funds only from other investors who hold and want to sell their shares; and you can sell, not to the fund management, but only to other investors who want to buy your shares!

This is a significant difference between closed-end and open-end mutual funds. Closed-end funds provide liquidity throughout the market day and the ability, at times, to buy these funds at what may be significant discounts from their actual share net asset values. They also sometimes provide the opportunity to sell shares at prices above their actual share net asset values.

Closed-end funds also involve brokerage commissions and bid-asked spreads when they are purchased and sold but are not subject to redemption fees and trading restrictions. For the most part, there is ample liquidity for most funds, at least for the typical private investor.

The relationships between the net asset value of shares of closed-end funds and the actual trading prices of such funds are variable, depending on market conditions and general investor optimism or pessimism. For example, in September 2005, a number of closed-end funds that invested in China/India were changing hands at a premium above the net asset value of their shares. For every $100 of underlying value, purchasers were paying up to $120, if not more in some cases.

On the other hand, there were a number of closed-end bond funds whose shares were changing hands at up to a 15% discount from the actual value of their bond holdings, as well as a number of energy-related closed-end mutual funds whose shares were trading at more than a 10% discount from the actual value of their energy company holdings.

Discounts Mean Opportunity

Actually, the typical closed-end mutual fund often trades at something of a discount, perhaps 5% to 7% on average. Why should this be, if open-end mutual funds trade at net asset value?

There are a number of reasons why closed-end funds trade at discounts which, in many ways, really represents a more realistic pricing structure in comparison to owning actual shares of stock or actual bonds than the net asset value pricing of open-end funds.

You may recall, from our discussion of bond funds, that one disadvantage of such funds are the effects of fund management fees, which reduce the actual income returns to shareholders from the investments made by such funds. Shareholders of bond mutual funds, open-end, or closed-end, do *not* receive the full benefit of their bond holdings, a situation not reflected in the pricing of related open-end mutual funds. (Actually, if every shareholder of an open-end mutual fund decided to redeem at the same time, it is doubtful that the fund would be able to pay out the net asset value of the fund's shares to all shareholders.)

Closed-end funds have the same disadvantage: Management fees eat into the income produced by their stock and bond holdings, particularly the income flow of the latter. However, because closed-end funds usually sell at some discount, this disadvantage is often at least partially mitigated for the buyer by the often-discounted price of their shares. Inasmuch as it is not unusual for a closed-end bond fund to sell at a discount of 5% to 7% from its net asset value, a discount of that amount would not urgently indicate an available bargain.

Finding the Special Bargains

What would be the situation, however, if a bond fund were to trade at a discount, say, of 20%, from the value of its underlying holdings? Moreover, what would be the situation if a little investigation revealed that the normal discount for this particular bond fund over the years usually lay in the area of 6% or so? We will presume that general market conditions were not so unfavorable as to mitigate against taking bond positions in general.

Such a situation would represent opportunity!

> There is a tendency for discounts to normalize, particularly in bond funds.

Closed-end funds that invest in stocks, domestic and foreign, often trade at wide discounts and premiums for long periods of time, perhaps even years. It is often a good strategy to track current discount and premium levels in relationship to more usual levels, nonetheless. Market declines that bring about high levels of pessimism and heavy mutual fund selling often result in closed-end stock funds being priced at levels that are well below their net asset values, at greater discounts than usual. If you keep track of such discounts, *you will often find opportunities following market declines to purchase stock assets at truly discounted prices.* Such discounts often narrow rapidly as the stock market recovers, providing additional profit in addition to those generated by improvements in stock market conditions.

In fact, the presence of larger-than-usual discounts in closed-end stock mutual funds is often a favorable indication itself for the stock market because such discounts often reflect excess pessimism. (Remember the "media indicator?")

Closed-end bond funds, again more than closed-end stock funds, tend to be characterized by the tendency of their discounts/premiums to normalize to more average levels over relatively shorter periods of time—not days or weeks, but more usually months to a year or so. How might this translate into real opportunity?

Suppose that a closed-end bond fund has a portfolio of bonds whose average current yield is 6% after fund expenses based on the net asset value of its holdings, and that the net asset value per share of this fund is $10. We will presume that the fund, in this situation, might normally trade at $9.40, or at a 6% discount from the net asset value of its shares. In this case, the annual interest to new buyers would be $0.60 per share or 6.38%, based on the purchase price of $9.40 (not on the net asset value, $10).

We will now suppose that during a period of interest rate pessimism, the price of the fund falls to a level that represents a 16% discount from the net asset value of its actual assets, which remain at $10 per share. The bond fund would now be priced at $8.40 per share, 16% below the net asset value of $10. The $0.60 income flow per share would now represent a yield after expenses of 7.14%, approximately 11.9% greater than the yield prior to the price decline created by the discount expansion.

This would represent a benefit in and of itself—investors would be receiving a 7.14% income stream rather than 6.38%. However, there is more! The bond fund's price would have a tendency to return to its normal discount of 6%, or to rise back to $9.40, given stabilized market conditions. Should this take place within a year, investors would secure an additional return of $1.00 or of 11.9% of the buy price, $8.40, resulting in a total return over the year following purchase of +19.05% ($0.60 interest + $1.00 price gain = $1.60 return/$8.40 price = 19.05%).

In this sequence of events, the savvy purchaser of the bond fund as it reached a high discount relationship would have realized a total return of more than 19% from an income mutual fund whose assets did not change in value and that paid annual income dividends that amounted to 6.38% per year.

Suppose further that the discount required 2 years to normalize from 16% to 6%, the excess discount half recaptured the first year and half recaptured the second year. The fund price would rise during the first year from $8.40 to $8.90 on that basis alone, providing a first-year profit of $0.50 in price appreciation, $0.60 in income dividends, for a total return of $1.10 the first year, or 13.1% (again based on an investment whose underlying values did not change in value and which paid a constant income stream of $6.38%).

In the first of these two examples, taking the opportunity presented by the above-normal discount resulted in a return nearly three times the normal income return produced by this fund. In the second case, taking the opportunity presented by the larger-than-average discount resulted in a return approximately twice that of the normal income return of this fund.

Larger-Than-Average Discounts from Net Asset Value Provide Increased Safety as Well as Increased Opportunity for Profit

As a general rule, larger-than-average discounts, created by investor pessimism, already anticipate, at least to a certain extent, future price declines that may occur. The rise in the discount, as above, from a normal 6% to a high 16% already builds in a cushion against further price erosion.

Closed-end mutual funds that are already selling at deeper-than-normal discounts from their actual share net asset values will tend to hold their prices better than funds selling at average or below-average discounts (and especially those that are selling at premiums, prices per share above net asset value). This is particularly the case with closed-end mutual funds that invest in high-grade corporate, U.S. government, and municipal bonds, and is somewhat less the case with other classes of closed-end mutual funds such as overseas, lower-grade bond funds, and equity-related funds.

Figures 11-1 and11-2 show typical patterns of price movement for higher-grade bond funds as premium-discount relationships change.

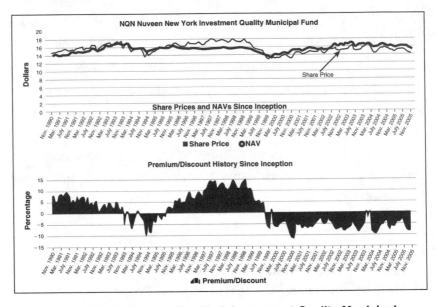

**FIGURE 11-1   NQN Nuveen New York Investment Quality Municipal
Fund**

This fund has, historically, tended to lie within fine buying areas whenever its share price has declined to below net asset value by approximately 8% to 9% or more. Discounts of this magnitude developed
during 1994, 2000, and 2004—all excellent junctures at which to
accumulate this investment. Large premiums developed between
1997 and 1999, in what proved to be a dangerous period in which to
own this fund.

Taking Advantage of Premium-Discount Relationships

1. Become familiar with the universe of closed-end mutual
   funds. There were more than 600 such funds in 2005, representing numerous geographic areas and investment objectives. The Closed-end Fund Association (www.cefa.com) and
   ETF Connect (www.etfconnect.com) are excellent sources of
   information about the closed-end fund spectrum, including
   premium and discount relationships. *Barron's Financial
   Weekly* carries extensive and useful information regarding
   closed-end mutual funds, as do numerous Web sites. (Search
   under "closed-end mutual funds.")

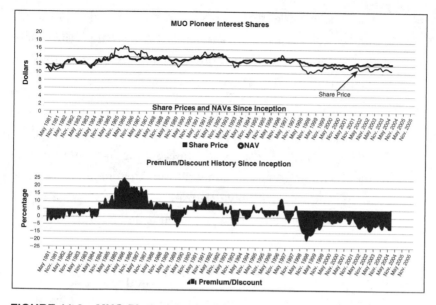

FIGURE 11-2 MUO Pioneer Interest Shares

Pioneer Interest Shares has, historically, proven to be a good buy at times that its share price has lain approximately 10% or more below the net asset value of each share. Good buying opportunities developed during 1981, 1990, 1994, and 1999. Periods in which premiums approached the 9% level (1985 to 1987, 1992, and 1997) have turned out to be precursors of decline in the price of this fund.

2. Identify those closed-end mutual funds with greater-than-normal premiums over net asset value (avoid buying) and those with greater-than-normal discounts from share net asset values (candidates for purchase).

3. Use tools that you have already learned to place such funds within your portfolios. For example, closed-end funds with greater-than-normal discounts may be candidates for your diversified-sector portfolio.

Closed-end funds may appear within the universe from which you select funds that lie in the highest deciles of relative strength, in which case the presence of large discounts, if any, provide additional reason for purchase if such funds rank highly in relative strength.

There is a wide selection of overseas closed-end mutual funds available for international investors. Emphasize those that are characterized by both favorable discount—premium relationships and superior performance.

4. Be alert to selling indications should the prices of any of your holdings rise to levels that represent a premium over their net asset value. Closed-end funds selling at premiums frequently incur greater declines in price than in net asset value when markets turn down. However, the presence of a premium is not, in and of itself, reason to sell a fund.

Barron's Financial Weekly, in addition to showing discounts and premiums, provides performance data for closed-end funds for the most recent 52 weeks. You can readily compare the performance of closed-end funds to other closed-end funds and to the general stock market.

Caveat

It does appear that, for whatever the reason, closed-end funds as a group do *not* perform as well as certainly the better open-end mutual funds and very possibly not as well as the average open-end fund. However, a number of closed-end funds do perform quite well by any standard, and you can often identify these by perusing rosters such as those in *Barron's.*

Do not purchase funds on the basis of large discounts alone! (High-grade bond funds, however, do tend to perform well when they are selling at above-average discounts based on longer-term historical data.)

Before purchasing any stocks, bonds, or equity mutual funds, you might want to check out the closed-end mutual fund area for funds that have been performing well and that also offer favorable discount-premium relationships.

Use the presence of such discounts as a basis for at least considering investment in funds that are favorably situated in this regard.

Caveat Emptor! (Buyer Beware!)

It almost never pays to buy closed-end mutual funds when they are first offered as new issues!

As you now know, closed-end mutual funds are initially sold to the public as IPOs, also known as new issues.

Here is what happens. The fund management company creates and makes available to investors a stipulated number of shares in the newly formed closed-end mutual fund. Suppose that the initial price is set at $10 per share. Prospective investors are asked to purchase shares at $10, the proceeds of the sale to be used for the purchase of investment assets. These shares are usually distributed by brokerage houses to their customers, who are enticed to buy, in part, by the assurance that there are no sales commissions involved in the purchase of new shares.

So far, so good. You will be putting $10 into the fund, with the expectation that savvy fund management will invest it wisely in a diversified portfolio of stocks, bonds, or whatever the specialty market of that fund might be. Even better, you are told that you can make the purchase without paying a commission.

What they do not tell you is that brokerage houses make more commissions on the sale of IPOs than they make on just about anything else they might try to sell to you. *As a general rule, companies that issue new securities pay approximately 5% of the proceeds of the sale to the brokerage houses that advertise and distribute these initial public offerings!*

This payment comes out of the proceeds of the sale. So for every $1,000 you spend for the new issue, $50 goes to your broker and only $950 remains available for investment. Therefore, your $1,000 investment actually represents purchase at a 5.26% premium ($1,000 selling price divided by $950 asset value = 1.0526) over the net asset value of the new closed-end fund—you are starting at a definite handicap.

More frequently than not, share prices of IPOs of closed-end mutual funds decline for some time after these offerings, generally from the 5% or so actual premium with which they start to some level of discount. Unless you believe that market conditions are extremely favorable and that there are no equally favorable alternative investments available, avoid purchasing IPOs of closed-end mutual funds.

Leverage Means Increased Opportunity but Also Increased Volatility and Risk

Apart from risks associated with IPOs, and the usual risks associated with the stock and bond markets in general, closed-end bond funds frequently involve extra risk because of the manner in which many managers in this area maintain their portfolios.

For one, to attract and to keep shareholders by maximizing potential profit, many closed-end bond funds use leverage to increase yield. For example, closed-end bond funds as a group often borrow money at short-term interest rates to finance investments in longer-term bonds that pay higher interest rates.

These positions, assumed with borrowed money, represent bonds carried on margin—possibly providing extra interest return, possibly extra capital gain if long-term bonds, in general, rise in price. However, the costs of borrowing to buy bonds do represent additional expenses to these mutual funds; the holdings purchased may rise in price (adding to profit) or they may fall (adding to losses).

Closed-end income funds tend to be more volatile than open-end mutual income funds, less stable in price, and not suitable for all investors. Similarly, closed-end equity funds, which may also involve leverage, tend to be more volatile than open-end funds, too.

Taken all in all, closed-end mutual funds provide some special opportunities for aggressive investors who can assume the risks involved. They also involve some special risks.

Strongly Performing Closed-End Mutual Funds

Table 11-1, based on data in *Barron's Financial Weekly*, September 12, 2005, illustrates some of the range of closed-end mutual funds available to the public.

The table shows the name of the fund, its price, premium or discount, and 52-week total return (price change plus dividend payout). For bond funds, the yield over the previous 12-month period is provided rather than total return.

To be included on this table, equity funds must have outperformed the Standard & Poor's 500 Index during this period and must have been selling at an above-average discount, which was also a condition for bond funds. This list, on its own, should not be taken as a recommendation of any particular closed-end fund. The performance data shown should be viewed as a snapshot at a particular point in time rather than as indicative of future performance. However, funds listed may be taken as a starting point for investors investigating the closed-end arena.

**TABLE 11-1   Representative Closed-End Stock and Bond Funds
September 12, 2005 General Equity Funds***

Fund	Net Asset Value (NAV)	Price	Premium/ Discount	12-Month Total Return
Royce Focus Trust	9.97	9.70	–2.7%	+25.0%
First Trust Value Line Ibbotson Equity Allocation	25.68	22.07	–14.1	+36.6
General American	40.08	34.80	–13.2	+23.5
Specialized Funds				
Cohen and Steers Quality Income Realty Fund	23.77	20.90	–12.1	+28.8
Evergreen Utility High Inc.	26.00	23.05	–11.3	+32.8

(continues)

TABLE 11-1 *(continued)*

Fund	Net Asset Value (NAV)	Price	Premium/ Discount	12-Month Total Return
World Equity Funds				
Europe Fund	13.04	11.66	–10.6	+29.0
Asia Pacific Fund	17.78	15.92	–10.5	+19.7
Mexico	31.14	27.20	–12.7	+62.7
Convertible Securities Funds				
Putnam High Income Bonds	8.76	7.85	–10.4	+8.0
TCW Convertible Securities	5.60	5.15	–8.0	+13.8
World Income Funds				
Scudder Global High Income	9.11	8.18	–10.2	+7.0
Salomon Global High Income	15.06	13.65	–9.4	+7.6

° The table is only a very partial list of what has been available in the closed-end area. In addition, there are numerous single-state municipal bond funds in the closed-end market as well as other income and equity specialties.

Discounts were somewhat restricted during September 2005 because of buying interest in the higher-yielding closed-end income funds at the time, a period when long-term interest rates in general were low and investors were pursuing whatever investments were paying higher-than-average interest. Discounts in closed-end bond funds are likely to be higher when interest rates are rising, bonds are falling in price, and assets are flowing from rather than into closed-end bond funds.

12

INFLATION— COEXISTING AND EVEN PROFITING WITH INFLATION

Like death and taxes, inflation seems always to be with us. Well, perhaps not exactly "always." Every so often, although rarely, periods of deflation (falling prices) show up, mainly during bad times for the economy.

Before we consider strategies for dealing with inflationary pressures, let's define and distinguish periods of "good inflation" from periods of "bad inflation."

What Is Inflation?

Inflation may be defined as a sustained increase in the costs of living, of goods, and of services—including not just the luxuries of life but also the essentials (food, clothing, housing, health care, education, and fuel). In recent decades, corporate managers and other highly paid workers and businesspeople have done just fine—their incomes rising as fast if not faster than the cost of living. Lower-paid workers have had a more difficult time, barely keeping up, if at all, with inflationary trends since the 1970s.

Inflation strikes retirees the hardest, year by year reducing the purchasing power of their life savings—a situation that has become more troublesome as life spans have increased. For example, the purchasing power of $100 in 1979 had declined by 2005 to an equivalent of less than $40. A person would have needed $250 in 2005 to purchase what $100 would have purchased in 1979.

The Benefits of Inflation

Although the general tendency is to think of inflation as a bad thing—the Federal Reserve Board seems to be frequently raising interest rates to fight inflation—the fact remains that, by and large, a certain amount of inflation benefits the economy, the general psychology, and many, although not all, investment markets.

For example, expectations of rising prices encourage individuals and businesses alike to undertake rather than to put off personal and business expenses. Deflation, with its promise of lower prices tomorrow, encourages the postponement of new purchases and investments, slowing business and consumer demand. Expectations of inflation encourage businesses to spend now, even to borrow for, rather than to delay expansions and other business expenses.

Inflationary pressures raise the value and prices of homes, encouraging home buying and other forms of real estate investment. The stock market prefers periods of *moderate* inflation to periods of deflation, which tend to be associated with periods of economic depression. Growth in the levels of corporate earnings (and to an extent, the prices of stocks) just reflects to some degree a byproduct of inflation, not necessarily real growth.

For many folks living on fixed assets/incomes, there is probably no such thing as "good inflation." However, even retired persons may achieve ancillary benefits from rising prices (to the extent that investment income tends to be augmented by rising interest rates to money market and bond investors during periods of moderate inflation, and to the extent that stocks and home values benefit from controlled inflation).

Runaway Inflation

The decline in the buying power of $100, 1979 money, to $40, 2005 money, is not quite as perilous as this comparison might seem. It actually represents a rate of inflation of approximately 3.5% per year over the 26-year period—slightly above average as rates of inflation have gone over the very long term. The stock and real estate markets produced fine rates of growth at above-average rates during this period, as did bonds starting in the early 1990s.

However, inflation did run rampant during the late 1970s into 1980 when rates of price growth surged to the mid-teens, prices advancing rapidly into the late winter, 1980, when runaway growth finally slowed. This was the period in which gold, a major beneficiary of inflation, rose to $800 per ounce, a period in which U.S. Treasury debt carried interest rates in the order of 13% to 15%, a difficult period, indeed, even for many well-financed investors.

This was "bad inflation"—if not quite as bad as the inflation which brought down the Weimar Republic in Germany during the great depression, or that has plagued countries in South America, including Mexico, from time to time. Runaway inflation creates panic and flights into known storages of wealth (gold). It adversely and seriously affects bond values, increases bank charges for mortgages and other loans, and even raises costs of stock market margin interest, thus negatively affecting the stock market.

It is difficult to find a really good defense against bad inflation, but investors can take steps to ameliorate the general effects of inflation, even to profit as a result of weakness in the dollar. (High levels of inflation that reduce the value of the U.S. dollar discourage foreign investment in the United States and negatively impact balance-of-trade relationships.)

Luckily, periods of runaway inflation do not occur all that often.

Measuring Levels of Inflation

- **The Consumer Price Index (CPI)** measures price changes in consumer goods and services such as gas, food, clothing, and automobiles.

- **The Producer Price Indices (PPIs)** are a group of indices that measure production and selling prices of goods and services produced by domestic producers.

Comparisons of price levels are usually made on a year-to-year or quarter-to-quarter basis and reported as year-to-year or quarter-to-quarter price increases or decreases.

Changes in the price levels reflected by PPIs usually translate eventually into the levels of consumer prices, although there are periods when stores and producers feel unable to raise prices lest customers back off and thereby reduce demand.

Dealing with Inflation

Income Investment—Borrow Long Term, Lend Short Term

As we know, interest rates generally rise during periods of inflation because the value of present money (money in hand) is considered greater than the value of future money (money to be collected in the future). Inasmuch as borrowers of present money will be repaying in future money, lenders will ask for higher-than-normal interest payments during inflationary periods to cover the losses of buying power that are anticipated between the time money is borrowed and the time that it is repaid.

If you are a borrower during periods of inflation, try to secure loans that carry fixed and predictable rates of interest rather than loans whose interest charges are tied to rates of inflation, rising as prices rise. (When interest rates start to fall, you can then try to refinance fixed-interest debt with new loans at a lower interest rate.)

If you are a lender or income investor, invest in short-term debt instruments or in bond investments whose rates of return are variable, rising and falling with inflationary trends. Long-term bonds are likely to continue to pay interest even during periods of inflation, but their prices are subject to decline as higher-yielding bonds come on the market. Prices for gold, collector coins, jewelry, and perhaps homes are likely to rise during periods of high inflation. However, gold, coin, and jewelry markets are generally more suitable for investors who are familiar with such specialized investments than for the typical investor.

Periods of runaway inflation do often end, it appears, suddenly. If and when you detect a reversal—interest rates spiking to a peak and then falling rapidly, the media writing consistently about the problems of inflation, a surge in the amount of investment schemes offering inflation-protective investments such as raw or processed gold and gold coins—take advantage of the opportunity to transfer your investments in short-term debt instruments to investments in longer-term debt, long-term bonds. By so doing, you can lock in high yields from such bonds, which are also likely to advance in price over the years as interest rates follow rates of inflation downward.

Treasury inflation-protected securities (TIPS) represent fine investments that protect against the ravages of inflation while offering the utmost in security, if not excitement. These have already been discussed.

Adjustable-Rate Bonds—Pretty Good, but Beware of the Joker in the Deck

Your brokerage will almost certainly alert you, if you so request, to opportunities to purchase adjustable-rate bonds issued by municipalities and corporations whose rates of interest are tied to the CPI or other measures of inflation—the higher the inflation, the more interest they pay, with adjustments usually made at 6-month or annual intervals.

Such credit instruments range from long-term bonds whose rates of interest are readjusted at longer intervals or may be of very short-term notes, whose interest rates may be reset weekly or monthly and which may be liquidated by investors at regular, short-term intervals. Such notes are often below the highest investment-grade quality but do tend to be rather secure, often paying more than money market rates. Some are issued by municipalities or government agencies and are therefore tax-sheltered.

One sort of offering, common during 2003 and 2004, when interest rates, although low, were beginning to rise, "step-up bonds" paid prevailing rates of interest at the time—usually around 4%—whose interest rates were scheduled to be increased at certain points in the future. For example, one such bond might pay 4% from 2004 through 2006, at which point its coupon would be scheduled to rise to 5% until, say, 2008, at which time the interest payments were scheduled to rise once again, this time to 6%.

Bonds of this nature were marketed at the time as having an average interest rate of 5% (4%, 5%, and then 6%) at a time that other bonds were paying 4%—but, in many cases, there was a definite catch to the deal. *The issuer of the bond (the lender) had the right to "call" the bond along the way (that is, to repay the loan prior to the bond's maturity).*

These deals left bondholders at a clear disadvantage. If interest rates were to rise rapidly prior to the times that these bonds were due to step up their interest payments, the bondholders would be left holding bonds that were paying less than alternative bonds, and whose market value was therefore likely to decline.

And suppose that interest rates were to decline rather than to advance? The bondholder would be stuck in another way. Call provisions allowed lenders to simply pay off the debts involved by calling or paying off the bonds and then issuing replacement bonds at the new, lower-prevailing interest rates. Bondholders might then have to purchase with the proceeds from the now-paid-off, formerly held bonds, newly issued bonds that would pay less in the way of interest income.

Buyers of step-up bonds that carry call provisions are unlikely to really come out ahead regardless of what happens to the direction of interest rates.

Moral of the story: Before purchasing any bonds, check out the "call provisions" of the bonds you are planning to purchase. Make certain that your bonds cannot be called in the near future, particularly if you are paying more than face value or par for these bonds. If call provisions appear disadvantageous, just back away from the deal.

Commodity Investment—an Ongoing Hedge Against Inflation

Certain types of inflation-protected/adjustable-rate bonds represent forms of defense against inflation, as do stocks over the long term, particularly stocks that represent industry groups such as real estate investment trusts (REITs). The direct or indirect ownership of commodities such as oil, gold, lumber, palladium, silver, iron ore, and even agricultural and other food products provide protection against rising prices, too.

Basically, the supply of commodities on Earth, which is finite, is being exhausted at an increasing (and somewhat alarming) pace to meet the exponential growth taking place in populations and consumption across the world. China, once an exporter of steel, now competes with other developing nations for raw steel, needed for its industries and housing. India, rapidly expanding its highway systems to accommodate increasing use of automobiles, requires concrete and other building materials, as does China. Japan, with relatively few domestic sources of raw materials for its needs, has been defoliating forests in New Guinea and elsewhere for decades; New Zealand is now among its major suppliers.

As I write in early 2006, oil prices, on one recent day alone, have risen by more than 4.5%, a significant 1-day advance. Natural gas supplies have recently been threatened by a Russian blockage of a gas line from the Ukraine. Drivers in the United States are relieved to see gasoline prices at the pump down to approximately $2.40 per gallon, forgetting that this remains a significant increase over prices below $2 less than a year previous.

Rising prices of commodities are, at one time, causes of worldwide inflation and the result of worldwide inflation. Debasement of paper currencies, which lose value with inflation, drive capital toward gold, the traditional refuge against weakening currencies and which has been the traditional hedge against inflation. (In 2005, gold broke upward out of a long trading range to move above $500 per ounce; still, however, far below its peak in the $800 area reached in 1980.)

You probably have the idea by now. Commodities, by their nature, are in limited and shrinking supply, whereas the demand for commodities, fostered by spreading industrialization and economic development, is increasing. Increasing demand, coupled with shrinking supply, almost inevitably leads to rising prices. Sometimes price increases are steady and consistent. Sometimes, as for gold, price increases take the form of intermittent, dramatic price explosions, interrupted by long periods of calm.

Commodities, incidentally, include foodstuffs such as oranges and other fruits—orange-based products rose sharply in price in the United States and elsewhere following hurricanes in Florida during 2005.

Benefiting from Rising Commodity Prices

Investors in raw materials may use commodity brokerages to place orders for them on futures exchanges at which contracts for the purchase and sale of commodities are traded, usually with the employment of heavy leverage or via various electronic-trading arrangements. Futures markets are not for the faint of heart, nor for the inexperienced. Newcomers to futures pits at the commodity exchanges have to compete against "locals," experienced traders often associated with industries represented by the various commodity futures, as well as with professionals associated with farming, mining, and other commodities.

Investors, however, do have avenues through which they may participate in price increases likely (in my opinion, at least) to take place in the various commodity markets over the years. There are not many yet, but some mutual funds' portfolios represent commodities in one form or another. Such commodity-based funds tend to be rather volatile, with relatively little history, and for the most part, not yet proven. *On the other hand, the relatively small number of such funds suggests that investors may have a fine opportunity at this point in time*—by the time every fund family sports its own commodity fund, the game may be nearly over (as per the "media indicator").

The following is a roster of commodity-connected open-end mutual funds and exchange-traded funds (ETFs) that were available in January 2006. I have not included mutual funds that specialize in gold stocks, to a large extent because gold, despite periodic bursts of strength, has not been a particularly profitable long-term investment. This is not to say that gold will not perform well in the near/long-term future—just that gold is not an essential commodity in the way that lumber, agricultural products, and energy resources are essential.

Nor have I listed any of the myriad open- and closed-end mutual funds that invest in the stocks of corporations that are related to energy, mining, metals, agriculture, food, and related drilling and

machinery companies, many of which may benefit from rising inflation (as energy-related companies have benefited in recent years
from rising oil prices). The following are mutual funds that actually
behave more like diversified commodity portfolios than investments
in U.S. and overseas stock markets.

Pimco Commodity Real Return Strategy/A

This open-end mutual fund, founded in 2003, did well following its
creation, with gains of 29.1%, 15.8%, and then 15.5% during its first
three years of operation. Its initial strategy involved using U.S. government bonds and notes as collateral to finance commodity investments made through the futures markets, a strategy sufficiently
appealing to bring assets to nearly $2.6 billion by the end 2005.

Pimco Commodity has been rather volatile as mutual funds go, if
not necessarily more so than other commodity-oriented investment
vehicles. The fund seems likely to represent a fine hedge against
other stock market investments and has virtually no correlation with
the Standard & Poor's 500 Index in its price movements. Redemption
charges have applied, however, and you should verify these prior to
investing.

Special caution: The IRS appears to be raising tax questions
about this mutual fund's use of futures contracts. These questions
may require the fund to change its methods of operation.
Therefore, carefully verify the type of strategies used by Pimco
Commodity prior to making any investment.

Oppenheimer Real Asset A

A longer-established commodities-based load mutual fund,
Oppenheimer Real Asset is basically an energy-related vehicle
designed to track closely with the Goldman Sachs Commodity Index
(GFSCI), an index whose construction is 78% related to energy associated commodities.

More volatile than most mutual funds, Oppenheimer, between 1998 and 2005 had price swings ranging from –44.7% (1998) to +44.4% (2000). The fund performed profitably in each of the 4 years between 2002 and 2005, its rates of return between 2001 and 2005 averaging 11.6%.

Like Pimco, Oppenheimer Real Asset uses leverage and invests at least partially in commodities as well as other derivatives.

The fund may be used as a long-term commodity-based vehicle for portfolio diversification. Inasmuch as large, taxable capital gain distributions tend to be made in profitable years, this vehicle may be best suited for tax-sheltered accounts.

Potomac Commodity Bull and Rydex Srs Tr: Commodities/A

These two funds are sponsored by the Potomac and Rydex families, each of which specialize in mutual funds that allow unlimited trading and which are now branching out into other investment arenas.

Both commodity funds mentioned started operations during 2005. Although both got off to a good start within a favorable commodities climate, their track records are too brief to allow for any real conclusions as to their suitability for most investors. Readers are advised to check these funds out starting, perhaps, after 2006.

Van Eck Global Hard Assets Fund/A

Van Eck Global is a well-diversified commodity fund whose top holdings are concentrated in energy-related investments but which also include timber and other resources. Geographically, the fund has large positions in Canada and Australia in addition to the United States.

Founded in 1995, Van Eck, experiencing both good and bad years, has actually done well on balance, with 3-year returns averaging more than 37% and 5-year returns averaging more than 19% (January 2006). This fund has been more correlated with the U.S. stock market than other commodity funds, its volatility more or less average for the typical mutual fund. The worst year for the fund was 1998 (−32.3%), but Van Eck has, otherwise, held its ground well since its inception, rated A for both return and risk-adjusted return by the Steele Mutual Fund Expert.

Morningstar, which has been negative on Van Eck Global's prospects for years, has been critical of Van Eck's high expense ratio, which has been reduced from approximately 2.6% over the years to 1.85% (still high) as of October 2005. Morningstar also questions the fund's relatively small asset base ($200 million) as well as the possible involvement of this fund in the mutual fund scandals of 2003 and 2004.

Whatever the caveats, Van Eck Global Hard Assets/A has achieved a longer-based and better track record than most other commodity-oriented mutual funds, and at the point of this writing at least appears to be among the best proven in its performance.

iShares Goldman Sachs Natural Resources Index Fund

The iShares Goldman Sachs Natural Resources Index Fund is a widely held ETF, managed by Barclay's Global, designed to mainly track the Goldman Sachs Natural Resources Index. The fund's net asset value declined by 13.0% during 2002, but rose by 33.6% during 2003, by 24.2% during 2004, and by 28.4% into early December 2005.

Considerably less volatile than the commodity funds listed previously, these iShares, which can be traded throughout the trading day, carry an expense ratio of just 0.5% annually. Although energy is its major sector, representing approximately 85% of fund assets, the Goldman Sachs Natural Resources Index Fund also holds positions in timber tracts, forestry services, producers of pulp and paper, and certain plantations.

The iShares Goldman Sachs Natural Resources Index Fund has maintained a steady price uptrend since 2002, with stable premium discount relationships (see Figure 12-1).

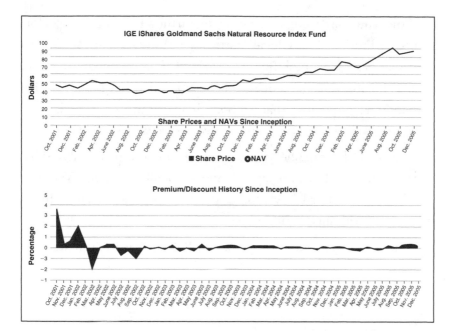

FIGURE 12-1   iShares Goldman Sachs Natural Resources Index Fund (source of chart: www.etfconnect.com)

The iShares Goldman Sachs Natural Resources Index Fund, an ETF, has been relatively stable in price compared to natural resource funds such as Pimco and Oppenheimer. You might notice that ETFs often do trade at premiums and discounts above and below their net asset values, but such discounts are generally moderate compared to the premiums and discounts associated with closed-end mutual funds.

The fund does provide investors the opportunity to purchase a natural resource portfolio that has at least some balance in a single transaction.

Summing Up

The investment vehicles listed here are presented more as a representation of the variety of inflation-fighting investments available than as specific recommendations, which I would hesitate to hazard given the period of years during which this work may be read.

Still, you may want to investigate further the ongoing performance of the Van Eck Global Hard Assets Fund/A and the iShares Goldman Sachs Natural Resources Fund, neither of which seem ideal as a natural resource hedge against inflation but both of which definitely have qualities that support their use in that regard. Most likely, assets divided between these two funds would do the job.

Pimco and Oppenheimer have performed well enough since their inceptions, but both appear more volatile than the Van Eck Fund, which seems somewhat safer in a high-risk group. These funds should be worth investigation, too.

The funds sponsored by Rydex and Potomac are simply too new to evaluate.

Final Thoughts

I hope that I have been able to convey my belief that *inflationary processes are neither inherently negative nor inherently positive* but do offer opportunities at times that inflation is rising and at times that inflation is declining.

Portfolios should contain ongoing hedges against inflation. These can take different forms, ranging from varieties of bonds designed to reduce the negative effects of inflation to mutual funds and individual stocks related to natural resources and energy that are likely to flourish as demand for raw materials intensifies across the world.

Remember to consider long-term invested positions in country-specific ETFs and mutual funds that represent the major providers of commodities to the rest of the world. Suggestions have been made in other parts of this book—New Zealand, Canada, and Australia are significant geographical areas in this regard.

We move along now to a final summation of many of the concepts and strategies you have learned throughout this book.

13

REVIEWING OUR ARRAY OF OPPORTUNITY STRATEGIES

This chapter reviews the key concepts discussed in this book. I suggest that you use these as an ongoing guide to your investment decisions.

Evaluate your own life situation, acceptable risk levels, and investment goals so that you can establish appropriate portfolios.

Ideally Achieved Investment Goals

At retirement, your investment portfolio should be of a size that is a minimum of 20 times the amount of your annual living expenses, after you deduct income from Social Security, pension plans, and any employment you may still have. Ideally, to allow for taxes and loss of purchasing power because of inflation and to avoid ongoing depletion of your capital, your investment assets should be 40 times the amount of income above Social Security and pension payments that you anticipate requiring annually.

In assessing the level of income that you are likely to require keep in mind the extension of life expectancies over the years, the fact that you are likely to remain active (traveling and such) for many years following retirement, and that medical costs (which increase with age) have tended to rise at high rates.

This achievement of a retirement asset level 40 times, or even 20 times, annual expenses is a difficult goal for most people to achieve but is more achievable for those who *start early and who maintain disciplined saving and investment practices.*

As a general rule, it is more important to avoid investment losses than to maximize investment returns, particularly if you are past your working years and dealing with irreplaceable assets.

Be realistic in your expectations. Over the long run, stocks have tended to provide returns of approximately 10% to 11% per year, bonds somewhat less (although their returns tend to be more predictable). I believe that your returns are likely to exceed average returns from the stock and bond markets if you apply strategies and investment principles that you have learned from this book.

Strategies to Control Risk

Allocate assets in a manner that reflects a realistic balance between your need to grow your asset base and your ability to tolerate risk.

- In your stock portfolio, emphasize mutual funds and other vehicles of no-greater-than-average volatility (risk), stocks and mutual funds that invest in companies with actual rather than mainly projected future earnings.

  Assess the balance of your portfolio in view of your risk tolerances. As a general rule, more favorable risk-adjusted results derive from portfolios that consist of 70% stock, 30% bond-related investments. However, conservative investors may opt for higher proportions in bonds to reduce risk. Should you already have sufficient assets to secure your projected lifetime retirement income, these should be protected as a first priority (and risks taken only with any surplus).

- Diversify, diversify, and then diversify some more! *Diversify* geographically. *Diversify* between stocks and bonds. *Diversify* among various industry groups. Diversify between investments that are likely to perform well during inflationary periods and investments that are likely to perform well during more stable price climates.

Diversify within each industry group and sector in which you invest, rather than investing in only one or two individual investments.

Review Chapter 1, "The Myth of Buy and Hold," and Chapter 2, "Putting Together a Winning Portfolio," for suggested diversification programs. For example, establish portfolios of stocks that represent different industries whose performances tend to show relatively little correlation with each other. *This form of diversification is likely to both improve performance and reduce risk. Example: A seven-sector stock portfolio based on domestic equities might include representation in mutual funds and exchange-traded funds (ETFs) whose portfolios mainly invest in real estate, energy, utilities, health, finance, technology, and natural resources.*

Your representation in each sector should include more than just one mutual fund. *Although it is not wise to maintain more positions in your portfolio than you can readily track, this layer of diversification is likely to prove useful in smoothing performance and reducing risk.*

Your portfolio of equities should include overseas-based mutual funds and other holdings as well as investment vehicles that represent domestic companies. *Investment holdings should be spread over several countries and geographical areas.*

Bond and other income investments should be diversified, too. You may use bond time ladders (Chapter 1) for time diversification. You may use overseas bonds as a form of currency diversification (Chapter 10, "Opportunities Abroad—Investing from Brazil to Britain"). You may use high-yield bond funds for maximum income (Chapter 5, "Securing Junk Bond Yields at Treasury Bond Risk"). As a general rule, bonds scheduled to mature between 4 and 8 years provide the best balance between risk containment and income.

- Monitor your portfolios actively to maintain their balance, reallocating and rebalancing your positions at regular intervals to provide more weight to those areas of your portfolio that are performing the best while still maintaining adequate diversification.

  Review the strategies discussed in this chapter as well as others that you have learned. Have exit strategies in place so that you can more rapidly close positions that are not performing as you hoped, before losses accumulate. In general, the more rapid and small the loss, the better. Better-performing positions should be maintained for as long as they are performing well (see Chapter 3, "Selecting Mutual Funds Most Likely to Succeed").

- Try to carry forth your investment program in a disciplined manner.

  It is not important to show a profit on each and every investment, and it is unrealistic to expect that to happen. It is important to try to put the probabilities on your side, so that profitable trades show gains that are greater than losses taken on unprofitable positions. It is important not to get caught up in speculative climates or to be influenced by friends, family or, as often happens, by the financial and other media.

If you can operate on your own (often against the crowd), if you can set reasonable goals and pursue clear investment plans, and if you can live with the awareness that there will be losses and that these are not a reflection on your character or personal worth, the chances of success will become considerably greater.

Investment Climates and Recommended Investments

Periods of Sharply Rising Prices

Favorable Investments

- Short-term debt instruments such as money-market funds, short-term bond mutual funds, and adjustable-rate bonds and bond funds (Chapter 4, "Income Investing—Safer and Steady . . . But Watch Out for the Pitfalls," and Chapter 10)

- Investments that tend to perform well during periods of rising prices such as commodity-related mutual funds and natural resource investments in general (Chapter 12, "Inflation— Coexisting and Even Profiting with Inflation")

- Tangible assets such as gold, coins, certain collectibles, and possibly real estate

- Investments overseas in countries where inflation is less of a problem and where currencies are retaining stable values that are likely to increase in relationship to the U.S. dollar

Unfavorable Investments

- Long-term bonds
- The stock market will often be adversely affected by rising interest rates if rates of inflation are very high

- Industries whose costs are likely to rise but which are not in an economic position to pass along rising costs in the form of rising prices (The U.S. automobile industry has been in this situation in recent years.)

Periods of Steady but Moderate Inflation

Usually not exceeding 4.5% to 5% (see Chapter 10)

Favorable Investments

- The stock market usually performs well in such climates, reflecting growth in the economy.

- Real estate tends to perform well, with home prices rising in a climate of moderate interest rates.

- Income investments are not likely to show outstanding performance, but their performance is likely to be adequate and predictable.

- Natural resource investments are likely to be more selective in their performance and on balance should prove favorable.

- Periods marked by consistent but moderate rates of inflation are among the very best for investors. A large portion of gains in the stock market develop during this type of inflationary climate.

- The U.S. dollar is likely to be supported by a positive economic climate.

Unfavorable Investments

- Investments whose prospects are linked to expectations of a weakening economy (for example, bearish positions, such as short sales in the stock market).

- There are no guarantees that stock prices will advance just because inflation is rising at a moderate, controlled pace. However, because the stock market fears deflationary climates far more than climates of moderate inflation, investment prospects are generally favorable during periods of moderately rising prices.

Periods of Deflation—Prices Decline
Favorable Investments

Investment-grade quality, intermediate- and long-term bonds are likely to rise in price as interest rates decline and investors seek investments that provide safety and predictability. Government bonds are particularly likely to be in high demand. (There were times in the early 1930s that Treasury bills actually paid a negative rate of interest! Fears regarding the safety of banks created a situation in which investors actually paid the government to hold their money for them.)

Real estate prices are not likely to advance during actual periods of deflation, but the area is likely to provide excellent investment opportunities as the deflationary period approaches its end.

Follow the price action of real estate investment trusts (REITs), which are likely to start to firm in price in advance of reversals in deflation as the stock markets look ahead.

Other defensive industry groups that usually outperform the stock market during difficult economic times include the drug and health industries, insurance, and utility companies that provide basic services. High-dividend-paying shares of well-established corporations are likely to outperform more speculative issues.

If economic distress appears to be worldwide, expect the U.S. dollar to remain a strong currency. If distress is essentially domestic, foreign currencies are likely to increase in value compared to the U.S. dollar, and foreign stock markets are likely to outperform domestic markets.

Unfavorable Investments

Prices of real estate (early in the deflationary process); many stocks, gold, and low-grade bonds (because of default risks) are likely to come under pressure.

Although some aggressively bearish stock market strategies may be profitably used during periods of declining prices, the typical investor is probably best off in cash or cash equivalents, keeping capital at the ready for major investment opportunities that will present themselves as prices and the economy ultimately firm.

Money market funds will be paying less in the way of interest to shareholders, but by and large their basic price structures and safety are likely to remain intact (except, perhaps, in the case of an extremely severe depression). For absolute safety, place a portion of your assets in U.S. Treasury bills or in municipal bonds issued by the most creditworthy of municipalities.

Specific Investment Strategies

Timing the Stock Market

- The NASDAQ/NYSE Index relative-strength indicator

  Chapter 1

  Stocks are more likely to advance when the NASDAQ Composite Index leads the New York Stock Exchange in relative strength.

- The 3-year, 5-year rate-of-change interest rate model
  Chapter 2

  Favorable for stocks and bonds when yields are lower than they were 6 months previous

- Comparing earnings yields from stocks to bond yields and other means of evaluating stock earnings data
  Chapter 7, "A Three-Pronged Approach to Timing the Markets"

  Stocks are undervalued when earnings yields are either higher or very close to interest yields of 10-year Treasury notes, or not too far below yields available from investment-grade corporate bonds. Stocks are overvalued when bonds provide yields that are considerably higher than the earnings yields from stocks.

- The 4-year opportunity cycle
  Chapter 7

  Identify the 4-year market cycle. The first 2 years of the cycle are likely to show much better performance (as has historically been the case) than the last two years, and especially the final year of the cycle. Recent 4-year cyclical lows have taken place in 1994, 1998, and 2002, with the next scheduled for 2006.

- "The New Highs Thrust Major Market Buy Signal"
  Chapter 7

  A sharp expansion on the percentage of issues reaching new highs in price indicates that continuing advances of the stock market are likely.

  Similarly, certain relationships between the number of issues making new highs and the number falling to new lows provide good indications of intermediate-term trend reversals.

- New highs/new lows entry and exit signals

  Chapter 7

  Certain new high/new low relationships suggest when to "hold 'em and when to fold 'em."

Timing Investments in the Bond Markets

- Time-diversified bond ladders

  Chapter 1

  Diversifying bond holdings by the length of maturity of your holdings can increase your long-term performance while reducing risk.

- The 3-year, 5-year rate-of-change interest rate model

  Chapter 2

  Bond prices are likely to advance when interest rate trends point down.

- Investing in bonds in accordance with trends in inflation

  Chapter 12

  During periods of high inflation, emphasize short-term bonds, adjustable-rate bonds, or TIPS (Treasury inflation-protected securities).

- The 1.25/0.50 timing model for trading in high-yield bond funds

  Chapter 5

  High-yield bonds have their risks, but the use of a trend-following timing model can smooth out the bumps. Readers can review specific timing rules and hypothetical performance data.

Selecting Mutual Funds and Other Investments

- Strategies

  Chapters 1, 2, and elsewhere

  The more diversified, the better (see above).

- Rebalance sector portfolios at regular intervals.

  Chapter 2

  While maintaining well-diversified portfolios, reallocate your portfolio mix so that strongly performing sectors are more heavily represented in your portfolio than sectors that are not performing well. You will benefit by rebalancing your holdings even as infrequently as once per year.

- Assemble a portfolio of mutual funds that qualify as outstanding long-term, tax-favored holdings.

  The Triple-Period Selection (TPS) strategy

  Chapter 3

  Look for lower-volatility mutual funds that have had continuous and successful management and that have featured favorable risk/reward relationships for extended time periods.

- Select outstanding mutual funds for intermediate-term investment.

  The Double-Period Ranking model

  Chapter 3

  Mutual funds whose performance has been standing in the top 10% of their peers should be purchased and held for as long as they remain in the top performance decile.

- Learn about and use ETFs.

  Chapter 6, "The Wonderful World of Exchange-Traded Funds"

  ETFs represent a serious alternative to traditional mutual funds. Learn the benefits and their drawbacks, and use related strategies. There are ETFs for all tastes and seasons.

- Purchase and maintain REITs as part of your well-balanced portfolio.

  A checklist for purchase

  Chapter 9, "Cashing In on the Real Estate Boom—Investing in REITs"

  High-yielding REITs provide fine diversification and stability of return as a counterpoint to many other sectors of the stock market.

- Closed-end mutual funds provide fine opportunity, but also additional risk

  Chapter 11, "How to Get the Most from Closed-End Mutual Funds"

  Deeply discounted closed-end bond funds provide extra opportunities for profit, although they can be quite volatile over the short term. Closed-end funds provide opportunities elsewhere, too, but for the most part, their high volatility may involve too much risk for conservative investors.

- Mutual funds and ETFs that invest in overseas equities and bonds represent fine diversification for portfolios largely invested in domestic stocks and bonds (and have the potential for very strong performance).

  Chapter 10

  Concentrate investments mainly in open-end mutual funds and ETFs. Diversify among different geographic areas.

Investments in overseas markets may be used to hedge against weakness in the U.S. dollar and the resultant loss of domestic purchasing power.

- Select those overseas funds that provide the best performance as well as the most effective diversification within your portfolio.

Chapter 10

Use similar relative-strength relationship strategies that you use with domestic mutual funds. For the best diversification, emphasize mutual funds from countries whose markets show little correlation with the U.S. stock market.

- Defend against inflation by maintaining portions of your assets in investments that tend to increase in value as prices rise sharply.

Chapter 12

A certain portion of your investments should lie in mutual funds that invest in commodities, natural resources, energy, timber, agricultural products, precious metals, and short-term debt instruments. Your overseas portfolio should include holdings from countries whose economies are commodity based, such as Australia, Canada, and New Zealand.

The Basic Five-Step Investment Sequence

1. Define your own life situation, risk tolerances, and income needs and decide on an appropriate over-all portfolio mix. If in doubt, opt to protect against loss rather than to seek maximum profit.

2. Apportion your assets among different general investment areas (for instance, stocks, bonds, commodities, domestic

investments, foreign investments), maintaining your positions in accordance with the rules of diversification and with your assessment of the general economic climate.

3. Within each broad investment category, define the mix of geographical and industry sectors that you will use. Review these periodically. Use relative-strength measurements to help you select which sectors you should overweight and which you should underweight in your portfolios.

4. After you have determined the mix of sectors within your diversified portfolios, seek out those individual mutual funds, ETFs, and perhaps individual securities that have been performing the best—for longer periods of time or for intermediate (several month) periods of time. Very short-term trading is probably best left to the professionals.

5. Assemble your portfolios. Use the tools at your disposal to reallocate your assets from time to time, and use the market-timing techniques and indicators you have learned to help you determine when you should be fully invested or, to at least some extent, in cash positions.

Try to remain objective, independent, relatively conservative, alert to shifts in the character of the various markets in which you invest, and flexible.

Remember that it is not important to be "right." Expect losing positions. It is important to try to keep your strong positions, to eliminate your weaker positions, and to avoid being overly influenced by your friends, family, fear, greed, and the media.

Suggested Reading

In addition to the many Web sites and other sources that I have already mentioned, you may want to explore the following material.

Periodicals

The periodicals listed here are likely to be of interest mainly to statistically sophisticated investors who have an interest in increasing their familiarity with technical analysis and statistical methods of tracking and forecasting price movement in the stock markets:

- *Formula Research,* by Nelson F. Freeburg, editor. 4646 Poplar Ave., Suite 401, Memphis, TN 38117 (1-800-720-1080 or 1-901-756-8607)

  This is a well-regarded, impartial source of research relating to methods of timing the general stock market as well as individual sectors therein. Research studies, generally based on long-term market history, have been well documented. Research reports do require a certain familiarity with statistical tools but are well worth the effort for investors who are interested in deepening their skills relating to market timing.

- *Technical Analysis of Stocks & Commodities,* 4757 California Ave., S.W., Seattle, WA 98116 (www.traders.com)

  A monthly publication of sometimes highly sophisticated articles relating to commodity, stock, and other investments. The emphasis is usually on timing strategies, but other areas are frequently discussed. This publication is of particular interest to mathematically sophisticated investors and market technicians, but many articles have been useful for less-experienced investors, too.

- *SFO Stock, Futures and Options Magazine,* 3812 Cedar Heights Dr., Cedar Falls, IO 50613 (www.sfomag.com)

  A monthly publication largely devoted to articles that present chart-based and other techniques that may be used for investment-timing purposes. Articles in *SFO* are generally not as statistically based as those in *Stocks & Commodities* but are, nonetheless, usually addressed to investors who already have some familiarity with technical analysis. SFO is a good source of ideas and concepts for investors who want to at least investigate strategies relating to technical approaches to investment as well as a source of reviews of other investment literature.

Books

The books suggested here should be of interest to both relatively inexperienced and experienced stock and bond market investors:

- *Trading for a Living,* by Dr. Alexander Elder (John Wiley & Sons, 1993)

  This fine general introduction by a well-known educator and psychiatrist covers technical analysis, money management, and the psychology of investing. A fuller work dealing with the same subjects, *Come Into My Trading Room* (Wiley, 2002), is recommended, too. Dr. Elder offers educational programs in investing at special seminars, both domestic and abroad, and sponsors investment groups for informal and formal discussion of investment experiences and strategies. Further information may be found at www.elder.com.

- *The Stock Trader's Almanac,* by the Hirsch Organization (Wiley & Co.)

  An annual publication since 1966, originally edited by Yale Hirsch and now by Jeffrey Hirsch, the *Almanac,* which is presented in the form of a calendar-based organizer, includes numerous articles relating to seasonal influences on the stock market, updates of the actual performance of seasonal patterns, year by year, as well as articles relating to other investment matters. The Hirsch Organization has been a pioneer and recognized leader in such research for approximately four decades. Articles are easy to read, even for inexperienced investors.

Newsletters

- *No-Load Fund*X,* 235 Montgomery St., Suite 1049, San Francisco, CA 94104 (www.fundx.com)

  An investment newsletter that recommends and follows mutual fund portfolios based on relative-strength concepts similar to those described in this book. The performance of its portfolios has received high marks from the *Hulbert Financial Digest,* a well-regarded publication that tracks the long- and short-term performances of stock market newsletters.

- *The Value Line Investment Survey,* 220 East 42nd St, New York, NY10017 (www.valueline.com)

  A long-established newsletter that monitors more than 1,700 stocks, about which it provides considerable fundamental data as well as its proprietary rankings for future performance. The service, most suited for long-term investment within well-diversified portfolios of individual stocks, has demonstrated long-term abilities to create portfolios that have outperformed the average equity. Trial subscriptions have been available.

- *The Chartist,* P.O. Box 758, Seal Beach, CA 90740

  In publication since 1969, *The Chartist,* still edited by its founder, Dan Sullivan, provides general predictions as to the direction of current and future market trends as well as a model portfolio, in which the editor invests his own capital on a real-time basis. One of the longest-published newsletters of its type in existence, the *Chartist* provides education in technical analysis as well as recommendations.

- *Ned Davis Research Investment Strategy,* 2100 RiverEdge Parkway, Suite 750, Atlanta, GA 30328 (www.ndr.com)

  A highly regarded publication, mainly directed at institutional and large private investors as well as money managers, the service provides numerous periodic reports, market data, charts, industry and stock ratings, and market outlooks. The various services and publications issued by the Ned Davis Research Group are likely to be relatively expensive for most individual investors but may well be worth the cost to investors with large portfolios or to trustees of company pension and profit-sharing plans.

The resources suggested in this chapter are hardly all inclusive or comprehensive. A search at Amazon.com for books about investing should turn up something of interest to almost anyone. Listings often include large excerpts from listed works as well as reader reviews.

A search on the Web for online investment newsletters will turn up a plethora of newsletters of more or less interest and more or less worth. (*Please* be leery of newsletters that advertise on the Web future performance expectations that are simply too good to be true or that offer to provide timing signals or security recommendations whose past claimed performance has been simply too good to be true.)

Online newsletters that offer to provide free subscriptions usually do so to secure your name, which they may either sell to advertisers or which they may use themselves, sending you advertisements for products that do cost. You may want to consider the use to which your name will be put before you send it out to anyone.

The above caveats notwithstanding, the Internet has become a treasure trove of information regarding investments. Within this book, I have provided you with numerous Internet sources from which you can access information on a wide range of subjects.

Inasmuch as successful investment is a lifelong project of self-education as well as self-discovery, you should try to keep abreast of new developments, new research, and new ways of exploring investment opportunities.

I believe that this book has been a good start.

There is really never an end to the process.

With my very best wishes for successful investing, throughout all the years to come.

— Gerald Appel

INDEX

Numerics

4-year (presidential) stock market
    cycle, 209-213
20-year Treasury bonds, yields, 38
28% major-term new highs buying
    signal, 224-227
401Ks, 86-91

A

A shares, 62
Aberdeen Australia Eq Fund
    (IAF), 266
accumulating capital
  growth target zones, 8
  "magic 20," 7
active asset management, 9
adjustable-rate bonds, 306-307
adjusting interest income, 144-148
Admiral, 1
ADRs (American Depository
    Receipts), 257, 260
advance-decline line, 218-219
aggressive portfolios, 176

agriculture, 36
Aim Energy (IENAX), 85
allocation of assets, ETFs, 159
Alpine Funds, 232
Alpine US Real Estate
    (EUEYX), 85
aluminum, 36
AM Best, 98
American Depository Receipts
    (ADRs), 257, 260
analysis. *See also* strategies
  bull markets, 185-186
  company earnings, 181-184
  measures of valuation, 180
  price/earnings patterns, 184-186
annual management of bond time
    ladders, 18-19
apartment buildings (REITs),
    selecting, 245-248
areas of income investment, 96.
    See also income
    investments
Asia Pacific Fund (APB), 266
Asia Tigers Fund (GRR), 266

asset management, 9
  allocation, 159
  bond time ladders, 18
  continuity of, 65
  diversification, 10
    geographic, 10-12
    sector, 13-16
    time, 16
  mutual funds, 73-74. See also
    mutual funds
  net values, 161-162
  returns, 45
  risk tolerance, 316, 319
Australia, 11

B
back-end loads, 62
Barclays Global Investors, 157
Barron's Financial Weekly, 21, 191
  closed-end mutual funds, 299
  Market Laboratory section, 37
  potential of foreign stocks, 256
basic five-step investment
    sequence, 327-328
bear markets, market breadth,
    220-222
below-average investment
    performance, 5
benefits
  of inflation, 302-303
  of mutual funds, 34
  from rising commodity prices,
    309-313
bid-asked spreads, ETFs, 160
bonds, 97
  20-year Treasury yields, 38
  adjustable-rate, 306-307
  consistency of markets, 32-33
  currency, overseas valuations, 278
  duration of, 100-101
  general-obligation, 123
  global, 42
  high-yield bond funds
    1.25/0.50 timing model,
      135-139, 146-148
    adjusting interest income,
      144-148
    calculating buy/sell levels,
      141-143

  comparing results, 148-150
  lower-grade (higher rates of
    return), 101-104
  markets
    foreign, 12
    timing, 324
  mood indicators, 20-21
  mutual funds, 109
    high-yield, 125-130
    intermediate-term, 113-114
    long-term, 115-117
    money-market funds, 109-110
    municipal, 122-125
    short-term, 111
    TIPS, 118-120
    U.S. Treasury bills, 110
    zero-coupon, 120-122
  performance over periods of
    time, 30
  portfolios, 43-44
  revenue, 123
  risk, 117
    foreign investments, 259
    tolerance, 316, 319
  time ladders, creating, 17-18
  trends, 49
  yields, 187
books, 330
borrow long term, lend short
    term (inflation strategies),
    304-305
bottom-finding parameters, 222
Brazil, 11
Brazil Fund (BZF), 266
breadth (markets), 214
  capitalization weighted, 214-215
  indicators, 217-227
  major market indices, 214
bubbles, speculative, 5
bull markets, 185-186
  Japan, 5
  market breadth, 220-222
buy portfolios, managing mutual
    funds, 73-74
buying
  28% major-term new highs,
    224-227
  cautionary conditions, 223
  patterns, 222
  signals, 220-222

stocks
  asset management, 9
  bond yields as a determinant, 187
  diversification, 10
  geographic diversification,
    10-12
  growth target zones, 8
  "magic 20" growth target, 7
  mood indicators, 20-21
  sector diversification, 13-16
  speculative bubbles, 5
  strategies, 6
  time diversification, 16
  timing, 19
  variable rates of return from,
    3-4

C

C shares, 62
calculating
  buy/sell levels, 141-143
  total returns, 140
Canadian World (T.CWF), 266
capital, accumulating, 7-8
capital gains, mutual funds, 154
capitalization, weighted, 214-215
cautionary conditions, 223
CEFA (Closed-End Mutual Fund
    Association), 265
Chartist, The, 331
Chile Fund (CH), 266
China, 11
China Fund (CHN), 266-268
Cisco, 1
climates (investment)
  periods of deflation, prices
    decline, 321-322
  periods of sharply rising
    prices, 319
  periods of steady but moderate
    inflation, 320
closed-end international bond
    funds, 275
closed-end international mutual
    funds, 265-269
Closed-End Mutual Fund
    Association (CEFA), 265
closed-end mutual fund strategies,
    287-288

discounts, 290-298
  performance, 299-300
closed-end REIT mutual funds,
    232-234
Cohen & Steers, 232
commissions, 48, 62
commodities, 307-313
company earnings, 181-184
comparing
  earnings, trailing/forward, 193-194
  stock prices to bonds, 188-195
  yields, 125, 195-197
conservative portfolios, ETFs,
    173-175
consistency of markets, 32-33
Consumer Price Index (CPI), 304
continuity of management, 65
corporate bonds, 115-117
corporate high-yield bonds, 41
costs
  commissions, 48
  management, 157
  transactions, 160
coupons, 97
  lower-grade bonds (higher rates of
    return), 104
  zero-coupon bonds, 120-122
CPI (Consumer Price Index), 304
currency
  bonds, selecting international
    funds, 274-276
  diversification, 278
  overseas bond valuations, 278
  risk, 258
current yield, 102, 125
  cycles, markets, 206-213

D

databases, Steele Mutual Fund
    Expert, 59
declines, performance, 82
declining prices, deflation, 321-322
default risk, 98-99
deflation, 321-322
DIAMONDS, 156
discounts
  closed-end mutual funds, 288-298
  premium, 268-269

diversification, 10
  currency, 278
  ETFs, 157
    creating portfolios, 165-170
    overseas-based, 262
  geographic, 10-12
  income investments, 96
  mutual funds, 34, 84-86, 105
  portfolios, 38-45
  REITs, 232
    closed-end, 232-234
    ETFs, 235-236
  risk tolerance, 316, 319
  sectors, 13-16, 46-56
  time, 16
dividends
  buy/sell levels, calculating, 141-143
  REITs, 231, 241
    closed-end, 232-234
    history of growth, 247
    minimum yield, 246
domestic income investments, 12
domestic market indices,
    ETFs, 164
Dominion Bond Rating Service, 98
double-period ranking models,
    80-82
Dryden High-Yield Bond
    Fund, 146
duration of bonds, 100-101

E

EAFE (Europe, Australia, and Far
    East) markets, 11, 253
earnings
  10-year Treasury bond yields,
    197-199
  company, 181-184
  forward earnings, 193-194
  forward operating yield, 190
  GAAP yield, 190
  price/earnings patterns, 184-186
  stocks, buying/selling, 200
  trailing, 190-194
  yield, 188
earnings per share, REITs, 247
Elder, Alexander, 330
emerging markets, 252

bond mutual funds, 274-276
currency diversification, 278
growth, 256-266
mutual funds, 271-273
opportunities, 279-281
performance, 254
risk, 276-277
timing, 270
energy, 36, 40
equal long-term gain, less pain, 77
equity, international, 40
ETFs (exchange-traded funds),
    153-154
  asset allocation, 159
  bid-asked spreads, 160
  development of, 155-156
  diversification, 157
  foreign markets
    growth, 256-266
    performance, 254
    timing, 270
  inflation, hedging against, 171-172
  liquidity, 159
  management costs, 157
  net asset values, 161-162
  portfolios, 159
    aggressive, 176
    conservative, 173-175
    creating, 165-170
    moderate, 175
  REITs, 235-236
  taxes, 158
  transactions, 160, 165
  types of
    domestic market indices, 164
    global investment, 163
    income, 163
    industry groups, 165
    overseas countries, 164
Europe Fund (EF), 266
Europe, Australia, and Far East
    (EAFE) markets, 11, 253
Evergreen International Bond
    Fund I, 275
excess return, 69
exchange-traded funds. *See* ETFs
expense ratios
  ETFs, overseas-based, 263
  mutual funds, 60

F

face value of bonds, 97
falling interest rates, selecting
    mutual funds during, 36
favorable investments
  periods of deflation, prices
    decline, 321
  periods of sharply rising
    prices, 319
  periods of steady but moderate
    inflation, 320
Federal Reserve Board, 3, 21
fees. *See also* costs
  commissions, 48
  no-load funds, 61
Fidelity, 157
Fidelity Real Estate Investors
    Class (FRESX), 46
Fidelity Select Brokerage
    (FSLBX), 85
Fidelity Select Energy
    (FSENX), 85
Fidelity Select Food and
    Agriculture (FDFAX), 46
Fidelity Select Insurance
    (FSPCX), 46
financial planners, sales charges (in
    mutual funds), 63
financial sector, 39
financial-based investing, 34
First Israel Fund (ISL), 266
Fitch Ratings, 98
fixed income, 97
flexible markets, overseas
    markets, 262
food, 36
foreign bond markets, 12
foreign markets
  bond mutual funds, 274-276
  currency diversification, 278
  growth, 256-266
  mutual funds, 271-273
  opportunities, 279-281
  performance, 254
  risk, 276-277
  timing, 270
forest products, 36
Formula Research, 329

forward earnings, 193-194
forward operating earnings
    yield, 190
France Growth Fund (FRF), 266
Franklin Utilities (FKUTX), 46
Freeburg, Nelson F., 329
front-end load funds, 61
future returns, predictability of
    past performance on, 31

G

gain, pain ratio, 64
General Motors (GM), 1
general-obligation bonds, 123
geographic diversification, 10-12
Germany Fund (GER), 266
global bonds, 42
global investment ETFs, 163
Global Natural Resources, 36
globalization, investment
    strategies, 10-12
GM (General Motors), 1
gold values, 6, 315
Goldman Sachs Commodity Index
    (GFSCI), 310
government
  bonds, 115-117
  stability of foreign
    investments, 258
Great Depression, 3, 303
Greenspan, Alan, 3
growth
  inflation, 303-304
  overseas markets, 256-266
  REITs, 247
  stocks, 32
  targets
    "magic 20," 7
    zones, 8

H

hedging
  commodities, 307-313
  against inflation, ETFs, 171-172
high-quality international bond
    funds, 275
high-velocity vehicles, 64

high-yield bond funds
  1.25/0.50 timing model, 135-139,
      146-148
  buy/sell levels, calculating,
      141-143
  interest income, adjusting,
      144-148
  results, comparing, 148-150
high-yield bonds, 125-130
Hirsch, Jeffrey, 330
historical performance records, 26
hold portfolios, managing mutual
      funds, 73-74
holding
  periods, tax-favored (mutual
      funds), 66-71
  stocks
    asset management, 9
    diversification, 10
    geographic diversification,
        10-12
    growth target zones, 8
    "magic 20" growth target, 7
    sector diversification, 13-16
    speculative bubbles, 5
    strategies, 6
    time diversification, 16
    variable rates of return from
        stocks, 3, 4

I

income
  bonds, 274-276
  domestic investments, 12
  ETFs, 163
  inflation strategies, 304-305
  interest, adjusting, 144-148
  investments, 16
    bond duration (as measurement
        of risk), 100-101
    bonds/bond funds, 109-118,
    default risk, 98-99
    lower-grade bonds (higher rates
        of return), 101-104
    mutual funds, 105-109
    portfolios, 95-98
  portfolios, 43-44

REITs, 230
  closed-end, 232-234
  dividends, 241
  ETFs, 235-236
  long-term performance of, 237
  timing entry and exits, 242-245
  trading, 245-248
  types of, 232
  retirement goals, 315
  strategies, 230
index funds, expense ratios, 61
Index Participation Shares
      (IPS), 155
India, 11
India Fund (IFN), 266
indicators, 195
  market breadth, 217-227
  price/earnings ratios, 210-211
indices, market breadth, 217-227
Indonesia Fund (IF), 266
industry groups, ETFs, 165
inflation, 7, 301
  benefits of, 302-303
  ETFs, hedging against, 171-172
  measuring, 304
  mutual funds, selecting during
      rising interest rate periods, 36
  periods
    of deflation, prices decline
        (investment climates),
        321-322
    of steady but moderate
        (investment climates), 320
  risk, foreign investments, 259
  runaway, 303
  strategies
    adjustable-rate bonds, 306-307
    commodities, 307-313
    income investment, 304-305
initial public offerings (IPOs), 287
interest income, adjusting, 144-148
interest rates
  inflation
    adjustable-rate bonds, 306-307
    benefits of, 302-303
    borrow long term, lend short
        term (inflation strategies),
        304-305
    commodities, 307-313

mood indicators, 21
mutual funds, selecting, 35-38
REITs, links between, 242-243
trends, 37
intermediate corporate bonds, 43
intermediate-term bonds, 113-114
intermediate-term investments,
    74-76
international equity, 40
international mutual funds
    closed-end, 265-269
    open-ended, 261-265
international small-capitalization
    companies, 41
investments
    basic five-step sequence, 327-328
    below-average performance, 5
    climates
        *periods of deflation, prices
            decline, 321-322*
        *periods of sharply rising
            prices, 319*
        *periods of steady but moderate
            inflation, 320*
    domestic income, 12
    grade (ratings), 98
    income, 16
        *bond duration (as measurement
            of risk), 100-101*
        bonds/bond funds, 109-118
        default risk, 98-99
        inflation strategies, 304-305
        *lower-grade bonds (higher rates
            of return), 101-104*
        mutual funds, 105-109
        portfolios, 95-98
    intermediate-term, 74-76
    portfolios
        consistency of markets, 32-33
        diversification, 38-44
        income, 43-44
        increasing returns, 45
        *performance over periods of
            time, 30*
        *predictability of past
            performance on future
            returns, 31*
        rebalancing, 49-53

sector diversification, 46-56
selecting mutual funds, 33-38
in small increments (mutual
    funds), 106
IPOs (initial public offerings), 287
IPS (Index Participation
    Shares), 155
IShares Dow Jones U.S. Real
    Estate (IYR), 235
iShares Goldman Sachs
    Natural Resources
    Index Fund, 313
isolating safer groups of mutual
    funds, 76

J–K

Japan
    bull market, 5
    Standard & Poor's 500 index,
        alignment with (Nikkei
        market), 5
Jennison Utilities (PRUAX), 85
Kensington Investment Group, 232

L

ladders, creating bond time, 17-18
large-cap markets, ETFs, 168-170
large-cap stocks, 33
lend short term, borrow long
    term (inflation strategies),
    304-305
leverage, closed-end mutual
    funds, 298
liquidity
    ETFs, 159
    overseas-based, 263
load funds, 61
long-term bonds, 115-117
long-term risk, 98
Loomis Sayles, 274
Loomis Sayles Global Bond
    Institutional Fund, 275
low-quality international bond
    funds, 275
lower-grade bonds (higher rates of
    return), 101-104

M

"magic 20" growth target, 7
MainStay, 274
maintaining market leaders,
        rotating portfolios, 74-76
major long-term risk, 98
management
  asset, 9
    diversification, 10
    geographic diversification, 10-12
    sector diversification, 13-16
    time diversification, 16
  bond time ladders, 18
  closed-end mutual funds, 287-288
    discounts, 288-298
    performance, 299-300
  continuity of, 65
  costs, ETFs, 157
  high-yield bond funds, 137
  mutual funds, 105. See also mutual
      funds
    401Ks, 86-91
    diversification, 84-86
    double-period ranking models,
        80-82
    intermediate-term investments,
        74-76
    outperforming typical, 77-78
    past performance, 78-80
    portfolios, 73-74
    statistical comparisons, 82
  open-end mutual funds, 284
  passive, 264
  returns, increasing, 45
  UITs, 285-286
Market Laboratory section
        (Barron's Financial
        Weekly), 37
market-reversal timing systems,
        135-139
markets
  bear, 220-222
  bonds
    foreign markets, 12
    timing, 324
  breadth, 214
    capitalization weighted,
        214-215

indicators, 217-227
    major market indices, 214
  bull, 5, 220-222
  consistency of, 32-33
  cycles, 206-213
  emerging, 252-254
    bond mutual funds, selecting,
        274-276
    currency diversification, 278
    growth, 256-266
    mutual funds, selecting, 271-273
    opportunities, 279-281
    performance, 254
    risk, 276-277
    timing, 270
  ETFs, 168-170
  stock, 322-324
  timing, 19
    10-year Treasury bond
        yields, 197-199
    bond yields as a
        determinant, 187
    bull markets, 185-186
    buying/selling stocks, 200
    comparing yields (with Aaa
        bond yields), 195-197
    earnings yield, 188
    measures of valuation, 180-184
    price/earnings patterns, 184-186
    REITs, 242-245
    stock prices to bonds,
        comparing, 188-195
  tracking, 28
materials, 40
maturity, 100
  dates, 97
  YTM, 103
measurements
  of inflation, 304
  of valuation, 180-184
Merck, 2
Merrill Lynch, 2, 274
Mexico, 11
MFS High-Yield Fund, 134-135
micro-cap stocks, 33
mid-sized stocks, 33
mining, 36
models
  1.25/0.50 timing, 135-139, 146-148
  double-period ranking, 80-82

moderate portfolios, ETFs, 175
money market
    investments, 36
    funds, 109-110
mood indicators, 20-21
Moody's Investor Service, 98, 190
Morgan Stanley, 157
Morgan Stanley Emerging Market
        Debt Fund (symbol,
        MSD), 275
Morningstar (mutual funds),
        selecting, 58
motion, objects in, 49-50
municipal bonds, 122-125
mutual funds, 96
    bonds
        *1.25/0.50 timing model,
            135-139, 146-148*
        *adjusting interest income,
            144-148*
        *calculating buy/sell levels,
            141-143*
        comparing results, 148-150
    closed-end
        discounts, 288-298
        performance, 299-300
        trading strategies, 287-288
    closed-end international, 265-269
    continuity of management, 65
    ETFs, 153-154
        aggressive portfolios, 176
        asset allocation, 159
        bid-asked spreads, 160
        conservative portfolios, 173-175
        creating portfolios, 165-170
        development of, 155-156
        diversification, 157
        domestic market indices, 164
        global investment, 163
        *hedging against inflation,
            171-172*
        income, 163
        industry groups, 165
        liquidity, 159
        management costs, 157
        moderate portfolios, 175
        net asset values, 161-162
        overseas countries, 164

        portfolios, 159
        taxes, 158
        transaction costs, 160
        transactions, 165
    expense ratios, 60
    foreign markets
        bonds, 274-276
        currency diversification, 278
        growth, 256-266
        opportunities, 279-281
        performance, 254
        risk, 276-277
        selecting, 271-273
        timing, 270
    higher-velocity vehicles, 64
    income investments, 105-109
    iShares Goldman Sachs Natural
        Resources Index Fund, 313
    Morningstar, 58
    no-load funds, 61
    open-end, 284
    open-ended international, 261-265
    Oppenheimer Real Asset A, 310
    performance, 77
    Pimco Commodity Real Return
        Strategy/A, 310
    portfolios, 66-71
        401Ks, 86-91
        diversification, 84-86
        double-period ranking, 80-82
        *intermediate-term investments,
            74-76*
        managing, 73-74
        outperforming typical, 77-78
        past performance, 78-80
        statistical comparisons, 82
    Potomac Commodity Bull, 311
    REITs, 232-234
    risk tolerance, 316, 319
    Rydex Srs Tr. Commodities/A, 311
    sales commissions, 62
    sectors, diversification, 46-56
    selecting, 33-38, 60, 325-327
    T. Rowe Price, 92
    Van Eck Global Hard Assets
        Fund/A, 311
    volatility, 63

N

NAREIT (National Association of Real Estate Trusts), 237
NASDAQ, 2
  100 Index ETF (QQQQs), 156
  Composite Index, 22
  historical performance records, 26
  identifying strength of, 25-26
  relationships of price movements, 23-24
National Association of Real Estate Trusts (NAREIT), 237
nationally recognized statistical ratings organizations (NRSROs), 98
Ned Davis Research Investment Strategy, 331
net asset values, ETFs, 161-162
Neuberger Berman Real Estate Securities Income Fund (NRO), 232
New York Stock Exchange. *See* NYSE
New York Times, The, 2
New Zealand, 11
newsletters, 331-333
Nickles, Marshall D., 212
No-Load Fund°X, 331
no-load funds, 61
nonfinancial-based investing, 34
noninvestment grade (ratings), 98
Norton, Leslie P., 256
NRSROs (nationally recognized statistical ratings organizations), 98
NYSE (New York Stock Exchange), 1
  historical performance records, 26
  relationships of price movements, 23-24

O

objects in motion, 49
oil, 36
one-in-a-thousand club, 70-71
open-end international mutual funds, 274

open-end mutual fund strategies, 284
open-ended international mutual funds, 261-265
Oppenheimer, 274
Oppenheimer Real Asset A, 310-311
Opportunities, overseas markets, 279-281
outperforming typical mutual funds, 77-78
outstanding long-term performance histories, 96
overseas markets
  bond mutual funds, 274-276
  currency diversification, 278
  ETFs, 164
  growth, 256-266
  mutual funds, 271-273
  opportunities, 279-281
  performance, 254
  risk, 276-277
  timing, 270

P

Pan Am (Pan American Airways), 1
passive asset management, 9
passive management, 264
past performance of mutual funds, 78-80
patterns
  buying, 222
  price/earnings, 184-186
pension plans, 315
performance
  1.25/0.50 timing model, 146-148
  below-average investment, 5
  closed-end mutual funds, 299-300
  mutual funds
    401Ks, 86-91
    continuity of management, 65
    diversification, 84-86
    double-period ranking models, 80-82
    maintaining market leaders in portfolios, 74-76
    outperforming typical, 77-78
    past, 78-80

ranking, 77
statistical comparisons, 82
TPS, 66-71
no-load funds, 61
overseas markets, 254
REITs, 237
periodicals, 329
periods
of deflation, prices decline,
321-322
of sharply rising prices, 319
of steady but moderate
inflation, 320
Pimco Commodity Real Return
Strategy/A, 310
portfolios
ETFs
aggressive, 176
conservative, 173-175
creating, 165-170
hedging against inflation,
171-172
moderate, 175
income investments, 95-98
bond duration (as measurement
of risk), 100-101
bonds/bond funds, 109-119
default risk, 98-99
lower-grade bonds (higher rates
of return), 101-104
mutual funds, 105-109
investments
consistency of markets, 32-33
diversification, 38-44
income, 43, 44
increasing returns, 45
performance over periods of
time, 30
predictability of past
performance on future
returns, 31
rebalancing, 49-53
sector diversification, 46-56
selecting mutual funds, 33-38
mutual funds, 66-71
401Ks, 86-91
diversification, 84-86
double-period ranking models,
80-82

intermediate-term investments,
74-76
managing, 73-74
outperforming typical, 77-78
past performance, 78-80
statistical comparisons, 82
risk tolerance, 316, 319
rotating, 74-76
specialized management (mutual
funds), 105
turnover, 60
UITs, managing, 285-286
visibility, 159
Potomac Commodity Bull, 311
PPIs (Producer Price Indices), 304
precious metals, 36
predictability of past performance
on future returns, 31
premium discounts, 268-269,
295-297
presidential (4-year) stock market
cycle, 209-213
prices
buy/sell levels, calculating,
141-143
commodities, benefiting from
rising, 309-313
declining (deflation), 321-322
market breadth, 217-227
movements, relationships of,
23-24
periods of sharply rising
(investment climates), 319
price/earnings
patterns, 184-186
ratios, 210-211
REITs, 237
stocks
changes in, 182-184
comparing to bond prices,
188-195
Producer Price Indices (PPIs), 304
profits
bull markets, 185-186
mutual funds, taxes, 154
public psychology mood
indicators, 20

Q-R

QQQQs (NASDAQ 100 Index
    ETF), 156

Radio Corporation of America
    (RCA), 1
ranking
    double-period ranking models,
        80-82
    mutual funds for performance, 77
rate of gain, sectors, 15
rate of return
    increasing, 45
    lower-grade bonds, 101-104
    mutual funds, tax-favored holding
        periods, 66-71
    predictability of past performance
        on future, 31
    REITs, 240
    stocks, variable, 3-4
ratings, 98
ratios
    expense
        mutual funds, 60
        overseas-based ETFs, 263
    Sharpe, 67-71
raw materials, 36
RCA (Radio Corporation of
    America), 1
real estate investment trusts. See
    REITs
rebalancing portfolios, 49-53
recordkeeping
    historical performance, 26
    mutual funds, 107
reduced prices, calculating buy/sell
    levels, 141-143
reducing risk, 13-16, 45
    bind time ladders, creating, 17-18
    stock market timing, 19
REITs (real estate investment
    trusts), 34, 39, 230
    dividends, 241
    income strategies, 230
    long-term performance of, 237
    timing entry and exits, 242-245
    trading, 245-248

types of, 232
    closed-end, 232-234
    ETFs, 235-236
relationships of price movements,
    23-24
resources
    books, 330
    newsletters, 331-333
    periodicals, 329
    REITs, 248
retirement
    401Ks, 86-91
    goals, 315
    municipal bonds, 124
revenue bonds, 123
reversing markets, 135-139
rising
    commodity prices, benefiting
        from, 309-313
    interest rates, selecting mutual
        funds, 35
risk
    bonds, 117
        foreign investments, 259
        measurement of, 100-101
    closed-end mutual funds, 298
    currency, 258
    default, 98-99
    inflation, 259
    major long-term, 98
    mutual funds, Sharpe ratio, 67-71
    overseas markets, 276-277
    reducing, 13-16, 45
        creating bond time ladders,
            17-18
        stock market timing, 19
    REITs, 232
        closed-end, 232-234
        ETFs, 235-236
    reward relationships, 64
    stocks
        foreign investments, 259
        type of value, 33
    strategies, 316, 319
rotating portfolios, 74-76
RS Investment Trust, 36
runaway inflation, 303
Rydex, 157
Rydex Srs Tr. Commodities/A, 311

S

sales charges
  commissions, 62
  no-load funds, 61
Schwab Health Care (SWHFX), 85
seasonal mood indicators, 22
SEC (Securities and Exchange
        Commission), 98
sector diversification, 13-16, 46-56
Securities and Exchange
        Commission. *See* SEC
selecting
  apartment buildings (REITs),
        245-248
  bond mutual funds, 274-276
  mutual funds, 33-38, 60, 325-327
    continuity of management, 65
    expense ratios, 60
    higher-velocity vehicles, 64
    Morningstar, 58
    no-load funds, 61-62
    overseas markets, 271-273
    sales commissions, 62
    tax-favored holding periods,
        66-71
    volatility, 63
separating volatile mutual
        funds, 76
SFO Stock, Futures and Options
        Magazine, 329
Sharpe ratio, 67-71
Sharpe, William, 67
short-term bonds, 36, 42, 111
signals
  buying, 220-227
  reversal timing systems, 136
small-cap markets, ETFs, 168-170
small-cap stocks, 33
Social Security, 315
SPDRS (Standard & Poor's
        Depository Receipts), 155
specialized portfolio management
        (mutual funds), 105
speculative bubbles, 5
spreads
  bid-asked, 160
  yield, 129

stability
  of governments, 258
  of REITs, 245
  of stock prices, 32
Standard & Poor's 500 Index,
        2, 5, 98
Standard & Poor's Depository
        Receipts (SPDRS), 155
State Street Global Investors, 157
statistical comparisons, mutual
        funds, 82
Steele Mutual Fund Expert,
        59, 312
Stock Trader's Almanac, The,
        212, 330
stocks
  asset management, 9
  buying, 200
    bond yields as a
        determinant, 187
    timing, 19
  consistency of markets, 32-33
  diversification, 10
    geographic, 10-12
    sector, 13-16
    time, 16
  growth, 32
  markets, timing, 322-324
  mood indicators, 20-21
  overseas markets
    growth, 256-266
    performance, 254
    timing, 270
  performance over periods of
        time, 30
  prices
    changes in, 182-184
    comparing to bond prices,
        188-195
  rates of return, variable, 3-4
  risk
    foreign investments, 259
    tolerance, 316-319
  selling, 200
  strategies, 6
  trends, 49
  value, 32-33
stop-loss orders, 143

strategies
 10-year Treasury bond yields,
  197-199
 basic five-step investment
  sequence, 327-328
 bonds
  market, timing the, 324
  time ladders, creating, 17-18
 bull markets, 185-186
 closed-end mutual funds, 287-288
  discounts, 288-297
  performance, 299-300
 diversification, 10
  geographic, 10-12
  portfolios, 38-44
  sector, 13-16
  time, 16
 earning yields, 188
 emerging markets, 252
 high-yield bond funds, 137
 holding stocks, 6
 income investments
  bond duration (as measurement
   of risk), 100-101
  bonds/bond funds, 109-119
  default risk, 98-99
  lower-grade bonds (higher rates
   of return), 101-104
  mutual funds, 105-109
  portfolios, 95-98
  REITs, 230
 inflation
  adjustable-rate bonds, 306-307
  commodities, 307-313
  income investment, 304-305
 measures of valuation, 180-184
 mood indicators, 20-21
 mutual funds
  selecting, 325-327
  tax-favored holding periods,
   66-71
 open-end mutual funds, 284
 price/earnings patterns, 184-186
 REITs, 245-248
 retirement goals, 315
 risk, 13-16, 316-319
 stock market timing, 19, 322-324
 stocks, 6
  buying, 187, 200

 comparing to bond prices,
  188-195
 selling, 200
 yields (comparing with Aaa
  bond yields), 195-197
 UITs, 285-286
StreetTRACKS Wilshire REIT
 Fund (RWR), 235
strength of NASDAQ, identifying
 of, 25-27
Sullivan, Dan, 331
Supershares, 155

T

T. Rowe Price, 92
targets, growth, 7-8
taxes
 401Ks, 86-91
 ETFs, 158, 263
 mutual funds
  capital gains, 154
  tax-favored holding periods,
   66-71
 REITs, 231
Technical Analysis of Stocks &
 Commodities, 329
Templeton, 274
timber, 36
timing
 1.25/0.50 timing model, 135-139,
  146-148
 diversification, 16
 markets, 19
  10-year Treasury bond
   yields, 197-199
  bond yields as a
   determinant, 187
  bonds, 324
  bull markets, 185-186
  buying/selling stocks, 200
  comparing stock prices to
   bonds, 188-195
  comparing yields (with Aaa
   bond yields), 195-197
  earnings yield, 188
  measures of valuation, 180-184
  price/earnings patterns, 184-186
  REITs, 242-245
  stocks, 322-324

overseas markets, 270
time ladders (bond), creating,
    17-18
TIPS (Toronto Stock Exchange
    Index Participations), 155
TIPS (Treasury inflation-protected
    securities), 118-120,
    171, 305
tolerance, risk, 316-319
Toronto Stock Exchange Index
    Participations (TIPS), 155
total returns, 138-139
TPS (Triple Period Selection),
    66-71
tracking
    markets, 28
    REITs, 243
    total returns, 138-139
trading. *See also* buying; strategies
    ETFs, 161
    mutual funds
        closed-end, 287-297
        open-end, 284
    premium discounts, 268-269
    REITs, 245-248
    UITs, 285-286
Trading for a Living, 330
trailing
    earnings, 193-194
    GAAP earnings yield, 190
    stop-loss orders, 143
Trans World Airlines (TWA), 1
transactions
    costs, 160
    ETFs, 165
Treasury inflation-protected
    securities. *See* TIPS
trends
    interest rates, 37
    stocks, 49
Triple Period Selection (TPS),
    66-71
trusts, strategies, 285-286
Turkish Invest. (TKF), 266
turnover, portfolios, 60
TWA (Trans World Airlines), 1
types
    of ETFs

domestic market indices, 164
global investment, 163
income, 163
industry groups, 165
overseas countries, 164
    of REITs, 232
        closed-end, 232-234
        ETFs, 235-236

U

U.S. small-capitalization value
    sectors, 40
U.S. Treasury bills, 30, 110
UITs (unit investment trusts),
    strategies, 285-286
unfavorable investments
    periods of deflation, prices
        decline, 322
    periods of sharply rising
        prices, 319
    periods of steady but moderate
        inflation, 320
unit investment trusts. *See* UITs
United States, 11
unlimited trades, 401Ks, 87
utility stocks, 36, 39

V

valuation
    measures of, 180-184
    overseas bonds (currency and), 278
Value Line Investment Survey,
    The, 331
value stocks, 32-33
values
    gold, 6
    net asset, 161-162
Van Eck Global Hard Assets
    Fund/A, 311
Van Eck Global Hard Assets
    Fund/Class A, 36
Vanguard, 157
Vanguard Energy/Inv (VGENX), 46
Vanguard Health Care
    (VGHCX), 47
Vanguard REIT Index Fund
    (VGSIX), 232

Vanguard REIT Index VIPERS
    (VNQ), 235
Vanguard Standard & Poor's 500
    Index Fund, 61
variable rates of return, stocks, 3-4
velocity, high-velocity vehicles, 64
visibility, portfolios, 159
visible markets, overseas
    ETFs, 262
volatility, 32, 63
    closed-end mutual funds, 298
    mutual funds, separating, 76
    raw materials, 36

W–Z

Weimar Republic, 303

year-by-year comparative results, 52
yield
    20-year Treasury bonds, 38
    bonds
        10-year Treasury bond, 197-199
        comparing using Aaa yields,
            195-197

buying stocks, 187
comparing, 125
corporate high-yield bonds, 41
current SEC yield, 125
earnings, 188
forward operating earnings, 190
high-yield bond funds
    1.25/0.50 timing model,
        135-139, 146-148
    adjusting interest income,
        144-148
    calculating buy/sell levels,
        141-143
    comparing results, 148-150
REITs, 246
spreads, 129
trailing GAAP earnings, 190
yield to maturity (YTM), 103
yield-high-yield bonds, 125-130
YTM (yield to maturity), 103

zero-coupon bonds, 120-122
zones, growth target, 8

THE SILK ROAD TO RICHES
How You Can Profit by Investing in Asia's Newfound Prosperity

Yiannis G. Mostrous, Elliott H. Gue, and Ivan D. Martchev

Asia is now the world's #1 growth story. Farsighted investors can realize enormous profits by investing in companies that benefit from Asia's historic transformation. In *The Silk Road to Riches*, the authors point you to the right companies, the right sectors, and the right strategies. You can learn ways to leverage Asia's accelerating integration into the world economy... profit from the pressure that Asia's growth is placing on commodities and resources... anticipate changing needs of Asian consumers in financial services, health and pharmaceuticals, communications, and many other industries.

© 2006 ■ 272pp. ■ ISBN 0131869728 ■ $25.99 US ■ $32.99 CAN

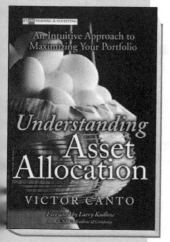

UNDERSTANDING ASSET ALLOCATION
An Intuitive Approach to Maximizing Your Portfolio

Victor Canto

It's not enough to rely on some investment manager's one-size-fits-all software to allocate your precious capital: you need to understand the process and take control. In *Understanding Asset Allocation*, economist, investment expert, and hedge-fund manager Dr. Victor Canto shows you exactly how to do that. Canto introduces a flexible, easy-to-use approach to asset allocation that leverages powerful business cycle information and investment vehicles most investors ignore. You can discover the right times to choose passive versus active investments, value versus growth stocks, and large-caps versus small-caps.

© 2006 ■ 336pp. ■ ISBN 0131876767 ■ $34.99 US ■ $43.99 CAN

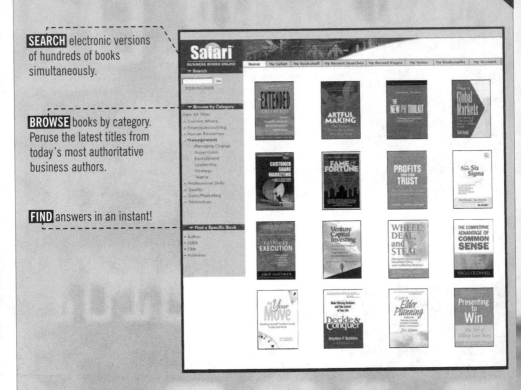